Disciples of the Desert

Disciples of the Desert

Monks, Laity, and Spiritual Authority in Sixth-Century Gaza

Jennifer L. Hevelone-Harper

Johns Hopkins University Press
Baltimore

Johns Hopkins Paperback edition, 2014
2 4 6 8 9 7 5 3 1

Johns Hopkins University Press
2715 North Charles Street
Baltimore, Maryland 21218-4363
www.press.jhu.edu

The Library of Congress has cataloged the hardcover edition of this book as follows:
Hevelone-Harper, Jennifer Lee, 1970–
Disciples of the desert : monks, laity, and spiritual authority in sixth-century Gaza /
Jennifer L. Hevelone-Harper.
p. cm.
Includes bibliographical references and index.
ISBN 0-8018-8110-2 (alk. paper)
1. Barsanuphius, Saint, 6th cent. Biblos psychāophelestatāe periechousa
apokriseis.   2. John, the Prophet, Saint.   3. Spiritual life—Orthodox Eastern
Church—History of doctrines—Early church, ca. 30–600.   4. Asceticism—
Orthodox Eastern Church—History—Early church, ca. 30–600.   5. Monastic and
religious life—Gaza Strip—Gaza—History—Early church, ca. 30–600.
6. Gaza—Church history.   I. Title.
BX382.B3734   1997
275.3′1—dc22
2004023565

A catalog record for this book is available from the British Library.

ISBN-13: 978-1-4214-1386-0
ISBN-10: 1-4214-1386-8

*Special discounts are available for bulk purchases of this book. For more information, please contact
Special Sales at 410-516-6936 or specialsales@press.jhu.edu.*

Johns Hopkins University Press uses environmentally friendly book materials,
including recycled text paper that is composed of at least 30 percent post-consumer
waste, whenever possible.

Frontispiece: Coptic monk with his hands raised in prayer. Limestone relief,
sixth–seventh century. Courtesy of Dumbarton Oaks, Byzantine Photograph
and Fieldwork Archives, Washington, D.C.

For my parents
and my husband, Colin

Contents

Preface

Recent scholarship on late antique asceticism has recognized regional contributions to the development of Eastern monasticism, taking advantage of archaeological findings, documentary papyri, and fresh approaches to analyzing written texts. Particularly fruitful has been the study of the sayings of the fourth-century Egyptian desert fathers and the way in which these monks understood scripture and community.[1] In the past two decades, monastic communities of the Judean desert have also attracted study, which has creatively revealed both the physical setting of the Judean monasteries and the personalities who inhabited them.[2] The monastic developments of the Gaza region, intimately connected to both the Palestinian and the Egyptian experience, have received considerably less notice.

This is a propitious time to undertake a study of two of the the holy men of Gaza, Barsanuphius and John. Publication in 2002 of a new translation of the discourses of their predecessor Isaiah of Scetis has begun to reveal the fertile setting Gaza provided for ascetic theology.[3] The collected Correspondence of Barsanuphius and John has recently been published (1997–2002) in a critical edition with a French translation, making the full text of the letters easily accessible for the first time.[4] John Chryssavgis' English translation of the letters completes the important unfinished work of Derwas Chitty, whose groundbreaking research on Palestinian monasticism provides the background for modern scholarship on the region.[5] The preparation of the critical edition and new translations of the rather unwieldy corpus of Barsanuphius and John's letters facilitate approaching the Correspondence from an historical perspective. Although enticing morsels from Barsanuphius and John's letters have, from time to time, appeared in the work of other historians, this is the first book-length study to examine the entire collection in its social context. I have organized the material within the framework of the development and exercise of spiritual leadership, examining spiritual authority within the monastery and also the means through which Barsanuphius and John touched both lay Christians in the surrounding neighborhoods and ecclesiastical leaders in Gaza and Jerusalem.

Much of the earlier work on the Correspondence focused upon the monastic wisdom recoverable from the letters of these holy men. Although I do not discount the intrinsic spiritual value of Barsanuphius and John's teaching, I am concerned here to reconstruct their relationships with disciples and with each other. Particularly useful for understanding the exercise of spiritual authority at the time is the manner in which the leaders of the monastery in Tawatha dealt with direct (and indirect) challenges to their carefully established system of authority. Barsanuphius and John's long tenure in authority was not due to an absence of conflict within the community, but to their ability to manage disputes. They redirected the energies of strong-willed monks, eventually transforming rebellious personalities into leaders within the structure of the monastic community. Investigating the training of leaders within the monastery yields insight into the operation of spiritual authority in Tawatha.

In the Correspondence of Barsanuphius and John, we are introduced to a crowded cast of individual fathers and disciples. In their struggles and doubts they serve as representatives of late antique Christians, not only in Gaza, but throughout the eastern Mediterranean world. The letters provide a window into the diverse world of sixth-century Byzantium, where we meet individuals from all walks of life whose stories have not yet been told. The attitudes, ambitions, and struggles of the monks, clergy, and lay Christians who became disciples of Barsanuphius and John animate the setting of the last century of Byzantine-ruled Palestine. This book situates these two anchorites within the recently Christianized society of the eastern Mediterranean during the rule of the overtly Christian emperor Justinian. It also moves beyond the holy men themselves, to explore the communities they inhabited. It is the writers of the nearly lost letters to Barsanuphius and John who serve as the focus of this book. The questions posed by petitioners reveal the anxieties and hopes of individuals representing a wide cross section of Byzantine society.

The first chapter of this book provides historical background for sixth-century Gaza and introduces Barsanuphius and John, connecting them with the monastic heritage of the Gaza region and the ongoing doctrinal disputes in Palestine. Chapter 2 explores the system of spiritual authority in place at the monastery in Tawatha for much of the first half of the sixth century. It examines the relationships between the anchorites Barsanuphius and John and the abbot Seridos, paying particular attention to the resolution of conflict between the leaders and disciples at the monastery. Chapter 3 presents a case study of Dorotheos, the best-known disciple of Barsanuphius and John. It follows his experiences as a monk, from his admission to the cenobium until his recognition as a spiritual leader in his own right. Departing from the earlier chapters' examination of spiritual direction within the monastery, Chapter 4 moves to the influence of Barsanuphius and John on the lives of lay Christians in the neighboring community. The correspondence between anchorites and lay people reveals both the anxieties facing those trying to live as Christians in "the world" and the concern of the leaders of the monastery to foster and control lay piety. Chapter 5 continues the analysis of the influence of anchorites' spiritual direction beyond the monastery walls, examining the letters relating to bishops and civil authorities. These demonstrate that, despite the physical isolation of these two holy men, they were involved in the controversies that preoccupied the inhabitants of the region and that they freely instructed ecclesiastical leaders on their proper relationship with secular power. Chapter 6 elucidates the radical changes that shook the leadership of the monastery upon the deaths of Seridos and John, and Barsanuphius' complete withdrawal from human contact. The chapter follows Aelianos, the layman newly appointed abbot, as he sought instructions on governing the monastery. From this final episode we learn about the transmission of spiritual authority from one generation to the next.

A rich community of people made this work possible. I am exceedingly grateful to my graduate supervisor at Princeton, Peter Brown, whose encouragement and vision sustained me in this project, and to William Chester Jordan for his trenchant criticism. The faculty and administration at Gordon College have offered support and encouragement, especially by granting me a sabbatical to pursue this work. Colleagues who offered practical support include Steve Alter, Graeme Bird, Dorothy Boorse, Martha Crain, Vanessa Crooks, Jennifer Fry, and Jamie Hokanson. My students, who read selections from the text, challenged me to consider the way in which Byzantium could best be made accessible to modern readers.

Other colleagues have aided me in my exploration of aspects of Barsanuphius and John's world, including His Grace Bishop Sava of Troas and Father John Chryssavgis. I would like to thank Scott Carroll and the Scriptorium Center for Christian Antiquities for making possible my visit to Egypt, where I saw the monasteries of Scetis and Sinai and learned something of the monastic culture from which Barsanuphius emerged. I also thank my colleagues Marilyn Cooper, Cornelia Horn, and Ute Possekel. My sincere appreciation goes to Henry Tom, Anne Whitmore, and Claire McCabe at Johns Hopkins University Press for their knowledgeable help and patient guidance.

My family has also invested in this project. It was my aunt and uncle, Martha and Joe Holeman, whose recollections of their sojourn in Gaza in the late 1980s first whetted my appetite to know more about the region. My parents, Nell and Jon Hevelone, and my husband's parents, Lillian and Bill Harper, lovingly supported me in countless ways during the writing of this book. My sisters, Suzanne and Christine, were dedicated proofreaders, while my brother, Nathanael, provided encouragement. My husband, Colin, has made his love visible daily in practical manifestations, making it possible for me to complete this project; and my daughters, Isabelle and Victoria, have been graciously tolerant of the demands on my time and attention.

Disciples of the Desert

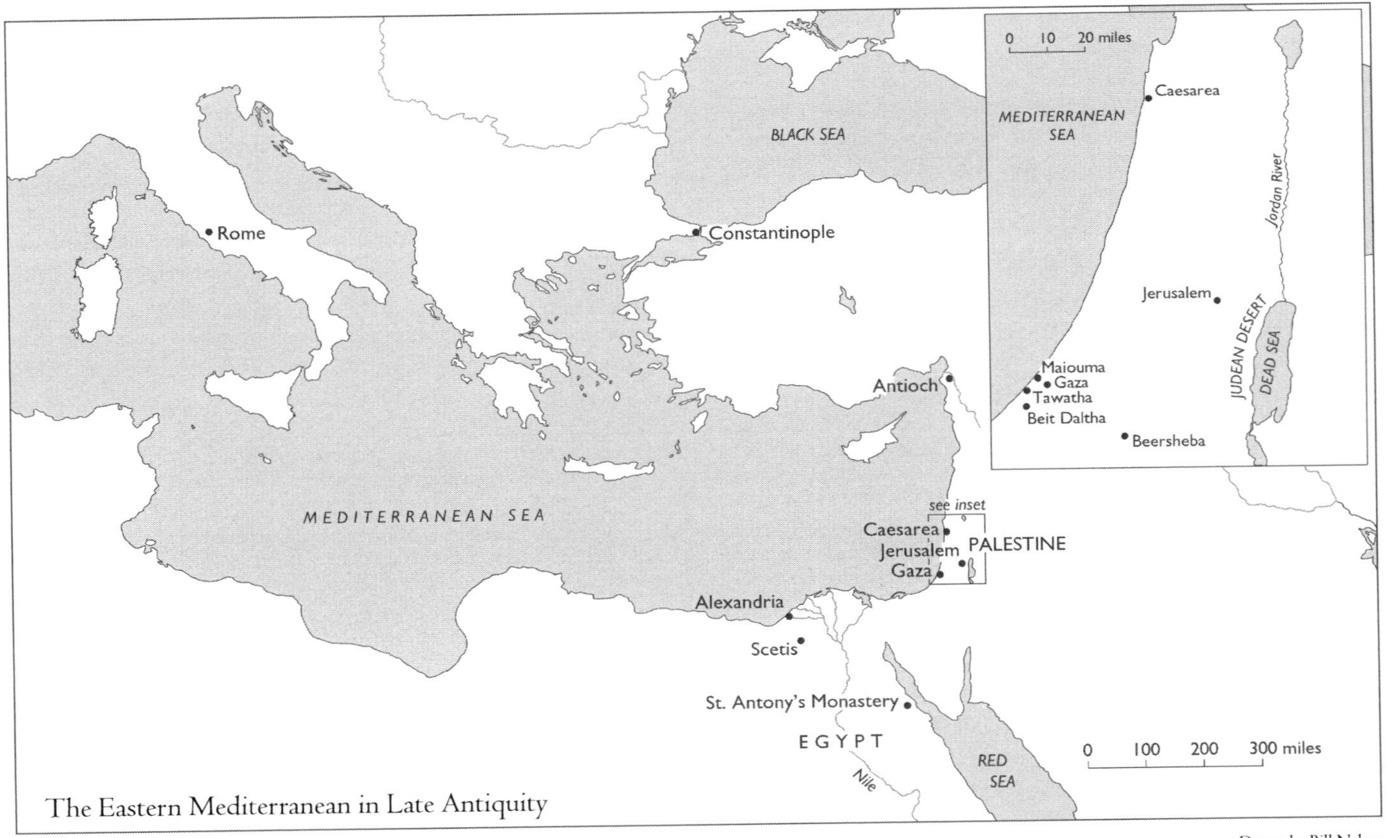
BLACK SEA
Rome
Constantinople
MEDITERRANEAN SEA
Antioch
see inset
Caesarea
Jerusalem
Gaza
PALESTINE
Alexandria
Scetis
St. Antony's Monastery
EGYPT
Nile
RED SEA
0 100 200 300 miles
0 10 20 miles
MEDITERRANEAN SEA
Caesarea
Jordan River
Jerusalem
JUDEAN DESERT
DEAD SEA
Maiouma
Gaza
Tawatha
Beit Daltha
Beersheba

The Eastern Mediterranean in Late Antiquity

Drawn by Bill Nelson

Introduction

A traveler journeying along the ancient road from Egypt to Palestine in the sixth century would have stopped for refreshment and supplies at the city of Gaza. Situated high on a hilltop overlooking the surrounding desert, late antique Gaza was a commanding cultural and economic center. In contrast to the political and religious strife that characterizes the region today, the sixth-century city was known for its bustling market-places, its lavish theater and baths, its resplendent churches adorned with mosaics, and all the other amenities of a prosperous urban center. With its port, Maiouma, a couple of miles away on the coast, Gaza served as a key commercial center, not only for its own province, Palestine I,[1] but for the entire eastern Mediterranean. The city was a major destination for spices, silk, and luxury goods coming overland by caravan from the East; these items would then be dispersed by sea to all parts of the western empire.[2] Local products, such as wine, dried fruit, and flax, were exported from Gaza to the rest of the Roman world, while wheat was imported from Egypt to feed the crowded city. Moreover, a road to the northeast led to Jerusalem, the chief center for Christian pilgrimage, only fifty miles away. Visitors to the Holy Land from all over the empire made sure to include a trip to Gaza in their itinerary, to see the ancient biblical city of Samson's last victory.

In addition to boasting urban amenities, the prosperity of late antique Gaza nurtured remarkable intellectual and cultural developments. The school of rhetoric in Gaza was famous throughout the Mediterranean world. Its distinguished orators were instrumental in bringing about a revival of rhetoric in the sixth century.[3] The rhetorician Procopius of Gaza (c. 465–528)[4] possessed both a commitment to the classical ideals of oratory and a keen interest in biblical and patristic writings. His student

Choricius used his oratorical skills to praise the splendor of Christian churches in the city, saying of one with a high, domed ceiling, "In attempting to look up to it, you will require an exercised neck, in order to stretch toward [such] a height; so it is lifted high above the ground . . . inasmuch as it imitates the appearance of heaven."[5] Choricius also defended such traditionally pagan entertainments as the theater and mimes, which Justinian would attempt to outlaw.

Alongside the flourishing rhetorical tradition and the bustling commercial activity, Gaza became the center of another late antique movement—monasticism. Had our traveler stayed in Gaza long, he might have noticed men and women making their way towards a village that lay in the southwestern desert just beyond the city. At his inquiry the inhabitants of Gaza would explain that the village of Tawatha boasted the monastery of Abbot Seridos, the home of the renowned anchorites Barsanuphius and John. Those seeking religious guidance and a life of ascetic discipline came from various parts of the world to Gaza, where they chose to live together deliberately in a spiritual community. The learning and writings generated by the inhabitants of the monastic community in Tawatha were based not upon the Greek classical works that inspired Gaza's great rhetoricians but upon the tradition of desert ascetic wisdom. With strong ties to Egyptian asceticism, monks in the Gaza region practiced both cenobitic and anchoritic monasticism. Cenobitic monks lived together, sharing in the "common life," and anchorites withdrew to live alone in desert cells but remained connected to the larger monastic community through spiritual ties and practical dependence.

The lay Christian inhabitants of Gaza and the members of the monastic community shared a common concern: they sought to apply the teachings of Christianity to the reality of daily life. Theological disputes over the relationship of Christ's humanity to his divinity and the controversial teachings of the theologian Origen (c. 185–255) echoed throughout the eastern Mediterranean in the sixth century, but within the walls of the monastery conflict also arose over the more mundane issues of preferential treatment, the abbot's authority, and monastic discipline. The surrounding lay communities, which were also frequently embroiled in disagreements (both petty and profound), looked to the monks to provide societal order and spiritual guidance. The monastic community was not seen as a retreat from the world but as a spiritual resource for the wider community. People from all walks of life came to the monks seeking answers to the dilemmas they faced each day. The modern reader will be tempted to sort their concerns into categories: familial, social, physical, and spiritual problems. For the lay Christians of the early Byzantine Empire there could be no such distinctions. They recognized that all of life was infused with the sacred. Even ordinary activities could have theological ramifications. The care of a physician did not replace a sinner's need for repentance. Patronizing pagan vendors at a festival might imply support for the accompanying religious observances. Chasing locusts from one's field could cause a broken relationship with a neighbor whose crops were subsequently devoured.

This book leads us from hilltop Gaza into the desert monastery at Tawatha, weaving together the stories of monks, bishops, city officials, and villagers. The abundant evidence of how spiritual authority actually functioned in Gaza allows us to understand better the interaction between spiritual fathers and their disciples throughout the early Byzantine world. It shows how members of spiritual communities organized themselves and constructed positions of leadership. It explores the ways in which spiritual fathers interacted with their colleagues and their disciples while engaging in the dynamic process of spiritual direction.[6] Frequent challenges to authority, a strong commitment to cooperative leadership, and ready interchange between lay and monastic Christians characterized the daily affairs of the Christian community in Gaza. The network of authority at Tawatha is a local expression of the system that undergirded spiritual authority in Christianity throughout the eastern Mediterranean.

Describing one fifth-century holy man from Palestine, historian John Binns writes: "The juxtaposition of such different environments as desert monastery, city church, and imperial court in the ministry of one man shows the close integration of the monasteries into the life and society of Palestine."[7] These diverse elements—monastery, church, and court— feature prominently in the sixth-century monastic sources from Gaza. In this region the boundaries between monastery and city appear surprisingly permeable. Lay Christians, monks, and clergy all had recourse to the same spiritual fathers. Some members of the laity embraced ascetic disciplines usually associated with monks. Anonymity was scarce in a place where everyone knew his neighbor's business. But the give and take among city, village, and monastery depended on more than just a lack of privacy; people chose to engage in conversation with one another. Communication flowed freely between the anchorites' cells and the homes of villagers and bishops. Even holy men who had made the radical vow not to see another human being face to face spent much of their time in correspondence with petitioners, willingly providing spiritual guidance to the community as a whole.

Spiritual direction was a cooperative endeavor, with both fathers and disciples actively involved as participants in a dynamic process. Monks, clergy, and lay people chose to become disciples of a particular father. Disciples were not passive recipients of guidance; rather they entered into a relationship of mutual obligation with a spiritual director. Just as fathers sought to guide their disciples, disciples sought to mold these relationships. The very act of becoming a disciple of a holy man conferred spiritual status on the supplicant. Frequently, spiritual fathers were also disciples; even renowned holy men with large followings of disciples sometimes based their authority on their own relationship with another spiritual father.

Spiritual directors belonged to a network of Christian authority. They rarely functioned as isolated leaders in a monastic community. Instead, most chose to work in concert with other leaders. In difficult situations competition between fathers could prove counterproductive for the well-being of their disciples. In more functional networks, spiritual fathers with different gifts could both complement and reinforce each other's teaching. Spiritual directors who worked together to oversee a community often assumed different roles within the leadership network. One might oversee novices, while another supervised solitaries; one might tackle interpersonal problems, while another dealt with questions of church doctrine.

Leaders faced the critical challenge of identifying the next generation of spiritual directors and developing in the new leaders the necessary skills and spiritual discernment to continue the work already begun. The choice of a successor could lead to jealousy and division within a monastic community, particularly if the person the brothers expected to be chosen was passed over.[8] A smooth transition required a period of training for the new leader and his clear identification with the established network of authority. Frequently, the monks chosen to assume positions of authority appeared initially as troublemakers, causing dissension in the community. However, a competent spiritual director could see past the early difficulties of a newcomer and recognize in his rebellion a leadership potential still undeveloped. The process of spiritual direction could accommodate challenges to authority, and with proper guidance trouble-makers could emerge as strong leaders. Successful transitions in spiritual authority from one generation to the next were critical for the continuation of monastic life and lay piety in the Eastern church.

Gaps in historical evidence are the perennial delight and frustration of an ancient historian. From fragmented records that were written in now-dead languages before the advent of paper and pen and which hint at relationships between two or three individuals, the historian extrapolates the possibility of hundreds of other human interactions. Interpreting the pieces of evidence, like rearranging the scattered tesserae of a damaged mosaic, is full of potential pitfalls and unexpected delights. From the particularly rich evidence that survives from sixth-century Gaza, it is possible to show how the components of Christian society developed in the eastern Byzantine world.

Historians who study monasticism rely on a variety of genres of texts that are often collectively referred to as hagiography.[9] Although creative work has recently been done utilizing hagiography, the nature of the material itself puts up barriers between modern historians and the people of late antiquity. Hagiographical writing was often highly stylized, with set conventions about the nature of sanctity and storytelling. The ancient audience's expectation of certain features in hagiographic accounts and the widespread ideal of the saint as imitator of Christ created an environment in which similar narratives flourished. Individuality and distinctive context were often sacrificed in the retelling of a saint's life. The task of discovering the interpersonal relationships behind the hagiography can appear daunting.

For the group of monks who lived in the desert outside the city of Gaza in the village of Tawatha, a remarkable corpus of evidence survives. Instead of hagiographical accounts of saints' activities or exhortatory treatises on asceticism, we have a collection of letters written by two anchorites, Barsanuphius and John of Gaza, to an assortment of petitioners: monks, bishops, and lay people. The letters, which number more than 850, were compiled by a sixth-century monk who belonged to the monastic community at Tawatha. This compiler selected and grouped letters by recipient, adding summaries of each petitioner's question. Through this contextualizing, the compiler certainly exercised some editorial shaping of the collection we have inherited. However, the letters of Barsanuphius and John bring us much closer to original interactions among members of the Christian community than most hagiographical texts permit. Although the letter collection preserves only one side of the original dialogue, it allows us to reconstruct the substance of many ongoing conversations. From these ancient voices we learn about the fears, concerns, and hopes of Christians living in the last century of Byzantine-ruled Palestine.

The Correspondence of Barsanuphius and John of Gaza is unique as an extant source preserving the voices of lay people, the challenges faced by monastic leaders, and the intimate interaction between clergy and ascetics. However, the often turbulent experiences of these spiritual fathers' disciples are probably far more typical than most sanitized hagiographic literature would suggest. The interaction between fathers and disciples at Gaza reveals as a dynamic process the spiritual direction prevalent throughout late antique Byzantium. Reading the letters of Barsanuphius and John allows us to hear ancient conversations between fathers and disciples, before they could be distilled by the hagiographer's pen into timeless, but static, pearls of wisdom.

The monastic community that serves as the focus of this book is the monastery of Abba Seridos. In the sixth century, at the same time when Gaza was being recognized throughout the empire for its thriving school of rhetoric, this monastery was the center of another renaissance.[10] Abba Seridos' monastery was the home of Barsanuphius and John, two of the most celebrated anchorites in Palestine and Egypt. Barsanuphius was known colloquially as the Great Old Man and his colleague John as the Other Old Man. Sought out as spiritual directors by bishops, monks, and laity, Barsanuphius and John maintained their ascetic practice by enclosing themselves in cells near the monastery. They refused to meet face to face with anyone save with the two disciples chosen to carry letters and food to and from the anchorites' cells. Although physically isolated from the crowds of disciples, the Old Men interacted freely with individual petitioners through their letters. By examining this correspondence, we can see, emerging from the anonymous crowds that flocked to late antique holy men in monastic literature, familiar voices, recognizable as individuals with distinct concerns. At the same time, these particular people serve as representatives of the larger Christian community of the sixth-century Byzantine world.

This book reconstructs the spiritual and ecclesiastical landscape of sixth-century Gaza. Historicizing monastic texts that have not been looked at before in their social and political context, this work delineates the manner in which spiritual authority was established in the monastery and the wider Christian community. In the dynamic process of spiritual direction, fathers and disciples negotiated divergent expectations and shared mutual obligations. Challenges to monastic discipline and spiritual authority were constantly voiced, requiring Barsanuphius, John, and Seridos to work to integrate dissenters into the community in order for the system of spiritual leadership they had established to flourish. Finally, for the long-term survival of the community the Old Men had to develop the next generation of monastic leaders and pass on to them their mantle of spiritual authority.

Inhabitants of Gaza in the sixth-century regarded Abbot Seridos' monastery at Tawatha as a central institution in their community. They petitioned the anchorites about practical and spiritual matters, supported the monastery's facilities with their offerings, worshiped with the monks in church, and sought help and healing from the two holy men in times of personal affliction. Having visited the city's churches, theater, and other public buildings, a visitor to Gaza might have been directed to the monastery to enjoy the hospitality of the monks in the company of other lay visitors, who had come from near and far to deliver their letters to the holy men.

CHAPTER 1

Gaza

Crossroads in the Desert

The citizens of Gaza venerated a multitude of deities. In the late fourth century, the Christian writer Mark the Deacon tells us that Gaza was adorned with many temples:

> Now there were in the city eight public temples of idols, of the Sun and of Aphrodite and of Apollo and of the Maiden and of Hecate and the temple called the Fortune of the City, which they called Tychaion, and the Marneion, which they said was the temple of the Cretan-born Zeus, which they accounted to be more famous than all the temples of the world. And there were also very many other idols in the houses and in the villages, whereof no man could reckon the number.[1]

Anyone coming into Gaza would have been impressed by these temples and, no doubt, the piety of its citizens.

Inhabited since ancient times, the Phoenician city of Gaza earned a reputation as a center for Greek culture in the Hellenistic period. As a result of Pompey's campaigns, the Romans added the city to their growing empire. The emperor Hadrian (117–38), who loved the Greek culture, visited Gaza on several occasions, and a new local calendar was established to commemorate his second visit in 129. Hadrian's attempt to impose Hellenistic culture in Palestine, by outlawing circumcision and building a temple to Zeus over the remains of the Jewish temple in Jerusalem, triggered a Jewish revolt led by the messianic figure Simeon bar Kochba. When the emperor returned to Palestine in 135 after the Bar Kochba rebellion had been suppressed, Hadrian brought captive Jews to Gaza to be put to death at newly instituted games; other Jewish prisoners were sold in the city's slave markets.[2]

The most prominent local cult in Gaza was that of the Semitic god Marnas, which gained an international reputation for the city. Marnas was a sky deity, credited with the crucial job of bringing winter rains to the arid region. His priests continued to offer public sacrifices until the end of the fourth century.[3] The Christian emperor Arcadius (395–408) was reluctant to give imperial support to efforts to Christianize the city, because the pagan landowners of Gaza paid their taxes quickly.[4] The ascetic Christian scholar Jerome in the late fourth century referred to Gaza as a recalcitrant stronghold of paganism: "At Gaza Marnas mourns in confinement, every moment expects to see his temple overturned,"[5] an event that finally came to pass when the Christian bishop Porphyry destroyed the edifice at the beginning of the fifth century.

The traditional strongly pagan character of Gaza contrasted with the largely Christian character of its smaller neighboring port, Maiouma, on the Mediterranean coast.[6] The emperor Constantine (306–37) had recognized the commitment of Gaza's harbor city to Christianity; he granted Maiouma status as an independent city with its own bishop and renamed it Constantia in honor of his sister.[7] Subsequently, the apostate emperor Julian (361–63) punished the city for its reputation as a Christian community by making Constantia/Maiouma subject once again to Gaza. Perhaps with the intention of encouraging discord among Christian leaders, Julian did permit Maiouma to retain its own bishop.[8] The fifth-century church historian Sozomen reports that some Christians in Gaza suffered martyrdom during this period.[9]

Gaza was notorious in late antiquity for conflict between pagans and Christians.[10] The struggle between Gaza and Maiouma became focused on the issue of Christianization. Crowds of Christians from the port accompanied Bishop Porphyry and a smaller group of Christians from Gaza as they marched to destroy the temples in Gaza at the beginning of the fifth century. Despite Mark the Deacon's effort to emphasize the unity of the Christians from Maiouma and Gaza behind Porphyry's leadership, the overall impression one derives from Mark's account is one of opposition between the two cities:

> At dawn we came into the seaport of the Gazeans, which they call Maioumas. And when we came ashore, the Christians there when they knew it received us with psalm-singing; and likewise also they of the city [the Christians of Gaza] when they heard it came out to

meet us . . . singing psalms. And the people from the two places were mingled together, and there was no small number; for they from the seaside [the Maioumans] were the more. . . . But they of the idol madness [the pagans of Gaza], were cut to the heart; but they dared not to do aught . . . because they heard the idols were to be over-turned; and they were sore disquieted and cast down.[11]

After the turbulent process of Christianization, which involved the suppression of public pagan worship, the two cities continued to express their rivalry in ecclesiastical affairs. Bishop Porphyry of Gaza tried to reassert the authority of his see over Maiouma, but the inhabitants of the seaport convinced a provincial council to protect their independence.[12] Long after the ferment between pagans and Christians subsided, the tensions between the two cities continued to disturb the Christian community of the region. Maiouma and Gaza took opposite sides in the christological debates that disturbed the region in the fifth and sixth centuries. The Council of Chalcedon (451), which decreed that Christ had two natures (one human and one divine) united in one person, caused serious divisions in the Eastern Church. Many Eastern Christians rejected the formula drafted at the council, because they feared it separated Christ's humanity too much from his divinity, succumbing to the Nestorian heresy. The lack of ecclesiastical concord threatened to undermine political unity in the Byzantine Empire, and emperors from the fifth to seventh century worked fervently, with little lasting success, to reach a christological position that would unify all their subjects. Throughout Palestine, ordinary lay people and monks, as well as bishops, voiced strong opinions about christological issues and the Council of Chalcedon. The rivalry between the cities of Gaza and Maiouma probably contributed to their leaders' taking opposite sides in the christological controversy. Maiouma boasted among her bishops two of the most outspoken opponents of the Council of Chalcedon in Palestine, while Gaza remained supportive of the pro-Chalcedonian patriarchs of Jerusalem.[13]

By the mid-sixth century, the large Christian community of Gaza was itself splintered into factions. Inhabitants of the city charged one bishop with corruption, accusing him of opposing God's will. Factions struggled for ecclesiastical control during an episcopal election, which sharply divided the city. Leaders from the monastery in Tawatha not only joined the debate over ecclesiastical politics but went on to rebuke Christian civil officials for their immorality and neglect of the poor.

Although Gaza had become a predominately Christian city by the sixth century, significant numbers of religious minorities remained. Christians lived in close proximity to Jewish and pagan neighbors. Social and economic ties continued to link closely members of the different faiths. Greek rhetoricians from the prestigious School of Gaza could, on the one hand, compose in classical genres that ignored the development of a Christian discourse, and on the other, praise the construction of a new church or the character of a Christian bishop. Pagans in Gaza continued to hold prominent governmental positions until the legislation of Justinian increased pressure on such men to convert to Christianity.[14] The ascetic Christian holy men Barsanuphius and John took for granted that their Christian disciples, whether in the city of Gaza or in neighboring villages, lived in religiously diverse communities. The two monks were remarkably untroubled about Christian interactions with Jews and pagans. (The presence of heretics worried them only slightly more.) No doubt these two anchorites felt a greater degree of security and self-confidence than had spiritual leaders in earlier centuries.

With concerns about Christianization in Gaza considerably dissipated in the sixth-century, the Christian population could turn to building a monastic community in which to pursue a life of prayer. In this new endeavor, Gaza joined a vigorous movement that was remaking Palestine, and much of the eastern Roman Empire with it, during late antiquity. Throughout the Mediterranean world men and women chose to leave their families and participate in new social arrangements. Anchorites lived as hermits in scattered groups of two and three, and cenobitic monks joined large well-organized monastic communities. Christian ascetics practiced a life of spiritual discipline, characterized by prayer, fasting, and celibacy.

THE MONASTIC MILIEU

Before the fourth century, Romans considered Palestine an obscure, out of the way province, notable only for rebellious uprisings if it drew attention for anything. With the conversion of Emperor Constantine to Christianity in 312 the status of the small province changed. After hastily executing his eldest son and wife, the emperor dispatched his mother Helena to the region to be a symbol of piety, and imperial patronage for the building of churches began in earnest. The Roman colony of Aelia Capitolina regained its ancient name Jerusalem and became the focus of a groundswell of Christian devotion. By the end of the fourth century, excavations had revealed what Christians of the time believed to be remains of the True Cross. As the Spanish nun Egeria noted, these relics became the focal point of the Easter liturgy in Jerusalem, which drew worshipers from across the empire.[15] Although patristic writers would continue to debate the theological question of whether an earthly place could be holy, the laity had already decided. Faithful men and women from all over the Roman world began to travel to see the land of the scriptures. Pilgrims flocked to the places associated with Christ's birth, life, death, and resurrection, as well as to many other places associated with biblical narratives from both the Old and New Testaments.[16]

Many visitors sought to extend their stay, trading their pilgrim status for settled monastic life. To house these newcomers, monasteries sprang up in Jerusalem, Bethlehem, and the surrounding areas. Monasticism in Palestine was, from the beginning, an international project, drawing men and women from Rome, Constantinople, and even Persia.[17] Aristocrats gave up comfortable lives in the empire's leading cities to embrace voluntary poverty in the land of Jesus and his disciples. Jerome, who left Rome to settle in Bethlehem in the fourth century with his ascetic colleague, the wealthy Roman widow Paula, wrote to another friend in Rome urging her to join them. He pictured "every band of monks and every troop of virgins" uniting in song to welcome her to the Holy Land where she would be taken to see the sacred places connected to the life of Christ.[18] In the mid-fifth century the Empress Eudocia, after making her first pilgrimage to Jerusalem as an imperial representative, retired from Constantinople to live in the Holy Land for almost two decades.[19] Although rumor had it that she left the capital in disgrace, her activities in Palestine earned her a reputation of great piety. She served as benefactress to many monks (even if a few accused her of disrupting their solitude). In the sixth century, a noble girl from Persia, who would later adopt the name Susan, ran away to Jerusalem, that "she should go and worship in the holy places, where the salvation of our lives took place."[20] Aristocratic women such as these valued lives of fasting and prayer more highly than the privileges and obligations of elite society. The existence of these high-status pilgrims demonstrates the attraction of the Holy Land for members of late antique society and underscores the diverse backgrounds of its monastic immigrants. Palestine was no longer a provincial backwater; it had become a place of special significance for Christians living in the Roman and Persian empires.

The Judean desert, a ten-square-mile strip of wilderness east of Jerusalem, became the center of a flourishing monastic movement during the fifth century. Two particular founders of monasticism in the region were Euthymius and Sabas.[21] The communities these men founded followed two different organizational forms. The *lavra* (literally "valley") was a loose association of monks who lived as anchorites in caves scattered along a natural ravine. They practiced asceticism individually during the week but came together in a central church for communal worship on Saturdays and Sundays. In a cenobium monks lived together in a single compound, sharing work, worship, and meals daily. The cenobium and the lavra were complementary institutions. Spiritual directors often required novices to spend time training in a cenobium before they advanced to a more solitary life in a lavra.

Monasticism in the Judean desert was closely associated with the ecclesiastical hierarchy of Jerusalem. Several bishops of Jerusalem had been trained in its monasteries, and the monks were not aloof from ecclesiastical politics. Although in the immediate aftermath of the Council of Chalcedon many lay people and monks in Palestine vehemently rejected the council for its christological settlement, the council did elevate the status of the bishopric of Jerusalem, making it a patriarchate (with Rome, Constantinople, Alexandria, and Antioch). The pro-Chalcedonian commitment of the monks of the Judean desert was instrumental in the ultimate reconciliation of the province to the church council, assuring that the see of Jerusalem would remain in communion with both Rome and Constantinople.

South of Jerusalem and the Judean desert, monasticism had another orientation. Asceticism in the region of Gaza was rooted in the deserts of Egypt. The tradition of monasticism in the village of Tawatha, where Barsanuphius and John lived, claimed for its foundation the authority of none less than the revered Egyptian holy man, St. Antony the Great (c. 251–356), through the hermit's disciple, St. Hilarion (b. 291). Hilarion's pagan parents, natives of Tawatha, had sent him to be educated by a respected grammarian in Alexandria. When Hilarion, "came to hear of the famous name of Antony which was talked about by all the people of Egypt, he was fired with a desire to see him and so he set off for the desert."[22] Hilarion embraced the lifestyle of St. Antony, but he quickly grew distressed by the crowds flocking to the holy man and returned home, distributed his wealth to the poor, and commenced a solitary monastic life in the region south of Maiouma.[23]

Like his spiritual father, Antony, Hilarion, because of his sanctity, attracted followers who disrupted his solitude. His presence encouraged the establishment of organized monasteries in the region, including the one founded by Epiphanius (c. 315–403) at Besandûk, near Eleutheropolis. After beginning the ascetic life in Egypt, Epiphanius became a disciple of Hilarion and eventually was ordained Bishop of Salamis in Cyprus.[24] Among those inhabitants of the Gaza region converted by Hilarion's healing miracles were the ancestors of the church historian Sozomen.[25]

Other figures in the fourth century linked the desert of Egypt, particularly the monasteries of Scetis, with the region of Gaza. Porphyry had traveled from his native Thessalonica to Egypt, where he spent five years as a monk in Scetis before settling in Palestine and becoming Bishop of Gaza.[26] Abba Silvanus, a Palestinian by birth, oversaw a group of monks in Scetis. He relocated his disciples first to Mt. Sinai and then established a lavra in the Gaza region.[27] Early in the fifth century many monks fled from Scetis to Palestine in the wake of internal doctrinal turmoil over Origenism and external attacks on monasteries by raiding desert tribes.[28] It may have been in Gaza that monks fleeing from Egypt first recorded the sayings of the early desert fathers.[29] Wishing to preserve the wisdom of their spiritual fathers, they compiled the *Apophthegmata Patrum*, an extensive collection of ascetic teachings, which continued to shape monastic spirituality for many generations.

Sometime between the councils of Ephesus (431) and Chalcedon (451), another Egyptian father from Scetis relocated to the Gaza region, having first tried to find a secluded retreat elsewhere in Palestine. Abba Isaiah (d. 491) settled near Tawatha in a place called Beit Daltha.[30] To achieve the seclusion he sought, Isaiah enclosed himself in a cell and refused to see any visitors. Communication with those who came to question him occurred through a disciple he had brought with him from Egypt named Peter (not to be confused with his later associate Peter the Iberian). Despite his physical isolation, Isaiah became the spiritual director for a cenobium that grew up around him.[31] This pattern of life, which Isaiah followed for almost fifty years, would become the model adopted in the next generation by Barsanuphius, also from Egypt, and his colleague, John of Gaza.[32]

Towards the end of Isaiah's life, a companion, Peter the Iberian (c. 409–c. 488), joined him, settling nearby in Tawatha for three years.[33] The two ascetics stayed in close contact, sharing food daily. Actively engaged in ecclesiastical politics, Peter the Iberian's experience differed dramatically from that of the secluded hermit. Named Narbarnugi at birth, Peter was a prince from Iberia in the Georgian region of the Caucasus, who had grown up as a royal hostage in Constantinople and had escaped to Jerusalem to become a monk. Having established a monastery between Gaza and Maiouma, he eventually became Bishop of Maiouma and an out-spoken opponent of the christological settlement reached at the Council of Chalcedon. When pro-Chalcedonian imperial policy resulted in his exile, Peter fled to Egypt.[34] Another important anti-Chalcedonian bishop, Severus of Antioch (d. 538), also spent time as a monk near Maiouma. The anti-Chalcedonian stance of many of the monks of the Gaza region contrasts strongly with the pro-Chalcedonian sentiments of inhabitants of the Judean desert. Monasticism in the region of Gaza was linked culturally and theologically with the anti-Chalcedonian monasteries in Egypt.

Living in a region steeped in monastic tradition, Barsanuphius did not boast of his own spiritual pedigree. We know that he came from Egypt, the cradle of Gazan monasticism, but neither Barsanuphius nor any of his colleagues ever mentioned the name of his own spiritual father. Instead, Barsanuphius appropriated a wider source of spiritual authority to buttress his own. He drew upon two categories of authority, that of scripture and that of the *Apophthegmata Patrum*.[35] He repeatedly quoted from these revered writings, using the phrases "as the apostle says" and "the fathers have said."

Barsanuphius so identified his own spiritual authority with that of scripture and the teachings of the desert fathers that he instructed one monk that he need read nothing except what Barsanuphius had written to him: "Meditate on these letters, and you will be saved. For you have in them, if you understand, the Old and New Testaments. And having these in your head you have no need of another book" (Letter 49).[36] The Great Old Man saw himself as part of a chain of spiritual authority, originating in Christ and passing from the apostles to the desert fathers to the fathers at Tawatha.

Barsanuphius interpreted an established tradition of spirituality in a new context. In his replies to correspondents, there are echoes of the dialogue between the Egyptian desert fathers and their disciples: "Give me a word, Abba" and "Abba, pray for me." These refrains are familiar rhetorical forms used throughout Egyptian monastic literature. However, the close links between content and form of the *Apophthegmata Patrum* and the Correspondence of Barsanuphius and John should not obscure the differences. The *Apophthegmata* represent a rich oral tradition; Barsanuphius and John communicated through written dialogue, because they had committed themselves to solitude. The *Apophthegmata* feature ascetic virtues, such as humility, obedience, and self-control, as timeless ideals shared by many monastic fathers.[37] Despite its deliberately traditional orientation, the Correspondence reveals the particularity of the two anchorites, who treated their disciples as distinct individuals. Their approach to spiritual direction demonstrated flexibility and a willingness to improvise. Monasticism at Tawatha was rooted in the earlier Egyptian practice, but Barsanuphius and his colleagues represented another stage in the development of father-disciple relationships, a stage organically connected with earlier experience but at the same time distinctive in its form.

THE LETTERS

The Correspondence of Barsanuphius and John of Gaza is a unique source for studying the dynamic interaction between spiritual fathers and their disciples, whether lay or monastic. One reason modern scholars have not fully utilized the abundant letters of Barsanuphius and John has been the lack of accessibility to the Greek text, but the recent publication of a critical edition with a French translation prepares the way for consideration of this evidence.[38] The letter collection has attracted the attention of translators, giving both historians and students better access to a critical primary source for the social world of sixth-century Byzantium.[39] Although the earliest surviving manuscript containing some of Barsanuphius and John's correspondence dates to the eleventh century,[40] the letters accurately reflect the social and religious worlds of their sixth-century composition. This portrayal is especially important because in the next century the Islamic conquests of Byzantine Palestine and Egypt would fundamentally alter the political and ecclesiastical realities of the region.[41]

A monk in the monastery during the period when Barsanuphius and John served as spiritual directors compiled the letters. This compiler claimed the rare opportunity of seeing the Great Old Man in person. When Barsanuphius became aware that some members of the community doubted his existence, he revealed himself by coming out to wash the feet of the monks (Letter 125).[42] In one public act, Barsanuphius set aside his radical physical isolation and revealed his intimate knowledge of the minds of his disciples, two themes reiterated by the compiler throughout the Correspondence. The compiler not only copied the letters of Barsanuphius and John, but he also commented upon each letter, occasionally naming the recipient, describing the situation that prompted the correspondence, and usually summarizing or quoting the original question addressed to the Old Men. This comment could be as brief as "Another pious layman asked the Great Old Man if he ought to leave his wife to become a monk" (Letter 662). In other instances the compiler volunteered far more details about the petitioner's specific situation. Many of the letters belong to series addressed to particular individuals. Thus, it is possible to reconstruct many individual narratives of suppliants seeking advice from their spiritual fathers.

The compiler brought these letters together after the deaths of the abbot Seridos and the Other Old Man, John, and the complete withdrawal of Barsanuphius from contact with the monastery (c. 543), events that will be discussed in Chapter 6. The new abbot and the community probably considered the letters a resource for advancement in spiritual discipline and perhaps even a guide for daily life in the monastery.[43] The compiler expected this use of the Correspondence by the community and warned in his prologue that the letters were written to a wide assortment of people—anchorites, cenobites, clerics, laymen, and novices—and, therefore, a response to one individual might not be applicable to another:

> For the same teachings do not suit all alike. For as in the ages of the body there are different foods for the suckling child, for the adolescent, and for one advanced in age, so also in the case of spiritual age. Often also [the Old Men] answered having regard to the infirmity of the thought of the questioner, coming down *oeconomically* to his level, so that he should not fall into despair. . . . And we must not receive as a general rule the things thus said by way of condescension

to particular people, having regard to their infirmity, but at once discern that certainly the answer given by saints was adjusted to the questioner.

A person might even outgrow advice that had been given to him at one time, "For it happens also that such a one, coming one day to his senses by the prayers of the saints, comes to a condition befitting monks, and then hears again what behooves him."[44]

The prologue draws attention to one of the striking features of the letter collection—the diversity of its audience. The compiler included letters addressed to monks, bishops, and lay Christians. The breadth of the audience gives a multidimensional portrayal of spiritual direction in Barsanuphius' circle. The perspective of lay disciples, in particular, expands on the traditional understanding of spiritual direction as an activity between monks. Individuals from all walks of life addressed the Great Old Man as "Abba" and trusted that he would provide guidance in the midst of their problems.

The Correspondence of Barsanuphius and John includes approximately 850 letters.[45] The majority of the letters are addressed to monks, either living in the cenobitic monastery or in nearby anchoritic cells. There are about fifty letters written to bishops or to others regarding episcopal elections. Over a quarter of the collection consists of letters addressed to Christians who were neither monks nor clergy. The Correspondence is almost evenly divided in volume between the two authors; it includes about fifty more letters from John than from Barsanuphius, but John's letters tend to be shorter.[46] Barsanuphius wrote in a more formal style than did his colleague, referring frequently to scripture and to the sayings of the desert fathers. John's letters tended to deal with more practical matters, offering concise, direct advice. Petitioners occasionally asked John for clarification of the more abstract spiritual direction given by Barsanuphius.

The compiler arranged the letters within the collection by recipient. Letters to named recipients, mostly anchorites, come first in the collection, followed by a larger number of letters to unnamed monks in the cenobium. Next are the letters to unnamed lay people, and the collection concludes with letters to bishops. Although, as a whole, the letter collection is not arranged in chronological order, within the collection there are many series of letters to individuals in which the letters are arranged chronologically and thus capture the unfolding interaction between spiritual father and disciple. Many of these series reply to a disciple's successive questions on the same subject; other letters cover unrelated topics and were grouped together only because the same petitioner brought the questions.

The letters of Barsanuphius and John provide a unique view of early Byzantine asceticism. Each letter captures both a specific moment in time and the response to the query of an individual petitioner. Although the compiler's summaries of the petitions often leave the historian hungry for more information, they constitute, nevertheless, an unusual window into the lives of sixth-century Christians. Indeed, there are few parallels for viewing lay spirituality in this period.[47] The letters provide insight into the process of spiritual direction. They more closely resemble actual dialogue between spiritual director and disciple than do the conversations preserved in hagiographic texts or ascetic exhortations.[48] The Correspondence also acts as a record of a system of spiritual authority, capturing the interaction between spiritual directors and their disciples in written dialogue.

LETTER WRITING AMONG THE DESERT FATHERS

Barsanuphius' decision to live in physical isolation with an active schedule of epistolary instruction was a new resolution to St. Antony's dilemma of whether to instruct the crowds or withdraw from social interaction.[49] Although separated from direct human contact, the Old Men of Gaza were intimately connected with the concerns of the inhabitants of the region. Their practice of spiritual direction through the medium of written correspondence was not new. Several fourth-century Egyptian desert fathers wrote letters to individual disciples and groups of monks under their direction, including John the Hermit, Paphnutius, and Nepheros.[50] However, the Correspondence of Barsanuphius and John contains a more detailed record of the method of spiritual oversight only alluded to in references to earlier letter-writing fathers.

John the Hermit's oversight of monasteries, mentioned in the *Historia monachorum*, serves as a precedent for the form of monastic governance practiced in Tawatha. As an anchorite in Egypt he wrote letters to hermitages, which were under his supervision but which also had superiors on site.[51] The letters to another Egyptian monk, Paphnutius, from petitioners requesting prayer and healing show a monk serving as spiritual father for a wide variety of lay people, as Barsanuphius and John did for the inhabitants of Tawatha.[52] Lay people also wrote to the Egyptian monk Nepheros who oversaw a "spiritual family" of disciples.[53]

Both Antony and Pachomius, the preeminent models for Egyptian monasticism, wrote letters. Pachomius wrote to the leaders of the monasteries he had established. He and his successors also wrote letters to convene the annual assembly of the Pachomian monks or to invite the brothers to come together for Easter.[54] In some of his letters, Pachomius used mysterious code to communicate with select disciples. This practice contrasts sharply with Barsanuphius' refusal to write in cipher (Letter 132) (see Chapter 2). Antony wrote to groups of monks whom he called "beloved sons in the Lord" and "beloved brothers," but his letters provide few details about the organization of the communities in which they lived.[55] One letter addressed brothers in a specific location, "at Arsinoë and its neighborhood," and also expanded the intended audience to include women and perhaps laity: "All of you who have prepared yourself to come to God, I greet you in the Lord, my beloved, the young and the old, men and women, Israelite children, saints in your spiritual essence."[56] Despite unanswered questions about the identity of the letters' recipients, it is clear that Antony expected his audience to recognize his spiritual authority. Indeed, he chose the highest source authority—scripture—as his model. His letters follow the structure and style of Paul's epistles, and Antony occasionally spoke with the actual words of the apostle.[57] The letters are open works of spiritual exhortation and do not appear to respond to specific questions posed by disciples.

Other ancient sources assumed that a father of Antony's stature must have written letters to disciples and on their behalf. Jerome attributed to Antony a correspondence with Hilarion, who had settled near Gaza.[58] Athanasius' *Life of Antony* depicts the anchorite reluctantly replying to the letters of emperors who had sought spiritual counsel and intervening by letter with a military commander on behalf of monastics suffering Arian persecution.[59] The Christian emperors desired Antony's advice, but the commander responded to it with insults, throwing the letter on the ground and spitting upon it. He refused to heed the anchorite's warning, and soon he suffered a gruesome death. The dramatically different attitudes of these powerful men towards the letters of Antony provided more humble recipients of the desert father's spiritual advice clear models for their own behavior. Athanasius' depiction of Antony as reluctant to engage in correspondence with the emperors is reinforced in other hagiographical writings. The author of the *Life of Pachomius* has Antony saying:

> When they heard that I had come to the outer mountain, many groups and crowds, besieging one another with importune requests, would come running to us and persist in demanding that I write the authorities and the judges concerning their requests. But I saw that there was no profit in this as far as our vocation is concerned.[60]

The saint's ambivalence about exercising power through engaging in correspondence with the political elite belongs to the *topos* of monastic humility essential to the conventions of hagiography. In late antique society letter writing was a tool that helped the elite to form networks and exercise influence. For hagiographical purposes it was sometimes necessary to construct the image of holy men as unable or unwilling to engage in such correspondence.

A different image of holy men emerges from the teachings of Barsanuphius and John. They were deeply involved in the lives of their disciples, including prominent lay and ecclesiastical leaders, responding to the various controversies of their time. They were not engrossed in dialogue for polemical purposes but remained primarily concerned for the spiritual condition of their disciples. A particularity of person, place, and time is clearly present in their correspondence but lacking in the letters of earlier spiritual fathers.

ORIGENISM AND THE COUNCIL OF CHALCEDON

The monks of Palestine were often actively involved in the theological controversies that disrupted the region during the fifth and sixth centuries. Monastic opposition was the first challenge leveled at the Chalcedonian settlement after the Bishop of Jerusalem, Juvenal, returned home from the Council of Chalcedon (with his new status as patriarch affirmed by the council). The monasteries of the Judean desert also became centers of the struggle over the teachings of the third-century theologian Origen. Teaching catechumens in Alexandria, Origen had freely speculated about the subordination of the Son to the Father, the preexistence of souls, and the possibility that even the devil could be redeemed. Trained in the doctrines carefully established by church councils since

Origen's time, many Christians in the sixth century found these early ideas heretical. The role played by Barsanuphius in these controversies is not as obvious as that of other monastic leaders, such as Sabas and Peter the Iberian. After the death of Barsanuphius, Byzantine writers defended the theology of the Great Old Man and members of his circle against charges of heterodoxy. A closer look at some of the letters from the collection will provide the information needed to situate Barsanuphius in the ongoing debates over the teachings of Origen and the Council of Chalcedon.

The controversy over Origenism disrupted monastic life in sixth-century Palestine. Cyril of Scythopolis is the major historical source for description of the conflict.[61] The charge of Origenism was first raised against some members of one monastery in the Judean desert, the New Lavra, whom Cyril described as being "more lettered" than the rest.[62] The Origenist monks were expelled from the New Lavra around 514 and went to the region of Eleutheropolis and Ascalon. There they were able to proselytize because of the relative weakness of the patriarch of Jerusalem in the area. It is possible that monks near Gaza heard of the teachings of Origen from the monks expelled from the New Lavra. The monks at Tawatha, however, did not depend on hearsay alone for their discussions on the teachings of Origen. They too were "lettered" and read for themselves the works of Origen and Didymus, the *Kephalia Gnostica* of Evagrius, and other writings by Evagrius' disciples (Letter 600).[63] When the brothers approached their spiritual father Barsanuphius with questions about these texts, they came armed with quotations, asking for explanation.

The Great Old Man refused to discuss preexistent souls or the duration of the final punishment, two topics avidly discussed in Origenist circles: "These are the teachings of the Greeks. These are the idle words of men who think they are somebody!" (Letter 600). In place of such speculation, he advised them to "walk in the footsteps of the fathers," practicing humility, obedience, tears, asceticism, poverty, and detachment (Letter 600).[64] Barsanuphius, according to his habit, brought the attention of his disciples back to the practical task at hand—their own spiritual formation. In the place of controversial writings, he suggested, they should read the *Sayings* and *Lives* of the fathers. Barsanuphius did not attempt to limit his disciples' exposure to controversial writings or persons; instead he maintained an open dialogue with the monks on their thoughts and readings.

The monks continued both to discuss doctrine with Origenists and to read from other church fathers in the monastic library in Tawatha. They wondered how Gregory of Nazianzus, Basil of Caesarea, and Gregory of Nyssa, church fathers with great reputations for orthodoxy, could discuss the preexistence of souls, the very doctrine associated with the heresy of Origenism (Letter 604). Barsanuphius explained, emphasizing the crucial relationship between master and disciple: even the most holy men, those saints who frequently spoke under the inspiration of the Holy Spirit, had absorbed certain teachings from their masters that were unreliable. By not recognizing which teachings came from human authority and which from divine, these men lent their names to unworthy doctrines. Thus Barsanuphius confirmed that the spiritual authority of the master was of great importance, no matter the degree of holiness attained by a disciple.

In contrast to his clear teaching against Origenism, Barsanuphius' stance in the ongoing christological controversy remained ambiguous. His widely acknowledged sanctity caused Greek and Roman churches to venerate him, although his reticence on the divisive issue of Christology created confusion about his orthodoxy. It is unusual in fifth or sixth-century Palestine to find an important Christian leader and spiritual director whose allegiance in the Chalcedonian debates cannot be easily categorized. More common is the Bishop of Maiouma, John Rufus, who in his writings drew explicit connections between ascetic sanctity and anti-Chalcedonian Christology, or the monk Sabas, who at the age of eighteen chose for his spiritual father the man who had recently convinced the empress Eudocia to be reconciled with the pro-Chalcedonian patriarch.[65]

Although Barsanuphius chose not to engage in debates concerning Christology, some of his disciples did. Both anchorites and lay Christians questioned Barsanuphius about the controversy. An elderly anchorite named Paul, whom Barsanuphius characterized as, "unable to examine the things concerning the faith" (Letter 58), wrote to the Great Old Man for help in his discussions with others about the true faith. Paul lamented, "Since the days of my childhood I have accepted the faith of the 318 fathers and never received any other teaching than this, and I am troubled" (Letter 58). The "faith of the 318 fathers" is a reference to the Council of Nicaea (325); it served as a slogan for the non-Chalcedonians, who refused to accept the authority of the new council on the grounds that it had added to the creed established at the first ecumenical council.

25

This reference to Nicaea situates these letters in the context of the christological debates. Barsanuphius recognized that some people were able to dispute with heretics without jeopardizing their inner peace, but he urged Paul to let "God judge the hidden things of men" (Letter 58; Rom. 2:16) and to focus instead upon his own sins. In making this recommendation, Barsanuphius followed his usual method of spiritual direction, not allowing theological speculations to distract his disciples from their task of personal spiritual discipline. While discouraging Paul from debating theological opponents, Barsanuphius revealed his own stance in the heated controversy: "For the rest, brother, since searching in other matters is above you, keep to 'the royal road,' I speak of the faith of the 318 fathers, in which you were also baptized. For it contains everything with exactness for those who understand its perfection" (Letter 58). Barsanuphius neither condemned nor defended the Chalcedonian settlement, although his rhetoric may have made him welcome in the group that opposed Chalcedon on the basis that it was a harmful innovation.

Barsanuphius also exchanged letters with a layman "concerned with his soul," who had inquired about participating in theological debate (Letter 693). The layman, whose high status as a disciple allowed him to sit with the fathers when they discussed the faith with one "whose thought was not orthodox," asked Barsanuphius if he could join the conversation (Letter 694). The Great Old Man did not allow him to dispute the faith and warned him not to condemn in his heart those who debated theology, since he did not know "if they spoke rightly or not or how God judges the thing" (Letter 694).

The man persisted in his inquiry, wondering if the same instructions held true if the heretic was winning the debate. Barsanuphius dissuaded him from speaking without authority and urged him to have recourse to God, praying for "the faith and for our brothers . . . that all men might be saved and come to the knowledge of the life" (Letter 695; 1 Tim. 2:4). Very determined, the man countered by asking if he might at least study the church decrees so that he should not doubt the faith. Barsanuphius warned him not to read these "dangerous sentences" and instructed the man to be satisfied with "the confession of the orthodox faith" (Letter 696). This exchange demonstrates the ongoing dialogue that characterized Barsanuphius' relationships with disciples.

Barsanuphius discouraged the lay person from involving himself in theological disputes between monastic fathers and those who were "unorthodox." This starkly contrasts with the attitude of earlier spiritual fathers from Gaza, such as John Rufus, who praised a layman who prevailed against a priest in an ordeal by fire to settle their doctrinal differences.[66] Barsanuphius' lay disciple must have possessed considerable spiritual status, if the fathers were willing to have him join in their theological dialogue. The disciple was confident in his own intellectual powers, since he assumed that he would understand the church decrees if he read them and would be able contribute to the debate when the heretics were besting the fathers. Barsanuphius' warning was twofold: not only did the layman not have the proper spiritual authority to debate theology, but he also needed to remember that God alone could judge some matters. Instead of trusting in the written decrees, Christians should cling to "the orthodox confession of faith," a reference to the Nicene Creed, with which the disciple would have been familiar from reciting it regularly in the liturgy.

Other questions from the layman strengthen the identification of this theological debate with the ongoing christological controversy. He asked if he should comply if someone demanded that he anathematize Nestorius and "the heretics of his party" (Letter 699).[67] Anti-Chalcedonians regularly charged their Chalcedonian opponents with having acquiesced to the heresy of Nestorius.[68] Barsanuphius replied to the layman: "It is clear that Nestorius and the heretics of his party are under anathema, but do not hurry at all to anathematize such a one, because the one who considers himself a sinner must cry for his sins without getting entangled with other things. It is not necessary to judge those who anathematize someone, because each must examine himself" (Letter 699; 1 Cor. 11:28). While acknowledging the heresy of Nestorius, Barsanuphius continued to instruct his disciples to focus on their own sins, rather than become obsessed with debate. They were to abstain from such disputes, but they were not to condemn those who chose one side or another. The disciple should not worry that men might judge him for not taking a position in the debate; instead he should worry that God might condemn him for failing to keep his commandments (Letter 700). Once again, the Great Old Man drew those in his circle away from controversial stances.

The lay disciple again protested: What should he do if he did not even know the person he was being told to anathematize? This question admits the possibility that Nestorius' name was being used to condemn a much wider group of individuals. In his response Barsanuphius revealed his own position in the ongoing controversy: "Tell him, 'Brother, I do not know

27

what that one of whom you speak thinks. To anathematize someone whom I do not know seems to me a matter deserving condemnation. This I can tell you: I know no other faith than that of the 318 fathers and that the one who thinks differently throws himself under the anathema' " (Letter 701).

Barsanuphius refused to be caught up in the debate over Chalcedon, affirming only his allegiance to Nicaea. In the context of christological perspectives in fifth- and sixth-century Palestine, this placed him firmly in the middle of the christological continuum, equally opposed to radical pro- and anti-Chalcedonian camps. Barsanuphius' rhetoric, constantly appealing to Nicaea and admitting that the "party of Nestorius" deserved condemnation, positioned him near the moderate non-Chalcedonian faction. However, his refusal to enthusiastically anathematize heretics associated with Nestorius allied him with the moderate camp that accepted Chalcedon but was loath to divide the church over the issue. Furthermore, in a controversial episcopal election in Gaza, Barsanuphius firmly supported the authority of a Chalcedonian patriarch of Jerusalem (see Chapter 5).

The example of Barsanuphius, who used the rhetoric of the non-Chalcedonians while urging others to follow the leadership of a Chalcedonian patriarch, reveals the complexity of the sixth-century christological debates. The well-known partisan commitments of monastic leaders like Sabas, John Rufus, and Peter the Iberian should not overshadow the less radical opinions of members of the monastic and ecclesiastical hierarchies. Barsanuphius disliked the innovation represented by the Chalcedonian settlement yet urged the people of Gaza to submit to the Chalcedonian patriarch. He discouraged his disciples from debating theology or condemning those suspected of heresy. Motivated by his deep belief that such debate disrupted the process of spiritual direction, he refused to become involved in the controversy. Barsanuphius' strong determination to help his disciples avoid doctrinal controversies grew out of his ascetic theology, which gave precedence to the individual Christian's struggle against sin.[69] This moderation regarding ecclesiastical controversy on the part of a powerful spiritual leader would later create suspicion about Barsanuphius' own orthodoxy.

BARSANUPHIUS IN LATER TRADITION

Little is recorded about the monastery at Tawatha after leadership passed to the new abbot, Aelianos, in the mid-sixth century, although the Old

Men of Gaza continued to be remembered in monastic tradition.[70] A brief reference to the monastery of Abba Seridos near Gaza appears in the seventh-century *Life of St. John the Almsgiver,* composed by Leontius of Neapolis.[71] In 600 John Moschus mentioned the monastery of Dorotheos near to Gaza and Maiouma; this may have been the monastery of Seridos at Tawatha or possibly another founded later by Dorotheos. When Evagrius Scholasticus wrote his *Ecclesiastical History* at the end of the sixth century, no one had communicated with Barsanuphius for more than fifty years, but many believed that he still lived. Evagrius recorded an incident that took place during the patriarchate of Eustochious of Jerusalem (c. 552–63). In an attempt to silence claims that the holy man was alive, the patriarch ordered that Barsanuphius' cell be destroyed. However, the project was abandoned when a mysterious burst of flame from the cell prevented the workers' approach.[72] That the patriarch, who was so busy suppressing Origenism in Palestine that he could not even attend the Council of Constantinople in 553, eagerly sought to disprove the rumors that the holy man lived demonstrates that Barsanuphius became a controversial figure within a short time after his complete enclosure.[73]

Barsanuphius' reputation in the East remained entangled with controversy. The names Barsanuphius, Isaiah, and Dorotheos were associated with heresy.[74] The defenders of the holy men of Gaza argued that multiple individuals bore each name. They distinguished the fathers of Gaza from other persons with the same names whom Sophronius, Archbishop of Jerusalem (634–38), condemned in his letter to Patriarch Sergius.[75] When Pope Leo III (d. 816) accused Theodore the Studite (759–826) of admitting the heretics (Isaiah, Barsanuphius, and Dorotheos) to the ranks of the saints, Theodore proclaimed that there were already three saints by these names, as well as three heretics.[76] Barsanuphius' ambiguity over christological issues probably caused some to charge him and his colleagues with heresy. An anonymous preface to the *Discourses* of Dorotheos cited Theodore's defense of the orthodoxy of the fathers of Gaza along with an affirmation of their orthodoxy by Patriarch Tarasios (c. 730–806).[77] The preface identifies the heresy in question with the "error of Severus," namely the rejection of Chalcedon. The author of the preface emphasized that both Greek and Oriental authorities affirmed the orthodoxy of Barsanuphius and Dorotheos, combating the argument that only local congregations accepted them. Furthermore, the preface claimed that an altar cloth in the Hagia Sophia Church in Constantinople bore the image of Barsanuphius, alongside those of St. Antony and St. Ephrem.[78] For Byzantine writers this was ultimate proof of the Great Old Man's orthodoxy and stature in the church.

Barsanuphius' reticence on Christology contributed to later speculations about his orthodoxy. Such reticence arose from his belief that theological debate was a source of distraction for many monks and lay Christians. As a spiritual director, he was acutely aware of the obstacles hindering true spiritual discipline. Rather than become entangled in dangerous debates, a disciple should depend upon his spiritual father for correct doctrine. Barsanuphius recognized that a well-founded system of spiritual authority guaranteed not only right doctrine but also progress in the spiritual life for all members of the community.

THE NATURE OF DIRECTION OFFERED BY THE OLD MEN OF GAZA

Barsanuphius and John addressed a wide range of practical issues associated with community life. Their spiritual direction was holistic; they dealt with the spiritual, social, moral, and physical dimensions of their supplicants' problems. Those who came hoping for quick answers to specific questions were often reminded of aspects of their situation they had not necessarily wished to bring to the Old Men's attention. Of highest concern to Barsanuphius and John as spiritual directors was their disciples' own awareness of sin. At a time when other spiritual directors placed great emphasis on correct christological statements as the ultimate proof of holiness, Barsanuphius and John were concerned that their disciples not be tempted into either anxiety or complacency concerning the ongoing disputes. Complex issues of doctrine, they stated, should be left to those who had already attained spiritual perfection. The Old Men urged their disciples not to be distracted from their task. Striving for sanctity was a long process that demanded perseverance. They wished their disciples to concentrate on this purpose alone, rather than allow themselves to be carried away with each torrent of controversy (theological or otherwise) that swept through the community. In his survey of spirituality, Simon Tugwell describes the spiritual direction of Barsanuphius and John as, "defusing one drama after another with relentless common sense."[79]

Glimpsing the comprehensive commitment required in submitting to spiritual direction, some disciples returned repeatedly with questions, trying to nail down piece by piece what exactly was expected of them. The repetitive character of some disciples' questions reveals the tediousness that can be part of the process of spiritual direction. No hagiographer molded the material to create climax and resolution for each disciple's spiritual journey. Barsanuphius and John's interaction with their disciples shows individuals succumbing to the same pitfalls over and over again. The Old Men were invariably patient with sinners caught in habits that were undesirable yet comfortable.

In the Correspondence, the petitioners appear to be ordinary people; so also the holy men seem less extraordinary than those presented in most saints' lives. In hagiography miracles demonstrate to the audience that God has granted authority to the saint.[80] Barsanuphius and John's spiritual authority was also confirmed by supernatural signs: they knew each other's thoughts, they knew what transpired in the monastery and abroad without having been told, and they occasionally performed miraculous healings. However, they were not primarily wonder-workers. Their spiritual power did not depend upon visible miracles. The spiritual authority of Barsanuphius and John was rooted in their relationship with God. Petitioners believed that the anchorites were the highest human authorities in a divinely based spiritual network. Supplicants regularly sought out the prayers of Barsanuphius and John, believing them to be efficacious, even without visible signs.

CHAPTER 2

Tawatha

Looking for God in the Desert

On the floor of a sixth-century Byzantine church in Madaba, Jordan, artisans constructed an elaborate mosaic map of the Holy Land.[1] The map includes cities and towns, geographical features, such as the Jordan River (complete with swimming fish), and holy sites, such as Oak of Mambre and Jacob's Well, where Jesus met the Samaritan woman. Cities are depicted with intricate architectural detail, including gates, colonnaded streets, churches, and fountains. To the south of the walled city of Gaza on the map, lies a small, square tower labeled Tawatha. The tower represents a village situated about five miles southwest of Gaza on the bank of the wadi. Travelers and merchants who passed between Palestine and Egypt came through Gaza, but beginning in the fourth century the village of Tawatha achieved fame for its own connections with Egypt. A number of ascetic luminaries with Egyptian pedigrees called the village home. Tawatha's most famous native son was St. Hilarion (c. 291–c. 371), who trained in the ascetic life as a disciple of St. Antony in Egypt. He later returned to the silence of the desert region south of Gaza in order to escape the bustle of crowds that flocked to see Antony.[2] In the fifth century the spiritual connection between the monastic circles of Egypt and Tawatha continued to grow. Abba Isaiah came from Scetis and lived near Tawatha for almost fifty years. Later his friend Peter the Iberian chose the village as his ascetic retreat.[3]

So, when Barsanuphius came to the Gaza region and settled in Tawatha, he had chosen a village with an established tradition of welcoming Egyptian ascetics. We do not know whether Barsanuphius built his own cell or found one left empty by another anchorite. Cells in the Gaza region probably resembled early cells excavated in Egypt, having two rooms, a smaller one for sleeping and a larger area, called an oratory, for

Detail from a mosaic map of the Holy Land in Madaba, Jordan. The large city depicted on the left, with its colonnaded streets and theater clearly visible, is Gaza. The small tower just to the right of Gaza represents the village of Tawatha. This map, like others from the period, is oriented with east at the top. Photo: Studium Biblicum Franciscanum Archive, Jerusalem.

prayer. The rooms had low, vaulted ceilings made of brick; wall niches held objects, such as a book or a lamp. Walls were sometimes decorated with images, including the cross, and inscribed with prayers to aid the monk's devotion.[4]

Already residing in a cell in the vicinity was an old anchorite named Euthymius. He and Barsanuphius began a lengthy correspondence and became close associates.[5] Barsanphius adopted the practice of his predecessor in the region, Isaiah of Scetis, and lived in complete physical isolation in his cell, relying on a disciple to convey his correspondence. For his disciple Barsanuphius chose Seridos, who at some point also

33

served as abbot for a cenobitic monastery in Tawatha. Although little is known about the origin of their partnership, Barsanuphius hints at how their relationship began: "For how many desired us old men, and they ran, and to them it was not given! And while [Seridos] was residing, God sent us to him, and made him our true child" (Letter 17).[6] If Barsanuphius' statement refers to geography, it may suggest that Seridos was living in Tawatha when Barsanuphius arrived, but it does not specify that Seridos was already an abbot. It is also unclear whether a cenobitic monastery existed in Tawatha before Barsanuphius settled there, or whether Barsanuphius himself attracted monks to the area.[7] It is certain, however, that by making the abbot his intermediary (or, if no monastery previously existed, by making his intermediary the abbot of a new cenobium) Barsanuphius established a system of spiritual authority that would prove quite durable.

The monastery at Tawatha consisted of a cenobium, where monks lived together, surrounded by scattered desert cells, where anchorites lived alone or with a disciple to serve them. Although there has been comparatively little archaeological excavation in Gaza, the remains of monasteries excavated in the Judean desert and in Egypt offer useful comparisons to supplement the documentary evidence.[8] The cenobium at Tawatha consisted of some central buildings containing common space. A church provided a place for communal worship, which was led by members of the monastery ordained as priests and deacons. A burial chamber may have been located near the church to house the tombs of deceased monks.[9] The church probably opened onto a central courtyard, which could be used for liturgical functions as well as provide a central meeting place. Cisterns, often located in the courtyard, collected rainwater, although new monks were often given the task of carrying water from a more distant source.[10] A library housed the monastery's books and may have had a separate room for use as a scriptorium, where some monks were given the task of copying manuscripts.[11] The sleeping areas of cenobitic monks consisted of either dormitories, where monks slept in a common room (as legislated by Justinian), or rows of individual cells, often located on the second floor of a monastery.[12] While anchorites ate alone in their cells, cenobitic monks gathered in a refectory to share a cooked meal together once or twice a day. A kitchen was probably attached to the refectory, where monks served for a term as cook, preparing lentils or other legumes for their brothers (in some communities this duty rotated weekly, in others yearly). Near the kitchen was a granary for storing wheat and a bakery with an oven (fueled by wood gathered in the desert) for baking bread, the staple of the monastic diet. Round loaves were baked in large quantities, and those designated for use in the Eucharistic liturgy were marked with a cross. Most monasteries had gardens to supply vegetables, and where conditions were favorable some had extensive orchards, which produced figs, dates, and olives, and vineyards yielding grapes. Monks worked together tending these crops and used stone presses to convert their produce to oil and wine.[13]

Seridos built a guesthouse at Tawatha to accommodate visitors, who were fed from the monastery's resources. Stables housed the horses, camels, or other beasts of visitors, along with the monastery's donkeys, which were used to transport grain and other supplies. An infirmary provided medical care to sick monks and lay people. The entire cenobium was surrounded by a wall, which may have been fortified by a tower. The monk who served as porter oversaw those coming and going through the monastery's gate.

Around 525 an old friend of Barsanuphius joined the monastic enterprise under way at Tawatha. In a striking gesture of hospitality, Barsanuphius gave the newcomer, John, his own cell and built another one nearby. John followed the pattern of Barsanuphius' life, living in complete solitude and speaking only through a disciple who served as his intermediary. The two anchorites lived in these neighboring cells in the desert for eighteen years (Letter 599b). Their reclusive lives of prayer and fasting attracted considerable attention. Local inhabitants eventually began to call Barsanuphius the "Great Old Man" and to refer to his colleague John as the "Other Old Man." Their holiness drew many disciples, and Barsanuphius and John became renowned as spiritual directors.

Because the Old Men communicated with the outside world (which included, but was not limited to the cenobium, the village of Tawatha, and the city of Gaza) only through letters, the "sayings" that people requested of desert fathers found a new mode of expression with these anchorites. The old custom of disciples asking their spiritual fathers for a "word" of exhortation took on tangible shape. The "words" of Barsanuphius and John were written in ink on plentiful Egyptian papyrus. Monasticism in Tawatha was a literate discipline; the hundreds seeking spiritual guidance had to address their petitions to the Old Men in writing. Barsanuphius and John, heirs of an ancient oral culture, preserved and transformed the dialogue of the desert by committing it to writing.

Spiritual authority in this community was a cooperative endeavor. Three men exercised spiritual leadership in Tawatha: the Great Old Man, Barsanuphius; the Other Old Man, John; and the abbot of the cenobium, Seridos. This rule by three spiritual fathers set the monastery at Tawatha apart; most monasteries in Egypt and Palestine were governed by a single abbot. In some cases an anchorite would found a monastery, appoint an abbot to direct monks there, and then withdraw to a more remote cell. However, Barsanuphius and John remained more intimately involved with the community at Tawatha than did most anchorites associated with cenobia.[14] Beneath the Old Men and Seridos were other fathers, experienced monks living as hermits in cells scattered through the area. These monastic fathers were associated with the cenobium, and some had their own disciples. Although the monks in Tawatha looked to Barsanuphius as the ultimate human authority in spiritual matters, as his title "The Great Old Man" implies, Barsanuphius worked in close cooperation with John and Seridos, delegating to them oversight of many practical affairs. The Correspondence of Barsanuphius and John presents as its ideal a stable network of leadership, in which the charisma of the anchorites upheld the abbot's rule, each father reinforcing the authority of the others. The governing hierarchy of the monastery, however, was not as unassailable as this idealized image. Members of the community frequently sought to challenge this system of authority. Some tried to bypass the abbot, seeking a decision directly from Barsanuphius and John. Others attempted to capitalize on possible differences of opinion between the two Old Men, wishing to obey the father who offered easier advice. Despite such challenges to their authority, the unusual system of leadership crafted by Barsanuphius and his colleagues remained surprisingly successful.

BARSANUPHIUS AND JOHN

The two anchorites Barsanuphius and John collaborated in their exercise of spiritual authority over the monastic community and the lay Christians of Gaza. John, who was referred to as "John the Prophet"[15] or "John of Gaza," was both Barsanuphius' colleague and his disciple. John acted independently as a spiritual director in Tawatha, answering questions with complete authority, yet he avoided all semblance of competition with his mentor by openly placing himself beneath Barsanuphius' authority. He frequently referred vacillating supplicants to the wisdom of the Great Old Man. His deference was self-imposed, since Barsanuphius never asserted his own authority over John. Despite living in separate cells and never discussing matters together, the two anchorites were always of one mind. Barsanuphius and John claimed to know the questions addressed to the other without reliance on oral conversation.[16]

The monk who compiled the Correspondence stressed that John and Barsanuphius knew each other's thoughts without speaking or the agency of a human go-between (i.e., the abbot). In pointing this out, the compiler wished to emphasize that their wisdom came from God.[17] The secluded anchorites' knowledge of specific details about human activity within the cenobium substantiated the claim that God spoke directly to Barsanuphius and John. The belief that they received regular divine revelations about members of the community strengthened the anchorites' authority, because, had the abbot been the one who had informed the Old Men of a dispute within the monastery, the monks involved might doubt the impartiality of his reporting. However, since God had chosen to enlighten the holy men directly, the participants did not dare to dispute the counsel subsequently given.

Communicating mentally reinforced the image of absolute unity that John and Barsanuphius cultivated and buttressed their claim to speak for God. In another example, a petitioner, dissatisfied with John's response, asked the same question of Barsanuphius without mentioning that he had already approached John on the subject. Barsanuphius instructed him to do what John had already advised. When the monk repeated this behavior on another occasion, Barsanuphius replied, "The God of Barsanuphius and the God of John are one!" (Letter 224).

This was not an isolated incident, nor was Barsanuphius always the one to reinforce John's advice. The two spiritual directors frequently referred their petitioners to suggestions the other had already made (Letters 224 and 225). John urged one monk not to neglect the commands of the Great Old Man, since although he himself may have spoken idly before, "all [the words] that the Old Man has said and says to you . . . are from the Holy Spirit" (Letter 462). When a layman questioned John's readiness to refer petitioners to Barsanuphius, John even dared to compare his relationship with Barsanuphius to that of Christ with God the Father (Letter 783).

Christ said, "My father is greater than I" (John 14:28); but he also said, "I do nothing of myself, but my father, who lives in me, does his works" (John 14:10). John of Gaza's bold comparison of himself and Barsanuphius to persons of the Trinity emphasized both his own willing submission to his colleague and the essential unity of the two Old Men.

The unified voice of the two ascetics was the product of long years of close cooperation supervising the spiritual development of monks and lay Christians. They instructed their disciples to recognize them as partners; they frowned on those who tried to play one against the other or who sought a lighter judgment from one father. The monk who compiled the Correspondence shared the anchorites' desire to present an image of unanimity. He depicted their partnership as timeless and unchanging. However, one series of letters sheds light on how the two old men began their partnership. Barsanuphius wrote to a certain John of Beersheba, assumed by most scholars to be a separate person from John the Prophet, of whom we have been speaking here.[18] Although the evidence ultimately remains inconclusive, there are enough hints that John of Beersheba is John the Prophet to warrant exploring the issue further.

THE IDENTITY OF JOHN OF BEERSHEBA AND THE BEGINNING OF THE PARTNERSHIP

The possible identification of John of Beersheba and John of Gaza as one person has significant implications for understanding the organization of spiritual authority at Tawatha. Barsanuphius' letters to John of Beersheba by name (Letters 1–54)[19] depict the dynamic process by which the Great Old Man directed the newcomer's transition from the cenobitic to the anchoritic life. They also show the unfolding relationship between John and the abbot Seridos, a relationship that was not always amicable. If John of Beersheba can be identified with John the Prophet, then this series of letters reveals the detailed process of spiritual direction of a man who reached the highest level of spiritual authority in the monastery. The series also depicts the forging of a new partnership that would become the basis for spiritual authority in Gaza.

Not only do the letters addressed to John of Beersheba open the collection of Barsanuphius' letters, but Seridos' explanation of how he began to record Barsanuphius' letters, in order to carry them to their intended recipients, indicates that the letters to John of Beersheba were the first dictated to him.[20]

> And I, Seridos, tell you a wonderful thing. As the Old Man spoke these things, I thought to myself, "How can I retain these things in order to write them? If the Old Man had wanted, I could have brought here ink and papyrus, and heard and written it down word by word." But he knew my thought, and his face shone like fire, and he said to me, "Go, write, fear not; until I tell you ten thousand words, the Spirit of God will not let you write either one letter too many, or too few. Not if you desire [this], but he guides your hand so you may write them in order." (Letter 1)

Barsanuphius thus claimed that divine revelation guarded not only the original content of his words but also the transcription of them. Seridos' role as scribe is more visible in the letters to John of Beersheba than in later ones. In these letters, Barsanuphius used phrases such as "say to John," while in later letters he speaks directly to the addressee. John of Beersheba first wrote to Barsanuphius when he was living in another monastery.[21] Although John was not yet a member of the community at Tawatha, Barsanuphius addressed him from the beginning with familiarity. It is certain that John of Beersheba eventually joined the cenobium at Tawatha, gradually adopted the anchoritic life, and came to exercise considerable authority within the monastery. He supervised building projects and traveled abroad during his cenobitic tenure, and as an anchorite he advised brothers, the abbot, and even a bishop.

The evidence against identifying John of Beersheba with John the Prophet is contained in only two letters in the series. One letter is addressed to John of Beersheba from "The Other Old Man" (Letter 3). Since this title is used throughout the Correspondence to refer to John the Prophet, the letter seems to indicate that the two Johns are different men. There is one manuscript, however, that names Euthymius as the author of this letter.[22] It is possible that John inherited the title "The Other Old Man" from Euthymius, Barsanuphius' first colleague in Tawatha. In another letter, Barsanuphius addressed Seridos: "Write, my child, to our brother John greetings in the Lord from me and you *and brother John*" (Letter 9, emphasis mine). This short reference is the only mention of a second John in the series of letters to John of Beersheba and may have been a later addition intended to distinguish John of Beersheba from Barsanuphius' colleague. Nowhere else in the Correspondence are John of Beersheba and John the Prophet mentioned at the same time.

Opposing these two phrases that appear to refer John the Prophet as a person separate from John of Beersheba are details in the letters that suggest they are the same man. In no other series in the Correspondence does Barsanuphius compose the vast majority of the letters. In fact, it is typical for John to write more letters in a given series than Barsanuphius. With the exception of the extremely short letter from the "Other Old Man" (Letter 3), Barsanuphius is the only author in this series. As noted above, the letters to John of Beersheba are among the earliest in the Correspondence and the first written with the help of Seridos. The compiler may have placed them first in the collection to show how Barsanuphius and John the Prophet began to collaborate.

As early correspondents and collaborators Euthymius and John of Beersheba shared a privileged place in Barsanuphius' circle of associates. At separate times each served as the Great Old Man's confidant. Barsanuphius addressed John of Beersheba in intimate terms, using the appellation "same-soul" (*homopsychos*), a term that aptly characterized Barsanuphius' relationship with John the Prophet (Letters 7 and 35).[23] Barsanuphius' letters to Euthymius demonstrate a similar intimacy. It is probable that John of Beersheba inherited the older monk's position as Barsanuphius' closest colleague in Tawatha.

When John of Beersheba joined the community at Tawatha, he entered at a relatively high level. Unlike laymen, who usually joined the monastery as novices, John arrived in Tawatha as an experienced monk. He did not become an anchorite immediately but undertook some administrative functions in the monastery. He oversaw building projects and made a journey by sea to Egypt with some of the brothers to obtain work.[24] There are indications that, even at this early point in his association with the community, John of Beersheba ranked as high or higher than the abbot in the spiritual hierarchy of the monastery. Once he asked Barsanuphius if he should tell the abbot to shorten the length of time the novices kept vigil (Letter 35). Another time Barsanuphius addressed a letter to both John of Beersheba and Seridos, "when they wanted to tighten the rule at once against the brethren," implying that the change was a joint decision (Letter 25). The high level of authority exercised by John of Beersheba supports his identification with John the Prophet.

There is another measure of John of Beersheba's high rank within the leadership network which supports his identification with John the Prophet: Barsanuphius' response to his quarrels with the abbot. John of Beersheba and Seridos had difficulty working together initially. John became easily irritated with the abbot and frequently disapproved of his supervision of the monastery. Not only did John openly argue with Seridos sometimes, but he also felt free to criticize the abbot to Barsanuphius, on one occasion saying: "The one who brings me this affliction is the abbot, because he is careless and overlooks matters, and they are ruined by his fault, and I cannot endure it. . . . And I marvel how that passion of love that I had for the abbot and the brothers has grown cold" (Letter 17). While there were others in the monastery who complained to Barsanuphius about the abbot, none did so as openly and with such self-confidence as John. More surprising than John of Beersheba's complaints about Seridos is Barsanuphius' unexpected response to John's accusations. When other monks dared to object to the abbot's manner of rule, Barsanuphius soundly rebuked them. He was quick to point out that Seridos was their spiritual father to whom they must submit in obedience. Barsanuphius consistently upheld Seridos as the spiritual and temporal superior of the other monks. Barsanuphius' reply to John's criticism of the abbot was much different. Instead of calling Seridos John's father, he referred to him as his "neighbor" (Letter 17). John of Beersheba had dared to dispute with the abbot about the interpretation of scripture and the manner in which he governed the monastery, subjects that related directly to Seridos' spiritual authority as abbot (Letters 17, 24, and 48). In each of these cases, Barsanuphius tried to arrange reconciliation, reminding John of Beersheba of the command to love one's neighbor. Barsanuphius reprimanded him for his general sinful attitude, but he made no specific reference to his "disobedience" to the abbot. At one point, Barsanuphius even declined to interfere in their argument, saying that the two would have to work out the misunderstanding on their own (Letter 49). It is clear from the tone of his correction that John of Beersheba was no ordinary monk. Rather than being under the abbot's authority like the rest of the brothers at Tawatha, he held authority similar to that of Seridos.

John of Beersheba's attitude of self-assurance towards Seridos even led him once to criticize Barsanuphius. The incident occurred when the abbot was slow in bringing a letter from Barsanuphius to John of Beersheba. While he was already irritated with Seridos, some monks came and complained to him about the abbot, reporting that "certain things occurred idly and unprofitably in the cenobium" (Letter 48). Instead of correcting the monks and upholding Seridos' authority, John openly agreed with them. Later the abbot protested that he had acted upon Barsanuphius' direction in the matter, to which John of Beersheba retorted, "The Old Man lets you write and walk according to your own will!" (Letter 48). In response, Barsanuphius reminded John that God had given them Seridos as a "true son," although John wanted to be rid of this obligation.[25] Barsanuphius chastised John but without invoking his own authority as father. Barsanuphius' measured attitude, combined with the classification of Seridos as their "son," makes the identification of John of Beersheba with John the Prophet more convincing.

Thus, the letters recording the quarrels between John of Beersheba and Seridos both offer us reason to identify the two Johns as one person but also provided the early redactor grounds to separate them. The monk who compiled the letters may have separated the two deliberately, in order to protect the reputation of John the Prophet, the Other Old Man. He may have thought it expedient to leave the identity of this querulous John ambiguous, since many later letters indicate that John eventually developed an effective working relationship with Seridos and supported the abbot's authority. On the other hand, the misclassification may have been accidental, since the letters to John of Beersheba do not reveal the spiritual maturity of the later letters, from John the Prophet. This series of earlier letters hardly presents a flattering portrait of John, and a compiler working much later would not necessarily have identified the recipient of these early letters with the holy man who guided the monastic community. To see the holy man in training in these early letters must have been disconcerting to later inhabitants of the monastery, who regarded his authority as a timeless reality.

If this identification of John of Beersheba with John the Prophet is correct, then we witness an unusually well documented transition from rebellious newcomer to senior spiritual guide of the community. Barsanuphius employed a dynamic process of spiritual direction in mentoring John of Beersheba, overseeing each stage of his development as a monastic leader. Having exercised administrative authority in the cenobium, John of Beersheba gradually relinquished this role and adopted the solitary life. Under Barsanuphius' guidance he began eating in his own cell, still joining the brothers for communion on Wednesdays and Fridays

(Letter 32). Finally, Barsanuphius signaled that John was ready for solitude: "And I say to you, the time for your entry has come with God's help. Set in order your new cell, and enter it having God as your guide. And when you are settled, have no care for anything" (Letter 36). Thus, John of Beersheba undertook the same manner of life as his colleague Barsanuphius.

The next step in the process of becoming a spiritual father entailed receiving permission to direct others. John of Beersheba undertook this responsibility prematurely, advising a layman before he had gained sufficient discernment. Realizing he had overstepped his authority, he apologized to Barsanuphius (Letter 37). John needed to learn to shed his administrative role and stop worrying about the brothers before he would be ready to offer them spiritual direction (Letters 38 and 41–43). One year, shortly after Easter, Barsanuphius granted John of Beersheba permission to guide others (Letter 51). The authority granted was far-reaching: Barsanuphius empowered John to advise novices, bishops, and even monks who were ashamed to confess before the abbot (Letters 51 and 54). The permission to instruct bishops strengthens the identification of John of Beersheba with John the Prophet, because the Correspondence includes a substantial number of letters from John the Prophet to the bishops of Gaza and Jerusalem.[26]

There is one more aspect of John of Beersheba's life that coincides with that of John the Prophet. As noted above, the monk who compiled the Correspondence presented John the Prophet as having no need to communicate with Barsanuphius through letters or conversations. Their perfection allowed them to see eye-to-eye and even to communicate mentally. Barsanuphius' letters to John of Beersheba reveal the latter to have been a man with a quick temper and a sharp tongue, who at first fell dramatically short of this degree of perfection. Nevertheless, Barsanuphius, through his correspondence with John of Beersheba, guided him steadily towards this goal. John of Beersheba frequently asked for assurances that Barsanuphius would continue to write to him, and Barsanuphius repeatedly replied that he had written him enough, that John should meditate on the letters he had already received.[27] Of the final letter in the series addressed to John of Beersheba the compiler recounts that John, not knowing how to advise a certain monk, "questioned the same Great Old Man mentally" (Letter 54). Evidently, John of Beersheba, whom Barsanuphius referred to in this last letter as Abba John, had reached the highest level of intimacy possible between spiritual father and disciple, possessing the ability to know the other's thoughts. Under Barsanuphius' direction it appears that John of Beersheba emerged as that powerful leader of the community and closest friend of the Great Old Man whom others remembered as the Other Old Man, John the Prophet.

This Correspondence grants us an in-depth view of the process of spiritual direction as practiced in sixth-century monastic circles. Not only does it portray the spiritual guidance of ordinary monks and lay Christians, but it also shows a system of authority under construction. The letters break from the model of other monastic texts, particularly vitae (e.g., those of Pachomius, Macrina, Rabbula, etc.), that propagate belief in the holy man or woman's unilinear development from a holy infant and accords us a rare view of the contentious struggle for cooperation that underlay truly effective leadership teams. When he had worked through his early struggles with Barsanuphius and Seridos, John of Beersheba became a trusted partner of the anchorite and abbot and a competent father for his disciples. Having challenged authority himself, he could guide others to submission.

The examples of spiritual immaturity from his early years at Tawatha enrich our later picture of John as a giver of advice. His own unguarded words and challenges to the abbot informed his patient dealings with young monks and laymen. He continually encouraged his petitioners, promising them divine aid to overcome temptation. At the same time he took a strong stand against gossip, recognizing from his own experience that even passively listening to malicious words could disrupt the harmony of the monastery (Letters 560–61). The portrait of John that emerges from the letters shows the practical results of the process of spiritual direction employed at Tawatha.

BARSANUPHIUS AND ABBOT SERIDOS

Barsanuphius and John the Prophet together served as spiritual directors for the entire Christian community at Tawatha. Beneath their general authority, Seridos governed the cenobium. The coordination of authority between Barsanuphius and Abbot Seridos was more likely to be challenged by members of the community than that in the equal partnership of the anchorites Barsanuphius and John. The abbot presided over the daily activity and decisions of the monastery, but the higher spiritual authority of Barsanuphius offered disgruntled monks the possibility of appeal. Many petitioners wished to exploit potential differences between the anchorite and the abbot. In some cases, members of the monastery hoped to conceal their questions to Barsanuphius from the abbot. This was not easy to do, since Seridos was Barsanuphius' scribe and letter carrier. One brother went so far as to construct an elaborate series of enigmas (in which a particular letter of the alphabet stood for a certain question), in order to keep his real concerns hidden from the abbot. The Great Old Man replied in an equally cryptic manner in order to teach the monk the futility of such unintelligible conversation (Letters 132–35). Finally Barsanuphius commanded him to explain his thoughts clearly to Seridos or to write them down; only in submission to the abbot would he achieve humility (Letter 136).[28]

Barsanuphius maintained his commitment to communicate only through Seridos even when circumstances might have led him to make an exception. For instance, when an old monk came from Egypt to live in the monastery at Tawatha, he sought out the Great Old Man Barsanuphius, writing to him in Coptic, asking for a "word" according to the tradition of the Egyptian desert. Barsanuphius responded in Greek, explaining that he had resolved not to write any letters by himself but only to dictate his responses to the abbot. Since the abbot did not know Coptic, they would have to confine their correspondence to Greek.[29] Barsanuphius would not exclude Seridos, even to address a fellow Egyptian monk in his native tongue. The monk also requested an interview, which Barsanuphius refused, according to his custom.[30] Despite measures that appeared harsh to potential disciples, Barsanuphius took pains to overcome the distance created by his seclusion: "You said in your letter, 'My sin has separated me from you, my master,' while by the grace of Christ, the Son of God, I am not separated from you, but I am always with [you] in the Spirit" (Letter 55).

Another unnamed monk, who served as a deacon in Seridos' cenobium, also had trouble with the Greek language. He wrote to Barsanuphius asking if it were really necessary to learn the Psalms in Greek: "I read Greek, and I do not understand what I say. Pray that the Lord might make me understand the reading!" (Letter 228). Barsanuphius responded that it was necessary to learn the language, because most books were written in Greek. If the student remained humble, God would aid his efforts, and he would receive recompense in heaven. The deacon did not use the question of language in this instance to challenge authority, although other interactions with the holy men reveal his resentment of the abbot's authority.

Barsanuphius and Seridos' relations with this deacon well illustrate their respective roles within the monastic community. The deacon challenged the hierarchy of authority in the community by seeking to circumvent both Seridos and John and go directly to Barsanuphius. Before the deacon first addressed Barsanuphius, he had already written to John with questions on ascetic discipline. Unsatisfied with John's response, he questioned Barsanuphius about abstaining from wine, sleeping sitting up (a common ascetic practice among Palestinian monks[31]), and seeing a doctor about his diseased eye (Letter 225). Barsanuphius urged the deacon to seek moderation and humility, and he took the opportunity explicitly to outline the hierarchy of spiritual authority behind his answer: "These things were dictated to you by me and written by my son Seridos. If then you do not struggle to set aside my words which were spoken by God, I pray that God will lead you to greater progress, and that you will not be separated from us, either in this world or the other" (Letter 225). Barsanuphius asserted that the advice he dispensed came directly from God and was delivered through the anchorite's spiritual son, Seridos. Ignoring these divinely sanctioned words could separate a monk from his spiritual director, in this case, Barsanuphius; from the official head of the monastery, Seridos; and ultimately even from God. Barsanuphius' prayers for the disciple's advancement would only be effective, he said, if the petitioner heeded the advice of his spiritual director, or at least did not actively rebel against it.

This deacon did not accept the guidance of Barsanuphius either. He rejected the order of spiritual authority that Barsanuphius described (from God to Barsanuphius to Seridos). He did not trust the abbot, and he even began to doubt that the advice he received came from Barsanuphius, and therefore from God, rather than the abbot. In his next letter he signaled his disbelief, "Tell me, if the first response was from you. Because the thought came to me, 'Was it not from the abbot under your name?'" (Letter 226). His question actually accused the abbot of forgery. Barsanuphius rebuked the man for his refusal to accept spiritual direction from the abbot and for his insistence on communicating directly with the anchorite. In his suspicion the deacon had neglected words that could have benefited his soul. The man's actions jeopardized the chain of command Barsanuphius had established at Tawatha, undermining the abbot's authority, and by implication that of Barsanuphius, who had appointed Seridos as his intermediary.

The dialogue does not end with this reprimand, as the reader might expect. The deacon's accusation was too serious for Barsanuphius to dismiss summarily. After comparing him to the Pharisees who demanded a sign from Jesus (Matt. 12:38–39), Barsanuphius acquiesced and gave the unbelieving monk a sign.[32] In an extraordinary development, Barsanuphius responded to the deacon's doubt by instructing the abbot to stand by the door to the Great Old Man's cell and repeat in a loud voice the words that had been dictated to him. In this way, the doubting deacon and Barsanuphius would both hear the actual words the abbot had recorded.[33] Barsanuphius explicitly linked the deacon's doubts to demonic influence. Under the modified procedure the devil would not be able to tempt him into thinking that the abbot had changed part of the message, for the Great Old Man himself would be listening.

This change of the established pattern of communication may give the initial impression that Barsanuphius had yielded to the deacon's attack. Still denying him face to face contact, Barsanuphius introduced an oral element to the dialogue, which brought a greater level of intimacy to the interchange. Although he was not using his own voice to address the deacon, Barsanuphius and the deacon were both simultaneously listening to the abbot read the response aloud. The shared activity of listening helped dispel the deacon's doubts about the abbot's role as intermediary.

In making the concession, did Barsanuphius undermine the authority of the abbot, by suggesting that he shared the deacon's doubts regarding Seridos' trustworthiness as a scribe? No, rather Barsanuphius acted on a bold plan designed to neutralize immediately the deacon's objections and to demonstrate with dramatic imagery the humility of both Barsanuphius and Seridos. According to his usual practice, Barsanuphius employed self-effacement to support a spiritual authority based on the supreme virtue of humility. Barsanuphius did not expect the abbot to read his letters aloud indefinitely; rather the rearrangement of procedure on behalf of the deacon would convict or shame him, delivering him from his stubbornness.

Barsanuphius also intended the arrangement to show the lengths to which he was willing to go to accommodate the weaknesses of his petitioners. By his participation in the plan, the abbot demonstrated his own humility and willingness to work for the deacon's salvation. Neither anchorite nor abbot expressed anger at the doubts that challenged their trustworthiness as spiritual directors. They attributed the distrust of the deacon to demons who had assaulted him. The task of the holy man and the abbot was to heal disbelief, not to castigate unbelievers.

The accommodation did not cure the deacon of his distrust of Seridos or his desire for more direct contact with Barsanuphius. Complaining of nocturnal phantasms, he beseeched Barsanuphius, "If it is possible, permit me to prostrate myself before you and to hear your holy voice. For I believe that if this happened, I would find great protection" (Letter 231). Once again, the man tried to bypass the intermediary. It was not enough for him to receive Barsanuphius' words via the abbot, or even to know that Barsanuphius was listening as Seridos read aloud. The deacon ardently desired to enter the holy man's presence and hear his voice. Only this personal encounter would satisfy him.

The deacon's earnest desire to have direct personal contact with Barsanuphius sprang from his distrust of the abbot Seridos. The relationship between the deacon and the abbot was seriously broken. Later in his correspondence with Barsanuphius, the deacon finally admitted the root of the problem: "I am distressed on account of the abbot, as he has greater regard for some brothers than for me, and I am offended by this so that I am struggling with hatred for him" (Letter 235).[34]

Barsanuphius counseled that by allowing such sinful thoughts to jeopardize his relationship with the abbot the deacon deprived himself of the spiritual benefits that flowed from father to disciple.[35] The abbot was the one who should nurture his spiritual progress, but the disciple's preoccupation with the abbot's treatment of others prevented him from fulfilling his role as spiritual father:

> The thoughts and demons trouble you wickedly in regard to the abbot . . . in order that you hate the one who loves you, and you afflict the one who desires to protect your soul. . . . Do you not understand what you do, my brother, when you often push your abbot to irritation, yet he endures your wickedness? Often he also exhorts you as a true and beloved son . . . and your heart weakens for a time, then once again you do not hold yourself firmly in the good, but you change as the moon. (Letter 236)

The correspondence does not reveal any resolution of the problems between the deacon and the abbot. This repeats a pattern in the letters of Barsanuphius: there is no easy solution to long-term difficulties. The compiler did not follow the model predominant in monastic literature, in which the holy man successfully vanquished the human frailties and demonic temptations in his community. Instead, the compiler attempted to show readers that spiritual direction was a dynamic and ongoing process. There was no single happy ending to the story, because temptation was a life-long struggle.

The obstacles that disrupted fellowship between the suspicious deacon and his abbot spilled over into the deacon's relationship with the rest of the community. His distrust of the abbot led to his jealousy of those whom he believed the abbot favored. Unable to remain in his cell to do penance, the deacon begged Barsanuphius for permission to retreat to the desert to pray for his sins, which Barsanuphius refused (Letters 237, 239). By seeking to withdraw temporarily from the monastery, the deacon hoped to participate in a common monastic discipline (hagiographers often describe fathers retreating into the desert for Lent). The effectiveness of penitential retreat depended on the monk's being a healthy member of a functioning monastic community before retreating. In this particular case, the deacon's discontent with the community would render retreat useless. His unrepentant attitude would reduce spiritual withdrawal to running away.

The unwillingness of the deacon to receive spiritual direction from the abbot and his inability to apply Barsanuphius' advice hindered him from exercising spiritual authority himself. A very young member of the monastery at Tawatha, having excessive confidence in the spiritual wisdom of the deacon, began to come to him for direction. The young man soon began attending to the deacon's physical needs, following a common pattern among Egyptian and Palestinian monks of acting as servant, as well as disciple to an older monk. The deacon saw no need to prevent the younger man's devotion, nor did he choose to consult Barsanuphius on the matter.

The Great Old Man did not remain long uninformed of the developments. Perhaps with the ongoing tension between the abbot and the deacon in mind, the compiler carefully explained that a vision had revealed the situation to Barsanuphius. (He may not have wanted the reader to suppose that the abbot had brought the matter to the anchorite's attention.) The Great Old Man saw this new relationship as not only useless but dangerous: "Listen, brother, have you become a paralytic that you should desire to be served by another?" (Letter 233). What Barsanuphius saw above all in the situation was an injury to the young servant monk, who might have been serving other brothers who merited such attendance and could offer him true spiritual guidance in return. Barsanuphius judged the deacon a child spiritually; he was in no position to direct the youth. The reason for taking a disciple was to offer spiritual direction to the disciple, not to make one's own life more comfortable. The Great Old Man added that before he had become a complete recluse, he had served himself, making his own fire and food even when he was ill.

The deacon's attitude hindered him from fulfilling his legitimate sacramental duty to the community. As an ordained deacon he was supposed to assist the priest who celebrated the Eucharist for the monks. Recognizing the great responsibility involved and his own inner turmoil, he hesitated to serve at the altar. Barsanuphius did not consider the deacon's rebellious attitude reason to excuse him from his liturgical functions. Instead, Barsanuphius comforted him, saying that only a fool would dare to think himself worthy of such service. He reminded him that since both his spiritual fathers (Barsanuphius and Seridos) remained with him, God would not abandon him (Letter 240).[36] Barsanuphius once more emphasized the connection between earthly representatives of spiritual authority and their heavenly source.

The deacon was rather easily reassured. His next letter to Barsanuphius posed a long list of questions: What should he think about when he stood at the altar, when he distributed the body and blood, and when he carried the elements to someone? Should he wear special liturgical vestments? Barsanuphius expressed disappointment in his disciple's lack of understanding: "Everything that is said spiritually, you hear in a carnal manner!" (Letter 241). A deacon should not dwell on such earthly concerns. His vestments should be spiritual and his earthly possessions few. A deacon's role was to serve as the cherubim and seraphim did in heaven, singing praise to the immortal King.

The prospect of carrying out the functions of the heavenly host terrified the deacon. He wrote to Barsanuphius in a more humble tone, asking his help in order that the diaconate might not bring about his condemnation. In his response, Barsanuphius linked the deacon's fears about serving at the altar with his trouble submitting to the abbot: "Acquire humility, obedience, and submission and you will be saved. Do not speak a single word of contest . . . but be very docile, above all towards your abbot, who having been entrusted with your soul, has care of you after God" (Letter 242). If the deacon were careful to place himself under the direction of the abbot, he would receive power from God and Barsanuphius. As a monk surrendered all his possessions to the abbot when he joined the monastery, so he should surrender to him the other burdens that weighed upon his soul (Letter 243). The scriptures demanded submission to human authority for the sake of Christ (1 Pet. 2:13). Ordination to clerical rank gave the monk no spiritual superiority over the monastic leaders of Tawatha.[37] In the organization of spiritual authority at Tawatha, there was no way to bypass the first step, submission to the abbot, and still reach the Great Old Man and the heavenly Father.

THE ABBOT AS DISCIPLE

Seridos not only referred those under his guidance to Barsanuphius and John, but he himself also asked the anchorites for help. At the same time that he acted as head of the cenobium at Tawatha, Seridos submitted himself as a disciple to the Old Men of Gaza. He turned to them when he was unable to manage the monastery's affairs on his own. Submitting himself as a disciple to the anchorites did not compromise the abbot's authority over the cenobium; rather his status as a disciple of the Old Men was the basis for his own authority. Being seen as a disciple of the Old Men was so important to Seridos as abbot that the compiler of the Correspondence chose to include an example of Seridos' submission to the anchorites in his eulogy of the abbot (Letter 570c). On one occasion Seridos attempted to purchase a nearby piece of land on which to build a church and a guesthouse for the monastery. These two buildings would facilitate critical components of monastic life, allowing for corporate worship and the practice of hospitality. The owner of the land refused to sell, and both monks and lay people were among those who severely criticized Seridos for his part in the failed negotiations. Doubting his own leadership, Seridos turned to John for assurance. John promised that when the monastery's need became acute, land would become available. John also instructed Seridos on ways to control his feelings of doubt and impatience. John's counsel proved correct when some time later the owner decided to sell the land.

Subsequently, other negotiations by Seridos provoked criticism, but this time John's promise emboldened the abbot. There was a hermit who lived on this particular piece of land. Before purchasing the land, Seridos

51

took the recluse aside and asked him if he opposed the monastery's building upon the land. If the proposed construction would disturb his solitude, Seridos promised not to proceed with construction. The hermit did not object, so the project went forward. A certain layman, a "friend of the monastery," heard about the abbot's conversation with the hermit and grew angry. He criticized Seridos, saying that the abbot should not have been willing to place the happiness of a single hermit above the good of all the brothers and their guests. This layman's interest in the affairs of the monastery and his willingness to openly criticize the leadership of the abbot may indicate that he planned to fund the building of the church or the guesthouse and, therefore, had a personal interest in the proceedings.[38] When the abbot explained that he had left the matter to God and considered the hermit's response a divine sign, the layman was reconciled. This incident shows that monks were not the only group to challenge the abbot's authority. Criticism of the abbot by a layman demonstrates the abbot's accessibility to the laity, and the abbot's gentle willingness to explain his position highlights the integration of certain laymen into the monastic community.

In addition to consulting the Old Men on the regular affairs of the monastery, Seridos had recourse to their aid in times of crisis. When the plague struck Palestine in 542, the inhabitants of Tawatha were not isolated from the fear that pervaded the empire. As the disease spread from the Egyptian port of Pelusium along major roadways north to Constantinople, it left many villages completely devastated.[39] The monastery at Tawatha was in close proximity to Gaza, a major metropolitan center for trade and a key stop on the road that linked Egypt to Palestine and Asia Minor. The village could have escaped neither the infection nor the panic that accompanied it. Some of the local hermits wrote to Barsanuphius on behalf of humanity:

> Since the world is in danger, we all call upon you, asking of the goodness of God, in order that he may avert his hand and return his sword to its sheath. Stand in the middle of those who have fallen and those who live with your holy incense and stop the destroyer. Lift up the holy altar in the holy court of heaven, and the wrath of God will cease. We pray and we beseech you, have pity on the world that is being destroyed. Remember that we are all members of you. (Letter 569)[40]

The fathers of the monastery appealed to Barsanuphius to assume the traditional role of the holy man as *patronus*, shielding them from evil.

All over the empire holy men interceded on behalf of humankind, asking for God's mercy. In Constantinople, Mare the Solitary, an ascetic from Amida trained in Egypt, "passed his time in affliction and great sorrow, and occupied himself with constant prayer and petition to God . . . kneeling and praying on behalf of the whole world."[41] At monasteries throughout Palestine, fearful disciples flocked to their spiritual fathers during the outbreak of the plague. Cyril of Scythopolis recounts that in the days of the "great and terrifying mortality" the fathers of the monastery of Chariton visited Abba Cyriacus who had withdrawn from their monastery to live in the "pure desert" of Sousakim.[42] He had served in the monastery for thirty-five years as baker, head of the infirmary, guestmaster, steward, treasurer, canonarch,[43] and finally priest. Now his disciples sought him in his role as a holy man who could protect them from God's wrath. In the midst of the crisis they wanted him physically present with them in the monastery. He acquiesced to their entreaties, and they gave him the cell of their holy founder Chariton to occupy.

In contrast to other holy men, Barsanuphius remained secluded in his cell, declining to employ his holiness to intervene supernaturally in the raging epidemic. Instead, he purposefully humbled himself, identifying with his wayward flock, whose sin, in his judgment, had provoked the terrible wrath of God. He left the role of holy man and deliverer to others, specifically naming three men who were perfect before God and whose prayers could move him to mercy: John in Rome, Elias in Corinth, and a third in the province of Jerusalem.[44] In naming these men whose prayers might stop the plague, Barsanuphius conflated the roles of intercessor and miracle worker, showing that he believed true spiritual power always flowed from a life of prayer.

As the hermits of Tawatha wrote to Barsanuphius corporately, seeking the salvation of the whole community, Seridos applied to John privately, asking for his intervention on behalf of the community: "Since the times are hard, father, pray that the Lord will make them pass, and that we, your servants, might be preserved from all the temptations of our sins" (Letter 568). John responded, offering the comfort of an ancient biblical symbol of protection from plague. God would send his angel to mark them with his sign, so that the one who carried the sword would pass them over (Exod. 12:13).[45]

In another letter, which may also belong to the time of the plague, a recluse who lived apart from the cenobium wrote to John, asking him to intercede with God on his behalf like Moses, who protected his people from divine wrath (Letter 567; Exod. 32:11–12). The recluse also begged John to tell the abbot to visit him soon. John encouraged the monk and solicited his prayers for Seridos. The abbot himself urgently needed divine protection. John conveyed the hermit's summons, but affairs at the monastery demanded the abbot's presence. It is uncertain if the abbot was ever able to visit the hermit. When the plague passed, life did not return to normal in Tawatha. Seridos and John both died within a year of the crisis. Events explored in Chapter 6 transformed the stable network of leadership in the monastery.

Especially in difficult situations, Seridos acted as both disciple and abbot. These roles did not conflict. Indeed, being a disciple enabled Seridos to become a better spiritual father. On one occasion John gave his disciple an object lesson in the qualities required of a spiritual director (Letter 570b). John asked Seridos to do something, but the abbot forgot the assignment as soon as he left John's presence. When Seridos returned, John repeated his request, but Seridos forgot again. This happened several times. Distressed at his own failure, Seridos finally turned to Barsanuphius for help. He explained that God had allowed Seridos to repeatedly forget John's instructions in order that he might observe the patience of his spiritual father and learn to imitate it. Seridos may have reminded himself of these events on subsequent occasions when negligent monks tried his own serenity.

In his eulogy of Abbot Seridos, the monk who compiled the letters of Barsanuphius and John articulated the belief that spiritual authority grows out of a life of discipleship. He emphasized the abbot's relationship with his spiritual fathers and the process of spiritual maturation as Seridos learned to exercise leadership. Adopting the conventions of hagiography, the compiler described Seridos as temperate from his youth. He related that Barsanuphius had intervened early in Seridos' ascetic training to stop excess in his practice of mortifying the flesh. With his characteristic commitment to ascetic moderation, Barsanuphius healed Seridos' self-inflicted wounds and ordered him to treat his body more gently in order that he might be strong enough to govern the brothers. The compiler specifically connected Seridos' observance of Barsanuphius' command to the abbot's ability to lead. Barsanuphius himself testified that Seridos' submission equipped him with authority. The obedience of the disciple and the prayers of the spiritual director forged the father-son relationship:

> He considered himself, not as an abbot, but as a disciple of the Old Man. And as he became perfect in obedience, this was also a proof of his profound humility, on account of which the Old Man regarded him as a true son, and prayed to God to give him grace and discernment, which once obtained, permitted him, with grace from above, to lead souls to life, to care for the afflicted, and to apply saving remedy, which is the word dictated by the Spirit, and to procure peace for the combatants. (Letter 570c)

Seridos' obedient discipleship was directly linked to the divine gifts that enabled him to carry out his responsibilities as abbot, including spiritual direction, nurturing, instruction, and mediation.

The compiler developed this model further in Seridos' eulogy, suggesting that a father's prayer could actually create obedience in an unsubmissive disciple. He related that Seridos, empowered by the prayers of Barsanuphius, changed the attitude of one of his own disciples. A monk was on the point of leaving the community, despite the abbot's arguments that he should stay. When Seridos prayed over the man, he suddenly lost the desire to leave. The compiler used this story to affirm Seridos' authority as a spiritual father. He did not attempt to apply the same test to Barsanuphius, whose spiritual authority was more firmly established; many of Barsanuphius' petitioners continued in their own purposes despite the holy man's prayers.

OTHER FATHERS

Barsanuphius, John, and Seridos were not the only human sources of spiritual authority in the monastic community. Many of the letters mention the "fathers" of the monastery. In contrast to the appellation "brother" (*adelphos*), which could refer to any monk (or even a layman), the title "father" (*pater*) was used for a monk advanced in the spiritual life. These monks were also referred to as the "old men" of the community. The monastery at Tawatha, like many other communities in Palestine, consisted of a cenobium surrounded by more isolated cells located beyond the monastery walls for those who had progressed in ascetic practice to a point where they desired to live as anchorites.[46] Living in an isolated cell did not make a monk a father, nor did all fathers choose to leave the cenobium, but very often fathers did opt for a more solitary form of life.

The abbot, in consultation with Barsanuphius and John, oversaw those moving from cenobitic to anchoritic life. Sometimes they concluded that monks seeking to take this step were not properly prepared for the transition. In the case mentioned earlier, Barsanuphius vetoed even a temporary retreat for the deacon who rebelled against the abbot (Letter 239). Barsanuphius told another monk who asked if he should live alone that his compunction and tears were transitory. The Great Old Man encouraged the monk to keep the commands he had already been given and assured him that when the time came for him to live alone, "I will send and tell you myself" (Letter 461).

Often, as part of his instruction in the ascetic life, a younger monk lived with an old brother in his dwelling. The older monk acted as the spiritual father of the younger monk, who served him as a disciple. Only an experienced and discerning monk could accept the heavy responsibility of another's guidance, as Barsanuphius was quick to remind the rebellious deacon.[47] Even with the instruction of the most qualified fathers, the transition from cenobite to anchorite could prove difficult. At the monastery in Tawatha a brother could consult Barsanuphius and John if he was uncertain about his new way of life or the advice of his spiritual father.

Seridos instructed a certain monk to leave the cenobium and to live with an old man in his cell.[48] At first the monk resisted the abbot's order, but then he reluctantly complied. After asking a rather abstract question of Barsanuphius about how to escape the passions, the young monk finally poured out to John his anxieties about the move: "How ought I to know, father, if it is according to God that I sit [in a cell], or if it is harmful to me not to be with the brothers in community, but alone?" (Letter 248). The monk's questions to the anchorites adhered to an established pattern: Barsanuphius discussed more abstract ideas, and John handled the nitty-gritty problems.

John reassured the monk that there was no intrinsic benefit or harm in living in a hermit's cell versus the cenobium, rather the good or evil depended on the monk's acting in obedience or rebellion. The unvoiced message was that the young monk should no longer contemplate disobedience to the abbot. John made this message explicit in a later letter when he reminded the young monk of his disagreement with the abbot about undertaking the solitary life (Letter 250). The abbot, John assured him, had acted in his capacity as spiritual director when he instructed the young monk to begin the anchoritic life; the monk needed no separate confirmation of God's will. John comforted the young monk that he was not really separated from his brothers. In his remote cell he remained a part of the spiritual community of Tawatha, which encompassed anchorites and cenobites and joined them through faith to the Great Old Man and his God.

John also addressed the monk's practical concerns, instructing him to continue saying the psalms as he had in the cenobium, a task which would help him regulate his sleep and unite him with those saying them in the cenobium. The monk's health was fragile, and he was unable to extend his fast until the customary time when the brothers ate together. John acknowledged that this was one of the reasons that the abbot had arranged for him to live with the old man. Just as Barsanuphius had corrected Seridos when his ascetic excesses had threatened his health, so now Seridos took measures to protect the young monk's physical well-being. John affirmed an earlier instruction from Seridos not to wait until the brothers' dinner hour but to eat earlier, so that he would not fall ill. Like the sick in the infirmary, the monk, at the abbot's instruction, could eat separately and at an earlier hour and still remain part of the community.

The young monk's early apprehensions lay with his physical separation from the cenobium, but in his final letter, this one to Barsanuphius, he began to focus on the relationship with his cellmate. The old man was ordained as a priest but had asked the younger monk to bless their meal. The young man's humility made compliance with this request difficult. He knew that the older man, by virtue of ordination and experience, should take precedence in leading their communal prayers. To set aside his own lower rank and offer a blessing over the meal, even upon a direct order, seemed presumptuous to the young monk. Barsanuphius affirmed John's refrain of obedience. The young monk's cellmate acted as another father to him, below Seridos, John, and Barsanuphius in the hierarchy of spiritual directors.

The young monk's problems adjusting to his new situation were not unusual. There are letters in the collection from other new anchorites seeking instruction on eating, sleeping, and prayer. Some also deal with problems that arose between spiritual fathers and their disciples.[49] One case grew to such proportions that others in the monastery became involved (Letters 489–91). The disciple of a certain old man asked him what he would like to eat. The old man flew into a rage at the question. The disciple was deeply troubled, and neither the abbot nor the other monks could comfort him. Unable to serve his father any longer, the monk secretly fled Tawatha. Some members of the monastery brought the dispute to Barsanuphius, who recognized fault on both sides. He refused to condemn the old man who had fallen prey to his passions, but he did add that it would have been better to eat whatever a disciple prepared, saying nothing. Likewise, patience would have been the best response on the part of a disciple. When others wrote asking the Great Old Man's permission to go find the monk and convince him to return, Barsanuphius replied that unless they had contributed to the cause of his departure, they should leave him alone for the time being. His wounded pride would subside, and he would remember "the peace of the monastery" and return (Letter 490). Barsanuphius' answer left open the possibility that the monk's own spiritual father would go to retrieve him, but this father's response to the dispute remains unknown.

Barsanuphius was unwilling to intervene actively or allow others to interfere in this conflict because he recognized the autonomy of the tie between father and disciple. Had either the old man or the disciple involved approached Barsanuphius about the altercation, he would have helped to reconcile the men. By doing so, he would have been acting in accordance with his position at the top of the hierarchy of spiritual directors. However, since the disciple refused the mediation of the abbot (who ranked above his cellmate in the order of fathers), there was nothing for the brothers of the cenobium to do. The problem stemmed from a breakdown in the system of mutual humility that undergirded spiritual authority in the community. The haughty old man had forfeited his authority over a disciple who in turn was too proud to accept criticism. Until both men relinquished their pride, the father-disciple relationship would remain severed.

Barsanuphius and John recognized that not every father could be an effective spiritual director for every disciple. Although the Great Old Man and the Other Old Man always acted in unison, refusing to undermine each other's advice by offering differing opinions and stringently supporting the authority of Seridos when members of the community challenged him, they did not uphold the authority of all spiritual directors to the same degree. John offered surprising advice to one monk who asked if it were permissible to consult an old man other than his own father and if it were necessary to first obtain his father's consent (Letter

504). A spiritual director who truly loved his disciple but was unable to dispel the disciple's troubled thoughts, replied John, should hurry, like a biological father bringing his sick child to a doctor, to bring his disciple to another old man with discernment. However, if a brother knew that his father was unable to live up to this ideal, he could, with God's permission, consult another old man. He could even go so far as to ask the other old man to keep the visit from his spiritual father, in order not to make him envious. Such seemingly deceptive behavior did not dissolve the bond that united disciple and father. Indeed, John assured the young monk that he would soon discover the special gift that the Holy Spirit had granted his own father, for each spiritual director was blessed in a different manner.

This unusual advice from John appears to disparage the ideal of obedience, one of the fundamental principles of spiritual direction upon which life in the monastery was based. Instead, this flexibility served as a safety valve for the pressures that built up in the close-knit hierarchical community. By granting leeway on the lowest level of the spiritual hierarchy, John strengthened the authority of those at the upper levels, the abbot and the anchorites. Although there were many sources of spiritual authority on the lower level, John sought to eliminate the possibility of competitive sources of spiritual authority at the higher echelon. This safety valve served to keep monks from becoming disillusioned with the principle of obedience, therefore, ultimately strengthening spiritual authority in the monastic community.

From their isolated cells, Barsanuphius and John exercised spiritual authority over all the monks of Tawatha, anchorites and cenobites. Although they refused face-to-face interviews, the old men wrote to their disciples prolifically. Barsanuphius named Seridos, the abbot of the cenobium, as his scribe and intermediary in order that the abbot might remain informed of all matters brought before the Great Old Man. Practical matters concerning the administration of the monastery were under Seridos' jurisdiction, while the anchorites supervised spiritual and interpersonal issues. The authority of John and Seridos sprang from their submission to Barsanuphius. Barsanuphius acknowledged his fatherly authority over his "true son" Seridos but elevated John as a brother. The power of all spiritual fathers in Tawatha was grounded in humility before God.

There is considerable circumstantial evidence that a certain John of Beersheba was the same person as John the Prophet, author of the Correspondence and Barsanuphius' colleague. Barsanuphius' direction of John of Beersheba reveals the formation of a holy man in progress, whether John of Beersheba eventually became John the Prophet or simply another leader in the monastic community. The letters provide an unusual view of the dynamic process of developing new spiritual leaders, a process usually shrouded in monastic literature by hagiographic conventions. John of Beersheba came as an outsider to Tawatha, assumed significant administrative authority in the cenobium, struggled with the abbot over how to run the monastery, and eventually adopted the anchoritic life. Barsanuphius granted him authority to direct monks, lay Christians, and bishops.

John of Beersheba's progress in fatherhood demonstrates that spiritual authority in Tawatha was reorganized over time. If he was not the same man as John the Prophet, then he was another monastic leader at Tawatha who exercised considerable power and even challenged the legitimacy of the abbot's authority. If John of Beersheba and John the Prophet were one man, then his experience reveals how Barsanuphius crafted the carefully balanced system of leadership at Tawatha. The three-person hierarchy, which the sixth-century compiler portrayed as static and unassailable, actually emerged only after significant internal conflict between John and Seridos. In either case, the letters to John of Beersheba reveal with frank precision the inner development of a monastic leader, largely unshaped by the hagiographer's pen.

Frequent challenges arose to the system of authority that Barsanuphius established at Tawatha. Although the monk who compiled the letters sought to portray a stable and peaceful environment, many petitioners registered clamorous protests against the status quo. Each link in the network of authority was challenged in turn: some appealed to Barsanuphius over Seridos, others tried to separate Barsanuphius and John. Even laymen ventured to criticize the abbot. Beneath the authority of Barsanuphius, John, and Seridos, monks quarreled with their own fathers. Each challenge to the system provides another opportunity to see how groups within the community understood, manipulated, and constructed spiritual authority. The next chapter will focus on a particular monk at Tawatha named Dorotheos, an idealistic newcomer who found the cenobium a hostile, unwelcoming environment. Despite his difficulties living with the others monks, he served in several official roles during his residence in Tawatha, including as the disciple of John, and he eventually exercised authority as a spiritual father in his own right.

CHAPTER 3

Dorotheos
From Novice to Spiritual Director

Among the many monks at Tawatha under the spiritual direction of Barsanuphius and John, one figure stands apart as an ascetic father in his own right—Abba Dorotheos. This famous disciple of the Old Men of Gaza began his monastic career as a hesitant novice in Seridos' cenobium but eventually exercised spiritual authority within the monastery and became John's means of communication with the monastery and the outside world. Dorotheos was both a product of the system of spiritual direction established at Tawatha and also an agent in the process of implementing spiritual authority. The various stages of Dorotheos' life are well documented, allowing us to trace his development as a spiritual director. His training in the monastery reveals the manner in which spiritual authority was transferred to a new generation of spiritual leaders. For Dorotheos the progression from disciple to spiritual director was not simple. His early years in the cenobium were characterized by difficulties with his fellow monks. He had trouble becoming a well-integrated member of the community and resisted new opportunities for service for fear that they would further distinguish him from his peers. Nevertheless, the spiritual fathers at Tawatha chose to give additional responsibilities to Dorotheos, intentionally preparing him for a position of leadership within the monastery.

We have the benefit of multiple sources to help us examine Dorotheos' life. His correspondence with Barsanuphius and John details his adoption of the monastic vocation and his early years in the cenobium.[1] The hagiographic life of his disciple Dositheos describes the spiritual direction Dorotheos offered the younger man. Although Dorotheos did not compose the text himself, the *Life of Saint Dositheos* probably reflects Dorotheos' own view of the life of his disciple.[2] Following the example of Barsanuphius and John, Dorotheos left letters of spiritual advice.[3] Finally, we have Dorotheos' recollections of his days at the cenobium of Seridos, retold in his *Discourses* for the benefit of his own disciples.[4] Far from remaining obscure, the *Discourses* of Dorotheos have proved substantially influential in the West, making Dorotheos better known to later generations than are his own spiritual fathers.[5]

A prosperous, educated, idealistic young man, Dorotheos expected life in the monastery to differ dramatically from that of the world, and he yearned for the solitary life. As a new member of the community, Dorotheos was assigned mundane tasks that threatened his spiritual retreat. Uncomfortable in many social settings, he was excessively concerned about appropriate interaction with the brothers. This social awkwardness when combined with his sharp intelligence alienated many of his peers.[6] Dorotheos did not make friends easily and he frequently worried that other monks would become jealous if he were given responsibilities within the community. His mental acumen made it difficult for him to submit to authority, particularly when he thought he knew better than the abbot how matters should be managed. Ignoring these shortcomings, the abbot found Dorotheos' quick mind, classical education, and medical knowledge useful to the monastery and promoted him to positions of responsibility. As the porter and later the head of the infirmary, Dorotheos exercised substantial authority within the monastery. He oversaw visitors, received donations to the monastery, and prescribed treatments for those who fell ill. Seridos eventually entrusted him with the oversight of others within the cenobium, including a young novice, Dositheos. After the youthful Dositheos died following a lingering illness, Seridos appointed Dorotheos to one of the most important duties within the monastery, serving as the disciple of the Other Old Man, John, where his literary and rhetorical skills facilitated John's communication with the outside world.

DOROTHEOS BECOMES A MONK

Coming from an upper-class Christian family, Dorotheos had received a classical education in rhetoric, either at the School of Gaza or in Antioch, where he was born.[7] Enthusiastically devoted to his studies, which included medicine, he could have practiced as a physician. Long after he had left the world where rhetoricians dazzled one another with their eloquence, he recalled with a certain fondness his early years of study, pursued with a single-minded passion that he would later transfer to the study of virtue:

> I became so engrossed with reading that I did not know what I was eating or drinking, or how I slept, I was so enthused about my reading. I was never drawn away to a meal with one of my friends. . . . When the master [sophist] dismissed us I used to take a bath— which I needed daily to counteract the exhaustion from excessive study—then I hurried to where I was staying without thinking about eating. . . . but I had a faithful companion and he prepared for me whatever he wished. I took whatever I found prepared for me, propped up a book beside me, and in a short time I was lost in it. . . . It was the same in the evening when I got back after lamplighting. I used to grasp my book and go on with my reading until midnight.[8]

By birth and upbringing, Dorotheos belonged to the elite of the Greco-Roman world, whose self-identity was based on a shared rhetorical education. The family wealth that allowed a young man the leisure to pursue these studies, while a slave attended his physical needs, fostered a way of life Dorotheos would abandon in order to adopt a monastic vocation that privileged voluntary poverty and prayer.

Dorotheos announced his desire to enter the monastery by inquiring of John and Barsanuphius how he should distribute his goods (Letters 252–54). Although this question marks the beginning of Dorotheos' formal association with the monastery as a postulant, the anchorites already considered the young layman a disciple. John wrote that previously he had given Dorotheos milk, but now he was ready for more (a reference to Heb. 5:12). John also spoke of Dorotheos' gratitude "to the one who carries your burden," a reference to Barsanuphius as the spiritual director of Dorotheos (Letter 252). The Great Old Man confirmed his acceptance of the role of Dorotheos' spiritual father by greeting him with a blessing and addressing him as "child" (Letter 253).[9]

The distribution of one's goods to the poor was an established way to announce one's intention of becoming a monk.[10] By divesting himself of family wealth, Dorotheos followed the model instituted by such saints as Antony of Egypt and Macrina, the elder sister of Basil of Caesarea.[11] In his transition from lay to monastic life, Dorotheos sought practical advice for the disposal of his goods. He turned to John, who advised him to decide how much of his property to give to the monastery and how much to distribute to the poor. The abbot could then carry out the dispersal. But John agreed that his books need not be sold but should go to the common library of the monastery (Letter 326).[12] Considering that Dorotheos' poor health might cause him some difficulty in his transition to monastic life, John specified the items of clothing that Dorotheos should keep for his own use (Letter 326).[13] Barsanuphius was also concerned for Dorotheos' health and suggested that he take a little wine (Letter 255). In an unusual decision, Barsanuphius conceded that Dorotheos could keep a small piece of land for his maintenance (Letter 254). Dorotheos made this request ostensibly because of his weak physical condition, although lurking behind it may have been a second reason: his family objected to his giving away all of his wealth (Letter 319). The concession was a temporary exemption, so that Dorotheos could turn his attention to the greater task of leaving behind his own will in order to become a monk.[14]

Onlookers might describe Dorotheos' entrance into the monastic life as a simple decision: "In all confidence Dorotheos abandoned himself to [Barsanuphius and John]."[15] The letters reveal it to have been a more complex process. Dorotheos' questions to Barsanuphius and John show the doubts and insecurities that accompanied his early development in the monastic life. Under the direction of his spiritual fathers, he faced the normal temptations associated with conversion from a life of luxury to one of ascetic discipline. He blamed his fragile health for preventing him from following through on the more severe ascetic practices that he adopted for penitence (Letter 257). This inability to adopt a strict asceticism may have made him self-conscious and slowed his integration into the monastic community. His social interactions with the brothers were at times strained; he worried that others would misinterpret his customary silence (Letter 258). Dorotheos considered fleeing the cenobium for the solitary life (Letters 259, 314). The anchorites provided a source of security, which sustained him during this troubled time. Later in his life, Dorotheos recalled the encouragement Barsanuphius and John provided him when he became discouraged: "And when such thoughts came upon me I used to take up my pen and write to one of the Ancients. On this occasion I wrote and asked Abba John, the disciple of Abba Barsanuphius, and while I was writing even before I was finished, I was sensible of help and relief, and this itself increased my freedom from care and my sense of peace."[16] Dorotheos' words provide explicit confirmation that the very act of writing to the anchorite could make a disciple feel less burdened.

Recognizing the young monk's capabilities despite his difficult transition to monastic life, the abbot entrusted and challenged Dorotheos with growing responsibilities. His assignments as porter and guestmaster required him to confront his uneasiness communicating with others, offering hospitality to visitors and informing the abbot of their arrival (Letter 288).[17] Entertaining guests required that he overcome the physical weariness from which he suffered and converse with newcomers: "Strangers would arrive and I would spend the evening with them or there would be cameleers and I attended to their needs; after that I would go to bed, but I was often awakened for some other emergency."[18] The work so overloaded Dorotheos that he asked Barsanuphius for an assistant (Letter 359). His new position required him to judge the character of guests, but Dorotheos was anxious that he might also be expected to inform the abbot of any questionable actions by the monks. Uneasy over his relationship with other brothers, he feared he might make enemies of those he reported to the abbot (Letters 294–97, and 301).[19] Dorotheos' concerns reveal his trouble fitting into the community, which made him reluctant to accept responsibilities that required him to interact with the public and supervise other monks.

The abbot utilized to the advantage of the monastery Dorotheos' experience in the world he had left behind. Seridos put Dorotheos' study of medicine to good use by giving him the task of constructing an infirmary for the cenobium. To finance this project Seridos turned to the young man's family. Dorotheos' biological brother, a lay Christian and "lover of monks," defrayed the expense of the infirmary.[20] When the building was completed, Dorotheos was put in charge of the infirmary and had the use of his own medical books now in the monastery's library.

The job of infirmarian could bring many hazards to a monk seeking the virtue of spiritual detachment (*apatheia*). This assignment, like that of porter, continued to force Dorotheos to interact with both brothers and lay visitors and to consult with the abbot regularly. He worried that this occupation would keep him from pursuing the very thing that had brought him to the monastery—a life of contemplation. Managing a busy infirmary frequented by monks and lay people might prevent him from having any time alone in his cell (Letter 313).

The abbot's growing approval of Dorotheos increased the hostility that some brothers felt towards him. Dorotheos was sensitive to this tension and went so far as to ask permission (which John denied) to stop associating with the brothers outside of the infirmary (Letter 286). He blamed his work at the infirmary for creating this jealousy; however, the level of animosity indicates more fundamental personality conflicts with his peers. Dorotheos later described his experience: "I know one brother walked behind me from the infirmary to the church, abusing me all the way. But I went on ahead without uttering a single word. When the abbot learned about it—I don't know who told him—he wanted to rebuke him. I fell at his feet saying, '[D]o not do so. . . . It was I who failed.' "[21] Dorotheos suffered worse than verbal abuse:

> And another brother, whether to provoke me or out of simplicity, the Lord knows which, during the night silence made water all over my head and soaked my bed. Similarly some of the other brethren began during the day, to shake their rush-mats in front of my cell, and I saw such a horde of flies and stinging insects coming into my cell that I could not kill them all. . . . When I came back to lie down they all settled upon me. . . . when I woke up I found my body bitten all over.[22]

Such acts of physical abuse reveal the dark side of cenobitic life, in which members of the community could act together to persecute one perceived to be different.[23] Dorotheos later drew on such incidents to instruct his own disciples on the necessity of bearing trials patiently, but they also reveal his own troubled time living in community.

Dorotheos had expected life in the monastery to differ in pronounced ways from life in the world. When he found himself in the monastery practicing medicine, which he had studied as a lay person, confusion ensued. His medical books offered the temptation to retreat to a great love from his previous life, which he thought he had renounced upon becoming a monk. He asked Barsanuphius if he should read works on medicine and put their theories into practice, "or if it would be better for me not to care for the things that distract the mind, and to flee them for fear lest I, being inattentive, allow them to create pride in myself. I could content myself with oil, and fire, and ointments, in a word, with the things that serve those who do not read medical works" (Letter 327). With gentle humor the Great Old Man replied that since no one was perfect, it was better to give oneself to medicine than to the passions. Dorotheos should use his medical books as the brothers used work manuals, always remembering that there was no healing without God, who gave both life and death.[24] Dorotheos found yet another source of unexpected temptation—the medical supplies donated to the infirmary. Dorotheos knew that he accepted bequests not only because of their benefit to his patients but also because they pleased him as a physician. As Barsanuphius had encouraged him to use his medical knowledge despite its tempting nature, John advised Dorotheos to accept what was necessary for the infirmary, at the same time rebuking himself for covetousness (Letter 336).

Dorotheos saw inherent conflicts between what he assumed to be proper monastic behavior and his role as a physician. As a monk he was supposed to flee from gluttony and thoughts of food. As the head of the infirmary, he had to carry tempting meals to the sick in his care (Letters 323, 328, and 330). As a monk, he was supposed to relinquish his own will in submission to others. As a doctor he had to force painful treatments on unwilling patients (Letter 328). Dorotheos was even torn by his desire to participate in the liturgy and his guilt over leaving his patients to the care of an assistant (Letter 334).[25] His early years in the cenobium at Tawatha forced Dorotheos to reconcile his idealistic expectations about ascetic life with the cumbersome realities of service to others.

An even greater challenge for Dorotheos than adjusting to the daily requirements of monastic life was learning to submit his own will to higher authority. Although he had a close relationship with both Barsanuphius and John, Dorotheos had difficulty relating to the abbot.[26] Perhaps the difference was due in some part to Dorotheos' ability to express himself well in written words (i.e., letters to the anchorites) and his problems with person-to-person interaction. He hesitated to reveal his thoughts to Seridos, because he thought the abbot would be troubled by his confessions (Letter 286). Dorotheos asked John if it were necessary to submit his will to Seridos' not only when the abbot's command seemed good or indifferent but also in cases when the abbot's word seemed to transgress God's commands. John explained that "the one who desires to be a monk" must submit to his spiritual father in all things (Letter 288). Even when his commands seemed to lead to sin, the abbot bore responsibility for his disciple before God. Dorotheos' concern that the abbot might give poor guidance was probably connected to his surprise at the differences between his previous expectations of monastic life and his actual experience of communal living.

Although initially the relationship between Seridos and Dorotheos was tense, the two were eventually able to forge a productive working relationship. Seridos began to integrate Dorotheos into the leadership structure of the monastery, even though the latter continued his habit of appealing to the Old Men when he doubted the abbot. The deliberate cultivation of Dorotheos' leadership skills in the face of the monk's own reluctance, the disapproval of his peers, and his resistance to the abbot's authority provides insight into the view of spiritual authority held by the abbot and the anchorites. Dorotheos' social awkwardness and difficulties bowing to authority did not disqualify him from being entrusted with responsibility. Rather, the fathers at Tawatha saw his intelligence and independence as attributes of a potential leader, who with careful training and experience in various positions of responsibility would be able to serve the monastery competently in years to come.

DOROTHEOS AS A SPIRITUAL FATHER

Despite his early difficulties relating to the other monks and submitting himself to the abbot, Dorotheos progressed in the monastic life to the point that Seridos gained sufficient confidence in him to entrust disciples to his care. As we have seen, the authority to direct another's spiritual progress was not granted lightly by the leaders of the monastery at Tawatha. A monk needed specific instruction from his own fathers to undertake the direction of those who came to him spontaneously. Dorotheos later recounted how he began to practice spiritual direction: "When I was in the cenobium, I do not know how it happened, [but] the brothers confided in me all their thoughts. It is said that the abbot at the advice of the Old Men charged me to listen to them."[27] In the setting of his infirmary, Dorotheos directed those who came to him, serving as an intermediary between these new disciples and higher authority within the monastery. When one young monk, who struggled with kleptomania, was ashamed to speak with the abbot, Dorotheos consulted Seridos on his behalf. Seridos permitted Dorotheos to make any necessary arrangements to help the monk.[28] This episode demonstrates that when Dorotheos did submit to the abbot it reinforced Seridos' growing reliance on him as one of the monastery's spiritual directors.

Dorotheos' most famous disciple was his first, Dositheos. One day some friends of the abbot who were in the service of the provincial military commander (*doux*) arrived with a youth dressed in military garb who sought admission to the monastery. According to the hagiographic text, the *Life of Saint Dositheos*, Seridos summoned Dorotheos from the infirmary to interview the new candidate. With evident trust in Dorotheos' judgment, Seridos confided his worry, saying, "I greatly fear that he belongs to some important person, and having committed some crime he wants to flee here, and we will have troubles."[29] When Dorotheos examined Dositheos and found him honest but uneducated in religious matters, he recommended that Seridos admit him to the monastery. Seridos agreed and instructed Dorotheos to take the boy under his direction. It may have been part of the abbot's long-term plan to find a helper for the infirmary, for Dorotheos had long complained of weak health and the many demands on his time. Nevertheless, the abbot added another practical reason for placing the youth in the infirmary under Dorotheos' care: "I do not want him to mingle with the brothers."[30]

Dorotheos rebuffed the abbot's instructions, protesting that he was not worthy to take charge of another's soul. This might easily be dismissed as an expression of conventional monastic humility common in hagiography if we had only the account in the *Life of Saint Dositheos.* However, from letters we know that Dorotheos often resisted the abbot's instructions when he disagreed with them and that he was uncomfortable in close interactions with other brothers. He found the idea of having someone constantly under his supervision very disconcerting. There is more evidence within the *Life of Dositheos* itself that Dorotheos was not merely adopting a modest stance of humility. When Dorotheos refused, Seridos asserted his own rank: "I bear the burden of both you and him."[31] Still not submitting, Dorotheos demanded that Seridos put the decision before the Great Old Man. The genuine tension of this verbal exchange captured in the *Life* was brought to a quick but artificial resolution when Barsanuphius replied that through Dorotheos' efforts Dositheos would be saved: "Then Dorotheos welcomed him with joy and had him with him in the infirmary."[32] We are left to wonder about the actual accommodations that Dorotheos was forced to make for his new assistant.

Dorotheos' new disciple knew almost nothing of the Christian life.[33] He had worked as a page for the provincial military commander and led a life of relative privilege. Hearing stories of the holy places, Dositheos had expressed an interest in seeing Jerusalem. The commander had quickly indulged his whim and made arrangements for him to travel there with a friend. At Gethsemane, Dositheos saw an image of hell depicted but did not understand its meaning. Then he had a vision of a "majestic lady dressed in purple," who explained to him the fate of the damned.[34] When he asked her how to avoid such chastisements, she replied that he should fast, abstain from meat, and pray. His companions noticed him acting upon these instructions and teased that he would make a fine monk. Still knowing little about the monastic life or about God, Dositheos asked to go to a monastery.

Dositheos' lack of familiarity with monasticism contrasted with Dorotheos' idealistic expectations about the monastic life. Unlike his own awkward attempts at strict asceticism complicated by weak health, Dorotheos found that his new disciple took easily to fasting. Dorotheos came to the monastery from the study of rhetoric; Dositheos came dressed as a soldier speaking "like a Goth."[35] There were also similarities between the two. Both men were strong willed and intelligent, excelling in the work of the infirmary. Dositheos struggled with his will even after he fell ill.[36] Dorotheos tried to protect his disciple from the very things by which he himself had been tempted. To limit Dositheos' enjoyment of equipment given to the infirmary, Dorotheos prohibited him from using a new knife he admired, asking him, "Do you want to be a slave to the knife and not a slave of God?"[37] Dorotheos also wanted to neutralize Dositheos' pride in his own accomplishments. When the young monk expressed pleasure in his ability to make comfortable beds for the patients, Dorotheos replied, "You are then a good servant. You are a good worker. But are you a good monk?"[38]

While still under the spiritual direction of the anchorites and the abbot himself, Dorotheos was beginning to guide his new disciple. The Old Men at Tawatha believed that directing a disciple was a critical step for Dorotheos' own spiritual development. The instructions given by this new spiritual father seem directed as much at his own shortcomings as at any flaws in his disciple's character. His sharp concern about Dositheos' appreciation of medical instruments contrasts directly with Barsanuphius' flexibility in responding to Dorotheos' apprehension about his fondness for medical books and supplies. The leaders of the monastic community may have hoped that overseeing Dositheos' spiritual development would help Dorotheos reflect on his own approach to the spiritual life.

After five years in the cenobium, Dositheos fell terminally ill. As his spiritual director, Dorotheos had taught him prayers that he had learned from his own fathers.[39] In the last stages of the illness, Dositheos turned to the highest spiritual authority within the monastery, the Great Old Man. The multiple layers of spiritual authority at Tawatha allowed recourse to increasingly mature fathers as the dilemmas faced by a disciple began to stretch the spiritual resources of his own father.

As the community grappled with the tragedy of Dositheos' approaching death, Barsanuphius addressed the spiritual needs of his disciples. He used the youth's passing to instruct the monks on the relative value of life and death. Instead of requesting healing, Dositheos had asked Barsanuphius to pray for his sins to be forgiven. Barsanuphius assured him that all his sins from his infancy until the present had been forgiven and also indicated that the end of his pain approached (Letter 220). Letters from the Great Old Man to individuals, particularly in times of crisis, were not always kept private. Rumors had circulated quickly among the anxious brothers, and they wanted to know what Barsanuphius had meant: would Dositheos live or die? They turned to John for an explanation of Barsanuphius' words. John answered that Barsanuphius had meant that Dositheos would die but added that if God inspired Barsanuphius, he could as easily pray for healing (Letter 221). The monks immediately demanded this of the Great Old Man, who explained to them that death was part of God's mercy and held many more rewards for their brother than life (Letter 222). Accepting this difficult lesson, the monks began to pray for death to come quickly and end Dositheos' pain (Letter 223).

In the *Life*, Dositheos himself asks Barsanuphius to pray that he might die. The Great Old Man finally granted his blessing, indicating that Dositheos' death was imminent: "Go in peace! Stand by the Holy Trinity and intercede for us."[40] In this text the brothers show more astonishment at the honor implied in this blessing than concern for Dositheos. They doubted his sanctity, since he performed his acts of asceticism in private. It required a visiting father's vision of Dositheos among the saints to convince them of his holiness.[41]

The *Life of Dositheos* depicts Dorotheos as a wise spiritual father, dispensing conventional ascetic instruction to his disciple. However, the sketch of Dositheos reveals some striking comparisons with the portrait of the young Dorotheos that emerges from the Correspondence of Barsanuphius and John. We see the same strained relations between the protagonist and the other brothers. But whereas the letters of Dorotheos show the real life awkwardness of a bright young man, who found the social interaction of joining an established community difficult, in the *Life of Dositheos* the awkwardness has been transformed into a sign of sanctity, distinguishing Dositheos from the other monks. Dorotheos worried that his talents would make his brothers envious and his misjudgments might make them angry. In the *Life* the brothers regularly made Dositheos cry for no other reason than to reveal his sensitive conscience.[42] Dositheos performed acts of asceticism but hid them from the brothers. Dorotheos, on the other hand, was unable to complete the ascetic practices he began. Dositheos' illness led to an early and sanctified death. Dorotheos' fragile health caused only frustration and embarrassment by keeping him from his ascetic ambitions. Although Dorotheos was not the author of the *Life of Dositheos*, the text expresses his version of the main events and his interpretation of the meaning of his disciple's life. Perhaps, in serving as a spiritual father, Dorotheos was able to reinterpret the memories of his own early years at the cenobium.

DOROTHEOS AS DISCIPLE OF JOHN

Appointment as a spiritual director was a clear acknowledgment of spiritual maturity, but becoming a disciple could also be a mark of spiritual advancement. This was certainly the case when Seridos designated Dorotheos to serve John, after the anchorite's previous disciple fell ill. Only two people spoke directly with the Old Men, the abbot and Dorotheos. Seridos recorded the letters Barsanuphius dictated, and Dorotheos carried John's letters to the brothers.[43] This elevation to the status of John's disciple created a functional bond between Dorotheos and Abbot Seridos, signified by their common task of representing the directives of the anchorites to the monastery. Dorotheos served in this role for nine years, until the deaths of John and Seridos precipitated the radical reorganization of the structure of spiritual authority in Tawatha.[44]

Later, speaking to his own disciples, Dorotheos described his reaction to this new assignment: "I used to reverence the door of his cell with as much devotion as one would pay the Cross of Christ. How much more reverently would I serve him? Who would not desire to be worthy to serve such a holy man?"[45] Others in the monastery desired this position. Once again, a promotion of Dorotheos by the abbot caused jealousy among his brothers. To alleviate this tension and to demonstrate his own humility,

Dorotheos asked the abbot to give the duty to another brother, one of those who coveted the position. Both Seridos and John refused this request.

Although some scholars have suggested that before this appointment Barsanuphius served as Dorotheos' primary spiritual father, it is clear that from this time on John directed Dorotheos.[46] In future years, Dorotheos would repeatedly recall the words of John from memory when he instructed his own disciples. The exchange of verbal communication between the two held particular meaning for Dorotheos, who recognized that hearing John's voice was a unique privilege. Their conversation made letters between the two unnecessary, bringing to an end one record of their interaction, just as their relationship reached a new level of intimacy. So it is upon Dorotheos' later recollections that we depend for information concerning this period of his life. He described for his disciples John's manner of speech. Following ancient tradition, each time he bid his spiritual father goodbye Dorotheos asked for a word from the Old Man.[47] Dorotheos confessed that their familiarity sometimes made him hesitate to confide his thoughts to John, since he did not wish to disturb the Old Man and he already knew what John would say.[48] Thus, as the relationship between disciple and spiritual father reached a more advanced stage, new temptations arose to jeopardize the process of spiritual direction. Serving as John's disciple helped Dorotheos become a better spiritual father. His experience as John's disciple provided him with a source of wisdom to draw upon when he mentored others in subsequent years.

ABBA DOROTHEOS

The course of Dorotheos' well-documented life becomes more elusive after his service to John ends, at the time of the Old Man's death. The events surrounding the death of John, which nearly coincided with the death of Seridos and the complete enclosement of Barsanuphius, are fully discussed in Chapter 6. Here it is necessary only to summarize them as they relate to Dorotheos. When Seridos' will was read after his death, it included a list of those who should succeed him as abbot. The list named senior monks from the community, each of whom declined the office, and the position passed to the last man named on the list, a layman named Aelianos. Barsanuphius and John supported both the monks' refusal and Aelianos' acceptance of the office.

It is probable that Seridos included Dorotheos among those named to succeed him, given Dorotheos' vast experience in the monastery, both in practical posts, such as porter and head of the infirmary, and in positions carrying substantial spiritual authority, such as directing novices and serving John. It is also not surprising that Dorotheos declined this responsibility, for although he excelled at administrative duties, he had long indicated his preference for the solitary life. The busy demands of the infirmary and guesthouse had always made him long for the peace of his own cell. The post of abbot would bring more responsibilities and leave him even less time for solitude. Dorotheos had enjoyed serving as John's disciple and may have hoped to emulate his father by becoming an anchorite after John's death.

Scholars have generally assumed that Dorotheos eventually left the monastery at Tawatha and founded his own monastery nearby.[49] This is a possibility, but it is necessary to examine the evidence behind this common assumption more closely. The strongest and most direct evidence that Dorotheos established his own monastery is the title given to the *Discourses* in manuscripts: "Discourses from our holy father Dorotheos to his disciples, when he withdrew from that of Abba Seridos and, with God, founded his own monastery, after the death of Abba John the Prophet and the complete silence of Barsanuphius."[50] This attestation was sufficient to convince Lucien Regnault of Dorotheos' departure from Tawatha.[51]

Two other pieces of early evidence may indicate that Dorotheos left Tawatha to found his own monastery. The first is a comment from Dorotheos himself in *Discourses:* "There was a certain brother in the cenobium before my withdrawal from there . . ."[52] The other piece of information used to support Dorotheos' establishment of his own monastery is a reference in John Moschus: "He took him to the community of Abba Dorotheos, near to Gaza and Maiouma."[53]

There is another argument for Dorotheos' leaving Tawatha, based not on specific evidence, but on characteristics of his personality. Obvious strife existed between Dorotheos and some of the brothers at the monastery in Tawatha. Despite this interpersonal tension, Seridos repeatedly elevated Dorotheos to levels of responsibility and authority within the monastery. Likewise, Barsanuphius and John both supported Dorotheos, and John even adopted him as his main physical link with the cenobium. Given his history of strained relations with other members of the community, perhaps Dorotheos' authority dissipated after Seridos and John died and Barsanuphius no longer oversaw the governance of the monastery. Without their support Dorotheos may have found life there too difficult, or he may have been unable to establish a productive relationship with the new abbot. Any number of problems resulting from the change in leadership could have caused Dorotheos to withdraw to another establishment, either alone or with a small group of brothers.

Despite the evidence outlined above, there is no certainty that Dorotheos left the monastery at Tawatha, as has been assumed. The manuscript title of *Discourses* crediting Dorotheos with founding his own monastery could have been added by a later copyist, unfamiliar with the final years of Dorotheos' life. The copyist might have based his title on Dorotheos' comment about his own withdrawal from the cenobium of Seridos. While this remark could be understood to mean that Dorotheos left the monastery at Tawatha, it could also mean that he left the cenobium and withdrew to practice the solitary life in an anchorite's cell. There were many fathers connected to the cenobium who lived apart in their own cells, and it would not be unreasonable for Dorotheos to have followed this pattern. In fact, given his early aspirations for the solitary life, his continued lack of ease interacting with others, and his close association with John, it is likely that Dorotheos eventually adopted the anchoritic life.

The reference by John Moschus to the community of Dorotheos near Gaza and Maiouma is also open to different interpretations. Some have understood this passage to designate a new monastery where Dorotheos served as abbot, but it could as easily refer to the monastery at Tawatha, which was close to both Gaza and Maiouma. John Moschus began his ascetic career at the Monastery of St. Theodosius sometime after Dorotheos' death but while the memory of the great spiritual father was still very much alive in Palestine.[54] The monastery at Tawatha had a long history of being under the direction of both anchorites and an abbot. There is no reason that the name of a well-known spiritual father and anchorite, Dorotheos, could not have been associated with the monastery, whose cenobium was governed by the lesser-known Aelianos or another abbot.[55] Dorotheos' letter to a person overseeing brothers in a monastery would be appropriate advice for an established anchorite to offer a nearby abbot.[56]

While intriguing for its attention to Dorotheos' personality and his interactions with others, the argument that Dorotheos left Tawatha due to personality clashes remains speculative. It is equally plausible to argue that he withdrew from the cenobium to live the solitary life in the manner of his mentor John without breaking his connection with the monastery. The evidence does not decisively exclude either possibility. After the change in leadership at Tawatha, Dorotheos might have left for any number of reasons, or he might have remained there as a hermit.

The debate about Dorotheos' later years has ramifications beyond the fate of one monk. The lack of certainty about Dorotheos' movements affects our understanding of spiritual authority in Tawatha. If Dorotheos maintained his relationship with the monastery, living in a nearby cell, his presence would have contributed to a sense of continuity between the leadership of Barsanuphius, John, and Seridos and that of the new abbot, Aelianos. He might have collaborated with Aelianos and other abbots in much the same way that Barsanuphius and John worked with Seridos. If this were the case, then Dorotheos' later writings would be the second volume of the story of monastic life at Tawatha. However, if Dorotheos departed to found his own monastery, particularly if this action was precipitated by conflict or followed his own refusal to become abbot, then we have an example of the failed attempt to transfer spiritual authority from one generation of leaders to the next within a monastery. Dorotheos would have been the spiritual heir but not the institutional successor of Barsanuphius, John, and Seridos, a position for which those three had certainly worked to prepare him. If Dorotheos had left the monastic community at Tawatha, the new leadership would have faced a sharper break with the past and had fewer spiritual resources on which to rely.

One final issue to consider is the possibility that Dorotheos himself was involved in the compilation of the letters of Barsanuphius and John.[57] He had the educational background and spiritual authority within the monastery to embark on such a task. As the disciple of John for nine years, he was second only to Seridos in his access to the Old Men.[58] We know that the compiler of the Correspondence had been a monk in the monastery at Tawatha during the active ministry of Barsanuphius and John. He claimed to have seen the Great Old Man himself on the rare occasion when Barsanuphius emerged from his seclusion to wash the monks' feet (Letter 125).[59]

Another reason for suggesting that Dorotheos had a hand in compiling the letters of the holy men is the lack of direct reference to him in the Correspondence. Although later manuscripts attach his name to some letters, these letters are not placed in the beginning, with the other letters to named correspondents. Since he was the most famous disciple produced at Tawatha, this silence is difficult to explain otherwise. Even if Dorotheos left the community abruptly following considerable tension with the new abbot, it is unlikely that his memory would be obscured by his departure at that point. A more reasonable explanation for the lack of reference to Dorotheos is that he compiled the letters himself. Neyt has suggested that the letters to the porter and others may have been written to Dorotheos. If Dorotheos were the compiler of the text he would have been motivated by monastic humility to leave off his own name and scatter his letters throughout the text. While this hypothesis about the compilation of the Correspondence cannot be proven, it remains an intriguing possibility.

The life of Dorotheos helps us to understand the manner in which the anchorites and abbot at Tawatha chose and trained new leaders for the community. The choice of Dorotheos as a potential leader for the community probably evoked mixed reactions from the inhabitants of the monastery. On the one hand, he was intelligent, hardworking, born to a wealthy family, and skilled in medicine—all attributes that were considered favorable in late antique society. Furthermore, he was idealistic and yearned to dedicate himself to the ascetic life. On the other hand, Dorotheos was reluctant to let go of all his personal possessions when he entered the monastery. He suffered poor health and ultimately had to give up any aspirations towards rigorous asceticism. His natural independence made it difficult for him to bend his will in obedience to the abbot. Above all these apparent shortcomings, however, loomed his social ineptness, which made him the target of verbal and physical abuse and prevented him from being fully integrated into the social network of the cenobium. Dorotheos' voice always retained the overtones of an outsider, no matter how many responsibilities the leaders of the community gave to him.

Barsanuphius, John, and Seridos looked beyond the difficulties Dorotheos experienced interacting with the other monks. They did not dismiss his gifts simply because he had trouble submitting to the authority of the abbot. As in the case of John of Beersheba, the fathers at Tawatha realized that an independent spirit, which caused initial difficulties, could ultimately be a valuable component in the make-up of a new leader. They recognized that Dorotheos' intelligence would serve the monastery well, once he had let go of his idealistic expectations and dedicated his talents to the real needs of the community. The anchorites and abbot directed Dorotheos' efforts towards practical tasks, such as running the infirmary or the guesthouse. They discouraged him from spending his energy in severe ascetic practices, and they did not permit him to withdraw as an anchorite. They made sure that Dorotheos experienced a wide range of leadership positions within the community.

Since spiritual authority at Tawatha rested upon the father-disciple relationship, discipleship was a key part of Dorotheos' preparation for leadership. Seridos arranged for him both to have charge of disciples and to serve as a disciple to John. Dorotheos initially resisted both assignments but eventually benefited from each experience. As a spiritual director, Dorotheos guided Dositheos through the transitions of becoming a monk and serving others in the infirmary. In his role as father to Dositheos, Dorotheos was able to reflect upon and perhaps resolve some lingering disappointments about his own early experiences as a monk. As a disciple of John, Dorotheos was able to observe first-hand a revered practitioner of the anchoritic life he desired to follow. Seridos and John believed this experience was necessary for Dorotheos before he was permitted to pursue the solitary life himself. Dorotheos' monastic career at Tawatha reveals a principle of spiritual direction consistently advocated by the Old Men of Gaza, that discipleship provided the basis of spiritual authority.

CHAPTER 4

Lay Disciples
Social Obligations and Spiritual Concerns

The Great Old Man's jurisdiction reached beyond the cenobium walls and the cells of the solitary monks. The advice of Barsanuphius and John permeated the boundaries of the monastery and exercised influence in the private homes of lay Christians in the region. Lay people found the anchorites accessible, as demonstrated by the fact that more than a quarter of the letters in the Correspondence addressed laity. Christians in the city of Gaza and its outlying neighborhoods questioned the holy men about the competing demands of friends, family, and property. Such worldly concerns of the laity offer a striking contrast to the contemplative life practiced by the anchorites. But these practical matters, which seem to draw a sharp division between the lay and monastic life, make up only a portion of the concerns that lay persons brought to Barsanuphius and John. There are questions, too, about church practice, asceticism, the spiritual life, and the theological disputes of the day. From the content of the petitions, it is not always easy to classify the petitioner as lay or monastic.[1] Many lay Christians were very closely associated with the monastery, and some appear to have been in the midst of transition from the lay to the monastic life.

LAY CHRISTIANS

The lay Christians who wrote to Barsanuphius and John were, in large part, people who took their Christian faith seriously. That is not to say that they were exceptionally holy. As in the correspondence between Barsanuphius and John and the monks, the questions posed by lay people display the full range of human frailties and imperfections. Still, it should be recognized that the very act of writing to an anchorite for spiritual direction gave a person the status of a disciple, not an altogether lowly position in sixth-century Palestine. Indeed, many holy men in this period based their own spiritual authority on being the disciple of a revered spiritual father. Those who chose to question the Old Men, therefore, deliberately assumed the position of disciple and voluntarily entered into a relationship with the anchorites. They accepted, in principle at least, that disciples owed their spiritual fathers obedience in return for the Old Men's wisdom and prayers.

Lay people from a cross section of Palestinian society appealed to the anchorites for advice. To compose a message to the holy men did not necessitate literacy. Although some petitioners did write their own letters (as the example of the monk who wrote in Coptic demonstrates [Letter 55]), it is likely that Seridos or his scribe would be available to record the questions of the illiterate.[2] In addition, some of the questions refer to situations involving particular women,[3] but no letter in the collection is attributed to a woman. While this may indicate a lack of female petitioners, it is also plausible that questions from women were not preserved or that the female identity of petitioners has been obscured, rather than that women were excluded from communicating with the anchorites.

The monastery was not an island, isolated from the bustle and clamor of life in sixth-century Palestine; rather the instructions of Barsanuphius and John to lay Christians reveal the many ways in which the monastery was intimately connected to the population outside the monastery. The rich detail of the letters presents various aspects of the social world not readily accessible in other texts from the period, elucidating the demands of kinship, property, and politics that competed along with religion for priority in the lives of ordinary people. Whether seeking to escape injustice at the hands of the powerful or requesting healing on behalf of a dying friend, lay people were confident that their most practical needs merited the attention of the Holy Men. The personal concerns confessed to the anchorites reveal the daily workings of the social, economic, and civic spheres of the region.

Some letters from the Old Men to lay people, however, could easily be mistaken for those written to monks. Many lay people possessed a deep level of spiritual insight and sought to engage the fathers on weighty theological matters. Barsanuphius and John's message to lay Christians did not differ substantially from that given to monks, although the letters do show an appropriate sensitivity to lay people's concerns and obligations. The same sins afflicted both monks and laity, and although some-times monks were required to maintain a somewhat higher standard of piety, both groups were measured against the same scale. The boundary between lay and monastic life in Tawatha was relatively permeable; in some instances this permeability caused confusion. Some lay persons sought the outward characteristics of monastic life, such as seclusion and fasting, without the inward commitment. Aspects of lay piety that most concerned the anchorites included ascetic practice, theological debate, and visions. On occasions when these activities became disruptive to spiritual development, Barsanuphius and John strove to sharpen the dis-tinctions between lay persons and monks, warning that laity should not be misled by false visions or adopt too rigorous an ascetic regimen.

NEIGHBORS: JEWS, PAGANS, AND HERETICS

Sixth-century Gaza was a diverse community, with Christians living side by side with pagans, Jews, and Samaritans. The intense pagan-Christian conflict that had characterized Gaza in earlier centuries seems to have subsided in large part, and Christians could write to the anchorites about mundane social interactions with their pagan and Jewish neighbors. The mingling of people of different faiths was typical in the cities of Byzantine Palestine, as historian Glen Bowersock describes:

> The ethnic and cultural communities with their broad range of religious observances and their local roots were integral parts of a larger Palestinian world. These communities did not exist with walls around them to keep them from associating with each other. Quite the contrary. Among educated persons bilingualism was common, and trilingualism not unknown. The communities enriched each other, and sometimes converted each other.[4]

Villages may have been more homogenous, some predominately Chris-tian and others largely Jewish or Samaritan, but trade still linked these smaller communities to one another and to the larger urban centers.[5] Even rural people, like their urban counterparts, consulted Barsanuphius and John about how to treat neighbors who belonged to other religions. To these concerns, Barsanuphius and John responded by advising open interaction on an economic level and more guarded behavior on social occasions that carried religious significance. John granted one man permission to press a Jewish neighbor's grapes in his press: "If, when it rains, God makes rain fall on your field and leaves [dry] next to it that of the Jew, then you may no longer press his wine; but if he is full of humanity for all and makes the rain fall on the just and the unjust, why would you, yourself, be inhuman and not merciful?" (Letter 686). This accommodation did not, however, extend to dining with Jews or pagans on their feast days. John wrote both to the Bishop of Gaza and to a lay disciple that the church canons forbade such fellowship.[6] This was not an easy prohibition for Christians in Gaza to accept, because of the close relations that flourished among pagan and Christian neighbors. The bishop had to reprimand the city's ruling citizens for attending pagan festivities (Letter 836), and the layman agonized: "But if it is an important person and my friend, and he is saddened if I do not accept, what should I say to him?" (Letter 776).[7] The question demonstrates both the intimacy and the unease that characterized interfaith friendships. John outlined the boundaries that had to be consciously maintained between friends who adhered to different religions: "Say to him: You know that those who fear God must keep all his commandments, and your own customs will convince you, because for the sake of your love towards me, you would never transgress the commandments of your tradition. And I would not think because of this that you had considered slight your love for me" (Letter 776).

After the Christian emperor Justinian issued his edict outlawing paganism in 529, the line between pagan and Christian grew further confused.[8] Peter, Patriarch of Jerusalem, was overwhelmed with converts seeking baptism (Letter 821). The influx of new members triggered by the imperial legislation strained the church's resources for discipling new believers in the faith, and some Christians were skeptical about the genuineness of politically coerced conversion.[9] One pagan, either wishing to pose as a Christian or perhaps not willing to wait until the appropriate time in the ecclesiastical year for baptism, was discovered "in the ranks of the faithful" at the eucharistic celebration (Letter 822). The furious crowd pressed for his death by burning, but the Other Old Man counseled the Patriarch of Jerusalem that this was not the correct Christian response. The trespasser should be fined and sent for proper instruction so that he might be baptized.

Although John did not permit pagans at the Christian mysteries nor allow his disciples to feast with pagan or Jewish neighbors, he did not forbid the commerce that accompanied pagan festivities. Christians could freely engage in business transactions with pagans, buying whatever they needed from merchants peddling their wares at pagan festivals (Letter 777). In a similar manner, pagans and Jews probably enjoyed the markets that accompanied the Christian festivals, with "booths . . . carefully executed with branches of laurel, with colorful fabrics and with gold and silver, [matching] well the abundance and luxuriousness of the merchandise."[10]

Interaction between Christian neighbors carried its own risk. The same theological controversies dividing the Eastern Empire threatened to separate the Christian community of Gaza. Lay Christians eagerly engaged in theological disputes despite the warnings of Barsanuphius and John. The anchorites believed that such activity ought to be reserved for experienced monks. The ability to offer spiritual direction to another required considerable discernment. A lay person needed to recognize his own limitations and judge when to seek help from someone with greater spiritual authority. John offered guidelines: "If it is a friend according to God and he is in danger for his soul's salvation or the destruction of his affairs, make haste to help him all that you can without injuring your soul. But if it holds harm to your soul, withdraw and do not throw yourself into it, but give the matter to God and pray to him concerning aid for your neighbor, for he is able to help him, in our place" (Letter 732).[11] A layman should exhort a heretical friend to study the orthodox faith but should not discuss doctrine with him, for fear that he might become infected himself with the "venom" of heresy (Letter 733).[12] Instead, the layman should send his friend to the fathers, who are capable of explaining such matters. If, after several exhortations, the friend refused to consider his errors, the man should flee his presence, according to the apostle's instruction (Titus 3:10).

An ascetic vocation did not guarantee orthodox doctrine. John cautioned lay Christians to be wary of heretical monks. The friends of a certain father who embraced heretical doctrines distanced themselves from the monk. Later they feared their behavior might encourage him to separate from the church. They decided to apologize to him but first solicited John's opinion. John said that they had done nothing to require repentance, but that they might apologize to prevent his leaving the church (Letter 734). If he did separate from the church and they met him on the street, they should treat him as they did all heretics (Letter 735).

Unfortunately, John did not elaborate on the proper greeting for a heretic, but his message was clear: communion with the church surpassed ascetic endeavors as a measure of spiritual authority.[13]

Religious difference was not the only variety of tension between neighbors that came to the attention of John and Barsanuphius. Laymen recognized that mundane problems carried spiritual implications when they threatened to disrupt social relations within the community.[14] One man whose field was being devoured by locusts hesitated to drive them away, for fear that he might anger his neighbors by driving the pests into their fields. John suggested sprinkling his field with holy water. If the pests would not leave peacefully, and he could not disperse them without causing strife, the man should resign himself to await God's will, which in this case could be the destruction of his harvest and hunger for the man and his family (Letter 684). This question illustrates another category of petitions from lay people to the anchorites, that is, solicitations of divine aid against the uncertainties of nature.

SICKNESS AND HEALING

Throughout the late antique world, people had recourse to holy men to combat illness. The Correspondence of Barsanuphius and John is filled with accounts of lay people seeking healing. Unlike the holy men in hagiographic works, however, Barsanuphius and John worked very few miracles. Their chief concern focused on elucidating the purpose of disease in God's divine plan. They also counseled their petitioners about which popular remedies were acceptable to use in fighting illness.

Christians in Palestine were attracted to the healing traditions of their Jewish and pagan neighbors. John recommended to one layman that he use holy water to anoint his sick animal and employ a physician's treatments. The man had asked if he could use an incantation upon the beast (Letter 753).[15] Magic seems to have been a well-used resource in this particular household, since the same man wrote to ask if God would hold him accountable if his sick servant went to a sorcerer without his knowledge (Letter 754). The man pushed the question of responsibility further, asking how he could dissuade others from seeking out a sorcerer's arts. John remained firm that, although he could only warn most people that such activities would harm their souls, it was his obligation to discipline a person under his authority who visited a sorcerer (Letter 755).[16] John drew a distinction between the man's obligation to his friends and that to strangers. He must warn a friend going to a sorcerer, but he need not interfere with a stranger unless the person asked his opinion. The different levels of responsibility for the misdeeds of servants, friends, and strangers reveal the complex structure of social obligation within the Christian community. Lay people had a greater sense of spiritual responsibility for those connected to them by other forms of obligation.

Many of the lay people who appealed to Barsanuphius and John wanted the anchorites to perform like sorcerers and miraculously heal their ills. While contemporary monastic literature often gives much attention to the dramatic cures of ascetic holy men, the letters of Barsanuphius and John have a different tone. God had the power to effect marvelous cures, but frequently the promise of heaven superseded mere physical healing. Spiritual healing was Barsanuphius and John's ultimate goal for their disciples.[17]

One layman whose servant had been bitten by a dog came to John to ask if the servant would die, since he had heard that a dog bite brought death within forty days. John replied, "It is no evil, do not fear anything, but think of what is written, 'A sparrow does not fall in a snare apart from your father in heaven'" (Letter 779; Matt. 10:29). The man took comfort and believed that his servant would live. Two days later the servant died. The master, who had great confidence in the Old Man, was so surprised that he refused to believe his servant was really dead. John wrote to the layman that the man was truly dead (Letter 780), but that his death came from God and was not evil. Even if he had died, "by ten thousand venomous serpents," it would not have happened without God's decision (Letter 781). The lack of healing appeared at first as a challenge to the spiritual authority of the holy man: the layman refused to believe his servant was dead because he did not want to doubt the message given by the holy man. However, John used the incident to redirect the petitioner's attention to God's ultimate authority over the natural world.

The absence of healing in the letters of Barsanuphius and John overshadows the few healing miracles recounted in the collection. Situations in which divine healing was not granted offered the Old Men greater opportunity for instruction. The issue of unanswered prayers for healing is explored in more depth in the correspondence between John and another pious layman, a teacher of philosophy. The man had two sons. When one fell gravely ill, the man went to John, who said that his son would live. The boy quickly recovered. The monk who compiled the Correspondence saw fit to dismiss this miraculous healing as a brief incident introducing a more important event. When his other son fell sick, the man once again consulted the Old Man who answered: "We are praying ourselves, but it belongs to God, to do mercy towards him. Conform your will to God's and give thanks to him in everything" (Letter 778a; 1 Thess. 5:18).

Like the man whose servant had been bitten by a dog, the philosopher understood John's words to mean that his son would live. But when he returned to his son's bedside, the young man had a vision and asked his father if he saw the saints that surrounded them:

> They say to me, "Why does his [biological] father come and go to torment us, in order that you should live in the flesh? Behold, we have prayed to God for you, and he has said, 'The time has come for him to leave his body.'" . . . and they have led me into a place shining very brightly and indescribable. There I see innocent children, and they say to me, "Because of the prayer of your father [John], we have asked God to admit you to this place." (Letter 778b)

In the sick boy's vision, the attitude of his biological father contrasted with the actions of his spiritual father. The earthly father fought to keep the son alive, while John's prayers worked to effect his salvation.

Reciting the Lord's prayer and the doxology, the son died. The vision signifying his son's salvation consoled the father. He was puzzled, however, that John had not spoken more clearly. The Old Man explained:

> Understand the matter according to your own experience: You are an instructor of philosophy [literally: the wisdom of the world] and you have your own disciples. If you dictate to one of them a letter, does the disciple write what you want or is he allowed to write what he wants, for himself? Clearly he will write what you say and not what he wants. It is the same with the saints: it is not they who speak themselves, but it is God who speaks in them as he wishes, sometimes mysteriously and sometimes clearly. (Letter 778b)

The metaphor here is unexpected. John did not compare himself (the saint) to the philosopher who exercised intellectual authority in his school, but rather to the philosopher's disciple. The holy man was merely a channel for the voice of God and did not attempt to sway God's will.

Basing his spiritual authority in submissive discipleship, John demonstrated that spiritual power overturned earthly hierarchies. The teacher of philosophy continued to question John on the manner in which God answered the prayers of holy men. John assured him that God did not grant even the apostles all of their prayers for healing (Letter 778c; Matt. 17:14–16). All human sources of spiritual authority yielded to divine omniscience. God knew what would benefit a person better than the one who asked, so there was no need for wordy prayers (Letter 778d).

Even more troubling than ambiguous prognoses were unfulfilled prophecies. On at least one occasion, a very clear pronouncement by John failed to be fulfilled. A layman had asked the Old Man to pray that God might heal him. John had given an unusually precise response: "The Lord will heal you quickly" (Letter 645). When this did not occur, the man was astonished, since he believed that God spoke through the Old Man and that the Old Man did not lie. Confused, the layman turned to Barsanuphius to learn why John's prophecy had not been fulfilled. According to the Great Old Man, this situation differed from the others in which desired healing did not come. Instead of saying that God did not intend physical healing or that John had misunderstood the divine will, Barsanuphius suggested that a lack of faith might have prevented the man from recovering his health. Then the Great Old Man pointed slyly to another possible obstacle: "I have asked you, for the love of Christ, no longer to drag me to the horse races, because I am getting old" (Letter 645). The man was delighted with Barsanuphius' clever manner of hinting at the problem. The sixth-century compiler of the text informs us that the man avoided the races—a spiritual impediment—from that point on, but we are left to wonder if his physical ailment disappeared with the spiritual one. Actual bodily improvement was not as important to the compiler of the text as spiritual health. Physical healing may have accompanied spiritual healing in this case, however, since the layman's next letter mentioned his recent marriage (Letter 646).

Sometimes one of the Old Men withheld information about a person's physical condition in order to protect his soul. When one sick man asked John if he would live or die, the Old Man refused to answer. Such knowledge could jeopardize a person's salvation. If he abandoned material concerns because he expected to die, he would be acting under the constraint of the fear of death. On the other hand, if he freely decided to pursue the good, his choice would be deliberate and not forced (Letter 637). Of course, to repent because one was going to die was better than not repenting, but it was still better to live righteously voluntarily, not knowing when the end would come (Letter 638). The ill man was sufficiently distracted from his physical pains to ask John several more questions about the salvation of the soul, including if God would give a person who truly repented on his deathbed a chance to live longer and if the end of the world was fixed (Letters 639–42).

While John rarely prophesied immediate healing for his disciples, Barsanuphius on several occasions worked miracles of healing. However, he wished these healings to be kept discreet. In one case a layman suffering from fever sent some water to the Great Old Man, asking him to bless it, so that the man might drink from it and be healed. Barsanuphius complied and the man was healed. It was not Barsanuphius' intention that others should know about this, but after his healing the joyous man began to tell everyone about the miracle, whereupon the fever suddenly seized him again. He wrote to Barsanuphius, who bluntly explained, "You suffer this in order that you might not be a babbler" (Letter 643). Barsanuphius prayed again, and the man's health was completely restored. The disciple had learned a lesson about the proper response to a miracle. From that day forward he kept silent about his healing and other blessings he received from the holy man. Barsanuphius rejected the image of a saint, known for his miraculous deeds, which has been popularized by hagiographers. Instead, he embraced the model of Christ presented in the gospels, that of a teacher who wanted to be followed for his words not his miracles (Mark 7:36).

Confusion over differing expectations for laymen and monastic leaders followed this incident. The layman whom Barsanuphius had healed learned the lesson about discretion so well that it led him to criticize the behavior of the abbot. When he overheard Seridos repeatedly praising the miracles of the Great Old Man to the monks, he became disturbed and wrote to John. He admitted mixed feelings about the matter; he rejoiced to hear the Great Old Man praised, but it bothered him that Seridos would so vocally glorify his own spiritual father. It was one thing to hear the praise of other fathers, but did the abbot not speak too easily, boasting about his own father?

John explained that the abbot had enough discernment to know who needed to hear of the Great Old Man's miracles. Seridos was not speaking to glorify himself by elevating his father, but to educate his disciples. His own position as father gave him the authority to proclaim the miraculous works. The layman was still unworthy to speak of the blessings he had received, as his willingness to criticize the abbot demonstrated. He could not impose the censure he had received from Barsanuphius on others of a higher spiritual rank (Letter 644). Not only had the Great Old Man authorized the abbot to speak, as the intermediary for communicating his words, but Seridos on his own authority could convey news of the holy man's wondrous deeds.

Humbly accepting physical healing and learning to cope with its absence both required submission to the divine will revealed through the prayers of the holy men. The requests for healing brought to Barsanuphius and John often had a communal aspect. They were requests on the part of powerful members of society—a teacher of philosophy, a father, a master—on behalf of their dependents. These self-sufficient men humbled themselves to become supplicants of the holy men. Instead of being rewarded with miracles, however, they were asked to accept that what appeared to be a lack of responsiveness to their petitions (that is, the deaths of those for whom they had sought healing) was actually a deliberate reply from God. Barsanuphius and John compelled their disciples to redirect their concern from physical well-being to spiritual health. When healing was granted, the recipient of divine aid faced a range of spiritual temptations. The natural desire to tell others of the miracle could become a cover for self-aggrandizement. If one overcame this hurdle, success could lead to the temptation to criticize the behavior of others. The goal of Barsanuphius and John was to use both healing and the lack of healing to cultivate humility in their disciples.

QUESTIONS OF LEGAL AND ECONOMIC JUSTICE

As many of the requests for healing involved one person asking for healing on another's behalf, so also other petitions to the holy men sprang from interpersonal relationships. Those with grievances against others and those to whom others appealed for mediation came to Barsanuphius and John for guidance. At times individuals were torn by conflicting social obligations. Their questions reveal a concern about the spiritual impact of economic relationships, an uneasiness about the appropriate use of secular courts, and an awareness that what the world acknowledged as justice might fall short of the standards of the holy men.

Lay people who brought their dilemmas to the anchorites often came with their own theological interpretations of their problems. A man whose home had been broken into explained to John that this had happened because of his sins (Letter 667). The robbers had not actually stolen any of his goods, but the man wondered if he should press a suit against them anyway. John accepted the man's theological interpretation of the events and built upon it. If the man truly believed that God had permitted the burglary because of his sins, then was it not God's mercy that prevented the loss of his possessions? The man continued his questions, constructing a hypothetical scenario (a common pattern in questions addressed to the anchorites). Had John's answer depended on the fact that the thieves had not actually taken anything; if they had been successful would legal recourse be appropriate (Letter 668)? John outlined two ways of life and urged the layman towards the higher. The imperfect, acting out of avarice, would quickly resort to the law to demand that their possessions be restored; the perfect would scorn worldly goods and remember Christ's command to give away the mantle with the tunic (Matt. 5:40). No matter what path the man chose, the courts could not change the outcome of divinely ordained events.

The man was apparently dissatisfied that John had discouraged him from taking the issue to court. If he were to give his goods away, would he not be left naked (Letter 669)? Was it not much worse if one had a habit of pressing lawsuits than if one did it on rare occasion (Letter 670)? John remained adamant that tribunals were dangerous to the soul, even if the punishment secured in court was justified.[18] The man pressed his point one step further. Suppose one witnessed a murder. Should he lie in order to let the murderer escape death? John dismissed lying in this case, as in all others; but he warned that if a person was not required to testify, he should remain quiet (Letter 671).[19] Judging another person was precarious business, and justice should be left in the hands of God.

The same man also asked about asserting his rights in another legal situation, debt collection. He asked if one could charge a rich debtor interest and if a needy lender could reclaim a debt from a poor man (Letters 672–73).[20] Another layman asked John what to do when he was tempted to cheat someone in a business transaction (Letter 749). John recommended that the man yield the other a little extra, in thanks for having escaped the temptation. If the man later discovered that he had cheated someone unintentionally, he should repay the sum if it was significant, and he should return even a trivial difference to a poor man (Letter 750). It was not necessarily wrong for a sales contract to contain an extremely high or low price if both parties entered into it freely; however, a person should not extort excessive gain for himself, especially if he exercised some sort of authority over the other individual (Letter 756). Throughout this discussion of debt collection and sales negotiations, John remained alert to the economic disparity between rich and poor and was concerned that those with less economic power not be exploited through legitimate commercial transactions.

Many sources of social obligation weighed upon the lay disciples of Barsanuphius and John. In some situations civic, familial, and spiritual allegiances competed; and lay people, torn between contradictory duties, turned to the anchorites for help choosing the best course of action. One man was in charge of selling land that belonged to relatives who lived some distance away. The potential buyers intended to use the land to build a place of prayer. The man was torn between the conviction that he should give the buyers a discount because of their holy purpose and the feeling of obligation to his relatives, that they should receive a good price for their land. Barsanuphius counseled the man to write to his relatives, naming the fair market price but suggesting that they offer a discount because the land would be used for a church (Letter 648). Barsanuphius added that it would be no great fault if they sold it at the market price. This diplomatic solution to the man's crisis of conscience shows the mildness of Barsanuphius' dealings with lay Christians. His own seclusion had not made him into a radical ascetic without empathy for the dilemmas of earthly entanglements.

This particular layman exercised authority outside his own family circle. He wrote to Barsanuphius on several occasions, asking what to do when the law of God contradicted the law of the world and how to practice justice towards the poor (Letters 650–51).[21] On one occasion a monastic father whom the man respected greatly asked him to use his authority in a way that did not seem just. Troubled, he turned to Barsanuphius. In other situations, such as with the father who embraced heretical doctrines, the Great Old Man had not hesitated to undermine the spiritual authority of certain fathers nor to distinguish between fathers who were able to discern God's will and those who could not.[22] In this case, however, Barsanuphius' trust of the father did not waver. The layman should explain the whole affair to the old man and follow his instructions: "The spiritual fathers say nothing in vain, but all [that they say] is for the salvation of the soul" (Letter 652).

Some spiritual fathers had asked another layman to arbitrate a legal case. The man felt unsure about the matter and asked John if he could refuse or if he should consult someone who was better informed about the situation. John told him to follow the order of the fathers, to consult whomever he wished, and to judge the case, not swayed by passion or seeking to please (Letter 720). If the affair required the swearing of an oath, he should refuse, unless a higher authority compelled him to swear. Then he should do so only after examining everything carefully (Letter 721).[23] The swearing of oaths was prevalent throughout late antique society, but the practice troubled many Christian leaders who recognized the seriousness of inadvertently committing perjury.[24]

The letters of Barsanuphius and John to lay people discussing questions of justice reveal a deep ambiguity towards formal legal practices. The anchorites did not approve of individuals' bringing lawsuits, testifying in court, or swearing oaths. However, if a higher authority compelled a person to do so, the person could cautiously participate in the proceedings. Despite this lack of approval for formal legal proceedings, the anchorites did encourage those laymen with authority in the community to exercise it wisely. They should not refrain from judging a case, particularly if monastic fathers requested their involvement. In questions of justice, Barsanuphius and John said, lay Christians could rely upon the guidance of spiritual fathers in the community.

FAMILY AND HOUSEHOLD

Lay people revealed to the holy men details of the intimate bonds of family and household that characterized life in late antique Palestine. The modern concept of "family" as related people living together, finds no exact parallel in Greek or Latin. Words such as *sungeneia* and *familia* refer not only to relatives but also to household slaves. Indeed, obligation between masters and slaves featured prominently among questions brought to the anchorites.

Nevertheless, the nuclear family was becoming increasingly important in late antiquity, in both rural and urban society. Classical Roman law had restricted the tie between husband and wife, in order to favor paternal authority. Kinship through one's father's line had carried more obligation than marriage: gifts between spouses were limited, and a woman's brothers, rather than her children, were her legal heirs. Later imperial legislation provided more support for the marriage bond, limiting divorce and remarriage. Despite this new focus on the nuclear family, extended families still provided the kinship networks that helped launch political careers among the elite and created bonds of mutual obligation at all levels of society. Even among men and women who entered the monastery, kinship ties could remain important, providing ascetic role models and practical support for monasticism. Pairs of famous monastics from the same family, such as Melania the Elder and her niece Melania the Younger, illustrate this phenomenon well.[25]

Lay people from Gaza, however, complained that relatives could test an individual's commitment to the spiritual life. A layman trying to lead a sober life complained to John that his father "according to the flesh" kept talking to him about worldly topics that held no benefit for his soul (Letter 767). John suggested that either the man keep his thoughts busy praying and meditating on God's word, or, if that were impossible, that he gently interrupt his father and introduce a more useful subject. The man also wondered how to deal with the rest of his family. He had wealthy, high-ranking relatives who lived nearby. When some poor relatives who lived far away came to visit him, he hesitated to introduce them to the rich branch of the family who would be ashamed of poor relations. John said that while it was not necessary to go out of his way to reveal the connection, if someone asked him who the visitors were, he had to answer honestly. To do otherwise would be succumbing to false pride: "Because we are all creatures of God, and no one is more elevated than another, except the one who does the will of God; but it is vainglory which creates a difference in the eyes of men" (Letter 764). John did not order the layman to publicly challenge the system that assigned the rich branch of the family more social status than the poor, but he was to be personally indifferent to such distinctions.

Change in a family through death or marriage could create anxiety within a household. Two laymen who were close friends lived together as brothers, sharing all they owned. When one man married, he feared he had disrupted the friendship by bringing a wife into the home. Barsanuphius responded to his concerns, saying that if the man wanted to know if his friend's feelings about the relationship had changed, he should examine his own heart more carefully (Letter 646). Another layman asked how one should help a friend who had lost a child or suffered some other disaster. John counseled that it was necessary to grieve with a friend to prevent him from losing all hope and contemplating suicide (Letter 676).[26]

Slaves were present in many elite late antique households.[27] Although their perceived function was to serve their masters, the needs of servants did from time to time make unusual demands on family resources. The layman who, as we saw earlier, sought to mediate between rich and poor relatives questioned John on his obligation to a slave afflicted with leprosy. The Old Man replied that though it would be a work of piety to care for the man at home, not every member of the household might be able to tolerate this. Therefore, the man could be installed in a leprosarium, and his master should provide him with food, clothing, and bedding (Letter 765). The layman then demanded to know if his slave were also entitled to a portion of the general alms that he and others sent to the leprosarium, in addition to his regular daily allowance. John said not to begrudge him his share of these proceeds as well (Letter 766).

There were others on the periphery of this man's household who did not enjoy the security that his slaves did. During the grape harvest, he allowed the poor to follow behind the harvesters, collecting grape leaves for their own use. The man was concerned that they were taking not only leaves but grapes as well. He asked John if he could prohibit the gleaners from taking grapes, and if he could search those he suspected. John permitted him to forbid taking grapes, but would not allow him to have anyone searched (Letter 768).[28]

John counseled another layman to dismiss a slave who had run away and later returned. The servant's behavior changed for the better and the man decided to keep him. John acknowledged that if the man could bear the servant's misbehavior it would be an exercise in patience but warned that if the servant provoked the man to wrath he should dismiss him. John's expectations that the slave would relapse do not seem to have been groundless, for soon afterwards he tried to steal from his master. The compiler adds that the servant's attempts at theft failed and he fled, "because of the prayers of the saints" (Letter 654). The layman blamed himself for not following John's earlier advice to dismiss the man. John explained that he had only suggested this course of action because he knew the man was unable to endure the trials the servant would bring him. The man should humbly correct his servants after his anger had cooled (Letter

656). He should not allow the recognition of his own failings to keep him from disciplining those in his charge. This was a temptation posed by the devil, which would work to the detriment of his servants and himself, since he was accountable for them before God (Letter 657).[29] John told another layman who was buying slaves to receive them in the name of the Lord, remembering that he also had a master (Letter 649).

PROPERTY AND CHARITY

One of the most prominent distinctions between lay and monastic life was the possession of property. Lay people wrestled with giving away their wealth as alms, or if they desired to become monks, stripping themselves of all their belongings. On the other hand, monks in principle possessed nothing of value, yet they were still expected to give alms, and communally they had great interest in the holdings of the monastery.

Laymen frequently consulted John about the best way to distribute alms. Should one distribute the whole amount at once, or give away alms bit by bit (Letter 617)? What should one give to beggars who passed by (Letter 635)? If someone asked a person for alms, but he had nothing, should he borrow in order to give (Letter 620)? What should a person do who desired to give alms but at the last minute had second thoughts (Letter 626)? How could a person who at first did not give easily develop the habit of giving (Letter 623)? John advised that if a person were confronted by two needy people but only had money to give to one, he should give to the weaker of the two (Letter 625). One question is particularly revealing about the process of distributing alms. A layman asked John if he should give equally to those who openly participated in the distribution process, to those who were ashamed because of their rank to receive the alms publicly, and to those who were sick and confined to their beds. John recommended that he reward those who did not try to disguise the fact that they accepted alms, even if they could not leave their beds, by giving them a little more than the others (Letter 630).

One common practice in late antiquity that John considered problematic was the custom of one person entrusting another with his money to distribute as alms. John discouraged a monk from distributing a layman's alms, even if the man threatened not to give anything if the monk refused (Letter 619).[30] By becoming a monk, a person gave up all concern over material possessions. Why should he willingly embrace such cares again?

John cited the example of a figure of great local importance, St. Hilarion, who, after healing a demon-possessed man, refused to accept the gifts the man brought for Hilarion to give to the poor, saying: "It is for you to distribute your goods, for you go about in the cities, and you know the villages. But how could I, who have abandoned my goods, receive those of another to distribute? It would be an occasion for pride or greed" (Letter 618).[31] Although the monk's relinquishing of earthly goods was an obvious reason for not accepting another's wealth, John also warned lay people from taking on the responsibility for distributing the alms of others (Letter 629). The person accepting such a charge would be required to render a full account of the money to God. A truly humble person ought to flee such a task. To impose such a heavy burden on another was unjust.

Arrangements of this type engendered all sorts of concomitant problems. Although he had counseled against accepting another's responsibility, John patiently helped to sort out the unexpected difficulties that arose when his advice was ignored (Letter 631–34). If the person distributing the alms learned of some needy people whom the benefactor had not been aware of, he could include them in the distribution of charity. The person distributing the alms might require assistants for this work. He should choose carefully those who seemed worthy of such confidence. If one of his helpers betrayed his trust and stole from the alms, the man could question him gently and ask for the sum to be returned. If the embezzler refused, he should be left to the judgment of God, since the money stolen belonged to God. If the helper stole only once and out of need or because of demonic temptation, he might be trusted again. If he took something a second time, he proved himself unworthy of such responsibility.

SOCIAL INTERACTION BETWEEN MONKS AND LAITY

Lay Christians practiced charity towards two groups: "the poor," who included beggars and other indigent people, and "the fathers," who had voluntarily embraced poverty. The quality of gifts offered to these two groups differed at times. One layman had a surplus of wine and some bread of an inferior grade. He had considered giving his own supply of high-quality bread and wine to the poor and making do himself with the inferior stuff, but he had decided against it. Then some fathers had come to visit him and, considering them more worthy than the poor, he had served them his best. Later, the man began to doubt if he had acted rightly and consulted John. The Old Man, acknowledging human weakness, did not rebuke him for loving himself more than the poor but did affirm that the fathers deserved special honor (Letter 636).

Lay Christians also offered the fathers lodging in their homes. One lay person accustomed to practicing hospitality in this manner grew distressed when a father came to his home and the host had no food to offer the old man (Letter 681).[32] He then began to worry about his own needs, imagining himself arriving somewhere tired and hungry to find no meal prepared (Letter 682). John comforted him, reminding him that it was God who provided sustenance. Whatever the host offered a guest was sufficient, as long as he gave freely and held nothing back.

Some laymen were concerned that offering hospitality to traveling monks entailed certain risks. It was not always easy to determine which visiting monks were fathers worthy of hospitality. One layman asked John if he had to welcome any strange monk who came to his door. If he admitted someone too quickly, it might prove necessary later to ask the guest to leave. John recommended that he question each visitor about where he came from and where he was going (Letter 727).[33] The layman was particularly concerned that if he invited a monk into his home, the man might overstay his welcome. What should he do if he had to go away on business himself? He did not dare tell the monk to leave. John wrote that it was reasonable to ask the monk politely about his plans and explain that he would be away and unable to continue serving his guest's needs (Letter 728). The layman was so concerned about the possibility of unscrupulous monastic visitors, that he asked if he could rearrange the furnishings in the guestroom to prevent anything from being stolen. John allowed this, in order to prevent temptation, but insisted that the man should try not to worry over material things (Letter 729).[34]

Other laymen were more concerned about their own behavior in the presence of spiritual fathers. One man asked how to excuse himself when pressing business required that his visit to the fathers come to a close. In response, John distinguished between those fathers who could discern the will of God and those who could not. It was best to follow the lead of the first group, remaining as long as they saw fit. When visiting the other fathers, it was acceptable to politely but firmly take one's leave (Letter 714).

Dining with monks raised other issues of correct behavior for the lay person. If a monk said a blessing over the food, a lay person should not add his own. To do so might imply that the layman lacked confidence in the original blessing (Letter 715).[35] Even if one of the fathers requested a lay person to say the blessing, he should refuse, saying, "I am not a priest, nor do I wear the *schema*, but I am a man of the world and a sinner" (Letter 716).[36] In the company of all laity it was appropriate for a layman to say the blessing at a meal. This blessing was not in the same category as that of a priest, but simply an opportunity to praise God before a meal (Letter 717). The host of the gathering should choose whomever he wished to say the blessing, and if everyone refused, he should say the blessing himself (Letter 718).[37]

Lay Christians worshiped together with monks in church. One layman asked John if he should rise to sing the Trisagion hymn,[38] even if those he was with remained seated. John's instructions took into account the company with him. If the man were with spiritual fathers he should do as they did. If he were seated with laymen of a higher social rank, who would be scandalized by his independent action, he ought to remain seated, but he could recite the Trisagion in his heart. If there were none present of a higher status, the man could stand and sing aloud. He could even invite those around him to stand and join him (Letter 712).[39]

John warned a layman who asked him about talking in church that not only was it necessary to be silent in God's house during the liturgy, but that the man's attention should be focused on praying and listening to the scriptures being read (Letter 737). If one of the fathers addressed him during the liturgy, he should reply only briefly, since even in these circumstances talking in church was an offense worthy of condemnation (Letter 738). The man also wondered if it was sinful to go to church but leave before receiving communion. John admonished him not to leave the liturgy until the final dismissal, unless it were absolutely necessary, in which case he should ask God to pardon him before he left (Letter 736).[40]

This layman, who had close interaction with monks, had incorporated ascetic elements into his own life. He cultivated an atmosphere of seclusion by remaining at home. This practice of withdrawal conflicted with steady attendance at the many church services held during the week. As his spiritual director, John approved of his withdrawal and encouraged him not to use the excuse of attending church as a reason to leave his retreat and go about the city (Letter 739). The bustle of a crowded church, where a person rubbed shoulders with many strangers, was not necessarily conducive to ascetic contemplation. The rhetorician Choricius described the crowded Church of St. Sergius in Gaza on a hot day: "The long colonnade of the church . . . is full of grace and allows a fair breeze, [blowing] sweetly and gently, and gliding softly beneath clothing, cools bodies, while the garments are billowing in the wind."[41] The anchorite thought passions could be cooled more easily by praying at home.

Even when compelled to go out to attend to his own affairs or those of the fathers whom he served, the layman should not fear missing a service but accomplish the business quickly and return to his solitude (Letter 740). On the other hand, if he went to the city for his own amusement, then he should certainly go to church. The mention of the layman's habit of taking care of the business of the fathers shows both his close association with the monks and the temptations that could arise even in the course of a laudable occupation.

John's practice of looking beyond an individual act to the underlying motivation in order to determine its moral value is evident in a letter to another layman, who asked if it was a sin to work on Sundays. John replied, "For those who work according to God, it is not a sin. . . . But for those who do it out of scorn, avarice, and cupidity, it is a sin" (Letter 751). Nevertheless, John added, it had been a tradition since the days of the apostles to cease all work and go to church on Sundays and on feast days commemorating Christ or the apostles. The advice given to the first layman that he could miss services during the week does not seem to have applied to Sundays and holy days. Night vigils, on the other hand, could be kept at home just as well as at church. John warned the layman who sought to live in retirement that when conducted at church these vigils were often accompanied by idle conversations (Letter 741). Acknowledging the potential for distraction at vigils in the church, Choricius admitted that married women and maidens attended night festivals, even laying aside the veils that were their modest attire in the day.[42]

This layman feared that John would similarly frown upon his visiting the martyr shrines to venerate relics. Visiting the burial places of saints was an popular expression of piety in late antiquity. Christians believed that those who had died testifying to their faith were immediately ushered into the presence of God. Churches called martyria were built to house saints' relics. Eager supplicants flocked to these holy places, seeking healing and other forms of intercession. John permitted the layman to visit such shrines, setting careful guidelines for the layman's actions within a martyrium. The man should enter the sanctuary humbly and take communion with the laity. He should not enter inconsiderately, but if a priest summoned him, he should prayerfully obey, guarding himself from vainglory and remembering his unworthiness (Letter 742).[43] Such precise instructions indicate the high spiritual status of this layman. His reputation for holiness created the potential for ambiguity about his proper role within the religious community, and John sought to remind the man of his lay status and of the need to yield to the clergy who oversaw the shrine.

The concerns of lay Christians about appropriate deference to monastic fathers reveal the close interaction between lay people and monks in sixth-century Gaza. Lay and monastic Christians practiced hospitality towards one another, ate at the same table, and worshipped together. In this intimate environment concern arose for proper etiquette. John and his lay questioners agreed that the fathers should be accorded the special respect that their position of spiritual authority merited, but in the close Christian community the manner in which this should be carried out occasionally needed clarification. Both anchorite and layman acknowledged that sometimes even those who apparently held the rank of "father" could prove to be unworthy of the designation. On such occasions the Old Men urged their lay disciples to follow the path of virtue, regardless of the behavior of those around them.

LAY ASCETICISM

As many of the questions posed by these lay people demonstrate, the boundaries between lay Christians and monks in Tawatha were fluid. Laymen gave the abbot advice about a variety of matters, including the purchase of land for the monastery and the construction of new facilities; the monks gave advice that mingled practical and spiritual counsel. This monastery was more open than others in the region to visits by relatives of the monks. The permeable boundary between monastic and lay communities is perhaps best proven by the succession of a layman as abbot following Seridos' death.

This flexibility of the boundary between the monastery and the lay Christian community occasionally caused Barsanuphius and John to feel the need to reinforce the distinction between lay and monastic status. As noted above, the anchorites expected lay Christians to yield to the leadership of monks and priests in church or private prayer. Barsanuphius and John encouraged laymen to convert to the ascetic life and formally join the monastery. However, they worried about laymen who, without the instruction of spiritual directors, began to adopt ascetic practices and an outwardly monastic demeanor. Such persons, like some monks in the cenobium, tried to bypass the proper channels of spiritual authority. Barsanuphius and John feared that lay people who practiced asceticism without the guidance of a spiritual director created confusion for their peers, because they sought the spiritual reward that accompanied monastic life without the obedience required of monks in the cenobium. Ascetic lay Christians also posed a potential challenge to the spiritual authority of monastic fathers. Without having participated in the process of supervision that allowed a monk to become a spiritual director, some lay Christians attracted followers because of their ascetic lifestyles. There was no formal system to hold such persons accountable for a disciple's spiritual welfare, as there was for their monastic counterparts.

One of Barsanuphius and John's lay correspondents caused the anchorites enough concern that they felt the need to distinguish for him the responsibilities of a lay Christian and those of a monk. This layman participated in all aspects of worldly life: interacting with his relatives, owning slaves, and farming his land (Letters 764–68). In addition to these activities, the man tried to maintain a semi-ascetic lifestyle. Once when he fell sick, a doctor recommended a bath, which would necessitate his going out to the public baths. The man expressed to John his worry that this might be sinful and his fear that he should not have seen a doctor at all. In his response John distinguished between what was permitted to a monk and to a layman: "A bath is not absolutely forbidden to people of the world, when it is necessary. If one is sick and in need of one, it is not a sin. . . . And concerning seeing a doctor, it is for the perfect to abandon everything to God, even if a thing is painful, but the weak see a doctor" (Letter 770). John's point was that whether they called upon doctors or not, both monks and lay people should recognize that health came ultimately from God.

The man had assumed a lifestyle that suggested a higher level of spiritual authority than he actually possessed. It seems that he was not merely concerned with correct behavior but was interested in protecting his reputation for sanctity. The man's distaste of going out in public, either attending to his affairs or visiting the baths, gave some the impression that he was exceedingly pious. The man was aware of this opinion, so that when he was forced by illness to go to the public baths, he worried how others would react. He was careful to add that people's inflated estimation of his piety came from the devil. John censured the man's pride in the ascetic image he had carefully cultivated: "If Satan suggests to some to consider you as a prophet, in order to lead your reasoning away in haughtiness, and for your part, you wish to corroborate this falsehood about yourself, for that you ought to be ashamed" (Letter 771).[44] John rebuked this layman for staying at home under the guise of asceticism, although on another occasion, he had encouraged a different layman to remain at home in semi-ascetic solitude (Letters 740–41). This man's prideful attitude and his desire to adopt ascetic practices without the supervision of a spiritual director led John to offer him different instruction.

This disciple's ascetic proclivities are even more pronounced in his subsequent questions. He asked if all food was harmful to a person, because it possessed flavor, and if cleanliness itself was inappropriate. John replied that God had given each food its taste, and in and of itself flavorful food caused no harm (Letter 773). It was attachment to food that he should guard against, since this could harm his soul. Likewise, the Lord loved cleanliness, but one should not require it, since all was destined to corruption (Letter 774). John repeatedly tried to shift the man's focus from the outward signs of sanctity to the inward condition of his soul.

The desire of this layman to live a disciplined life spurred him to ask John about the source of good actions, whether they came from divine providence or human effort. He wondered how to reconcile the age-old dilemma of the ascetic Christian: "God has made man free, but [scripture] says, 'Without me you can do nothing'" (Letter 763; John 15:5). The Old Man offered his explanation of the mystery: "If then the man inclines his heart towards the good and calls God to help him, God, considering his good desire, provides him the power necessary for the work. So the two go forward together, the liberty of man and the power of God" (Letter 763). When the man confessed that he sometimes took pride in repairing an injustice that he himself committed, John reminded him of the impossibility of accomplishing anything good without the power of God: "If then we cannot take pride when we do good, how much more when we turn from evil! For it is a great folly to believe that there is glory in not sinning" (Letter 769). Barsanuphius and John feared that a lay person, who practiced asceticism without the oversight of a spiritual director might be tempted to cultivate a false appearance of holiness. Like a monk, a layman needed a spiritual director to guide his thoughts and behavior and to keep him from pride. Many signs of sanctity could be used to assert spiritual authority; false displays of sanctity could challenge the organization of spiritual authority and have a detrimental effect on the wider community.

VISIONS

Just as a miraculous healing could distract a person from pursuing the health of his soul and an ascetic demeanor could convey a false appearance of holiness, so visions had the potential to mislead those who saw them or heard about them from others. The sixth-century inhabitants of Palestine believed that visions could be either revelations from God or the devil's temptations to pride. The majority of those who consulted Barsanuphius about the reliability of visions were lay people. Just as he was concerned that lay people not appropriate ascetic practices in a piecemeal fashion (without the proper oversight of a spiritual director), because such practices could lead to pride, so he considered visions dangerous to a lay person's spiritual life.

Barsanuphius recognized the ability of visions to convict the individual of his sin. One monk had overlooked a certain sin he had committed, when, "suddenly by the permission of God and for his correction there appeared to him a fearful apparition" (Letter 44). But more often Barsanuphius spoke of visions as instruments of temptation. One layman wrote to Barsanuphius, saying that he had had a vision of his evil thoughts attacking his soul like wild beasts, yet incapable of harming it. Barsanuphius quickly exposed this vision as a trick of the enemy (Letter 419). The man's pride was trying to persuade him that evil thoughts could not hurt him.[45] Barsanuphius insisted that the spiritual state of the person receiving visions was paramount, regardless of whether he was a layman or a monk. He explained that when a vision comes to a sinner, "it is evident that it comes from evil demons, in order to lead the unhappy soul to its ruin" (Letter 414). Sinners should never trust their own visions.

Christians in Palestine believed that there were tests that could validate the legitimacy of a vision. One layman consulted Barsanuphius about these, asking if a vision were reliable if it contained the figure of Christ:

"How does the devil dare to appear in a vision as the Lord Christ or the holy Communion?" (Letter 416). Barsanuphius did not consider these tests very useful for proving that a vision came from God. He explained that the devil could not appear as Christ or the Eucharist but could fool a person by appearing as an ordinary man or as plain bread. There was, however, one symbol that Barsanuphius believed the devil could not imitate and could, therefore, be used as a test of a reliable vision: "He cannot appear as the holy cross, because he cannot find the means to present it in another form. As we know its true image and shape, he does not dare use it. His power flees from it and by it he receives the mortal blow. . . . when you see in a dream the shape of the cross, know that it is true and that the dream comes from God" (Letter 416). Barsanuphius dismissed another popular test of the authenticity of a vision, that is, seeing the same vision three times. If the devil was able to fool a person once, then why should he not succeed three times or even more (Letter 418)?

The spiritual condition of the person seeing visions could help determine the reliability of a vision. Rather than testing the vision, Barsanuphius recommended critically appraising one's own heart: "The saints had divine visions, but they always proceeded from calm, from peace, and from the confidence in their hearts. And although they recognized the truth, they judged themselves unworthy. How much more it is necessary for sinners never to trust [their visions], knowing their own unworthiness?" (Letter 415). Although a sinner was unlikely to receive a vision, Barsanuphius did not completely rule out the possibility that God might speak to a lay person in this way. Upon hearing that Barsanuphius believed the appearance of a cross validated a vision, a layman questioned him, fearing that he might see a cross in a vision and then be pulled into the sin of pride. Barsanuphius comforted him, saying, "Do not worry yourself about this. For if the holy cross appears to you, it altogether deflates the exaltation of haughtiness. It is, indeed, from God, and not from evil" (Letter 417). The real test of a vision was whether it resulted in pride and sinful exaltation. Those that came from God brought only good to the visionary, lay or monastic.

Barsanuphius and John invested a considerable portion of their energies in discipling lay Christians. Despite their own choice of seclusion, they were ready to help lay people manage the day-to-day concerns of worldly life. They counseled moderation in relating to Jewish and pagan neighbors, caution in dealing with heretics, and compassion in serving the poor. They urged their disciples to uphold justice but to flee from legal entanglements. Obligation to family and the state needed to be balanced by an unswerving dedication to biblical principles. Barsanuphius and John expected lay people to revere monastic fathers; at the same time, they recognized that not all monks merited blind trust.

The anchorites held lay Christians to high standards of behavior, believing that the monk and lay person pursued the same goal: the imitation of Christ. When appropriate, Barsanuphius and John also encouraged lay people to make the transition to monastic life or adopt ascetic practices in their own homes.[46] Nevertheless, when lay Christians became preoccupied with the outward trappings of the ascetic life and were distracted from their own spiritual obligations, the holy men sought to remind them of the temptation of pride. The fluid boundary between monastery, village, and city enabled lay Christians to have monks as spiritual directors. The Old Men were concerned, however, that lay Christians not challenge the established hierarchy of spiritual authority by assuming the outward characteristics of monastic life without the inward commitment to obedience.

CHAPTER 5

Bishops and Civil Authorities
Rulers of Church and Empire

In the eastern Mediterranean in late antiquity, the title "bishop" invoked the image of the city. A bishop was based in each of the urban centers, where bustling marketplaces, noisy amphitheaters, crowded apartment blocks, sumptuous villas, and resplendent basilicas made up the life pulse of the Eastern Empire. Bishops wielded considerable power, both temporal and spiritual. Sophisticated and urbane, they interacted with civic officials, revealing by their cultivated rhetorical style that they belonged to the educated elite of Roman society. At the same time they displayed their piety by feeding and protecting the urban poor. In contrast, anchorites retreated from the cities, taking up residence in the deserts and wastelands on the peripheries of civilization. They made a point of using plain speech and were known for divinely inspired wisdom, embracing a life of poverty for its spiritual rewards. Despite these outward appearances, the occupations of bishop and anchorite were not as disparate as they might initially appear.

The relationship of episcopal authority to monastic spiritual authority was never straightforward. Occasionally bishops and monks engaged in open conflict.[1] At other times latent tension existed between the two sources of power.[2] Often, however, bishops and anchorites managed to unite their spiritual authority, working together to achieve common goals. In these partnerships it was sometimes difficult to determine which party held controlling power.

A famous early example of intertwined episcopal and monastic authority involves Athanasius, Patriarch of Alexandria, and the desert father St. Antony, the subject of Athanasius' popular fourth-century hagiographic account. In this work, the patriarch co-opted the holiness of the anchorite to support his own anti-Arian agenda: "When the Arians falsely claimed that [Antony] held the same view as they, he was quite irritated and angry at them. Then, summoned by the bishops and all the brothers, he came down from the mountain, and entering into Alexandria, he publicly renounced the Arians, saying that theirs was the last heresy and the forerunner of the Antichrist."[3] Athanasius depicted the ascetic anchorite leaving the seclusion of the desert to confront heretics in the city—all at the request of the bishops.

In sixth-century Palestine the bishop's palace and the anchorite's cell were still closely linked. Bishops appointed monastic leaders and served as patrons for monasteries. Anchorites advised bishops on choosing clergy and directed disciples who would eventually be elevated to episcopal authority. Ecclesiastical politics were fierce in Palestine then. Controversy raged over the validity of the Council of Chalcedon, the church council that in the mid-fifth century had determined that Christ had two natures, one human and one divine, and that these two natures were united in one person. Bishops and anchorites were actively engaged in theological struggles, and even emperors frequently became involved in trying to sort out these ecclesiastical conflicts. When one bishop was summoned before the emperor because of doctrinal controversy, he wrote to Barsanuphius for help. For encouragement, the anchorite offered the prophet Daniel as a model for maintaining integrity under royal pressure (Letter 792).

Although secluded in their cells, Barsanuphius and John remained attuned to the problems that troubled the citizens of Gaza, the provincial leaders, and even the emperor in Constantinople. Members of the community sought insight from the anchorites concerning events at hand. Independent of civic and ecclesiastical leaders, the Old Men of Gaza acted as a third source of authority. Yet, from the very nature of their writings—letters of guidance from anchorites to bishops—it is clear that the holy men saw themselves as having spiritual authority over bishops. Barsanuphius and John freely offered advice, both solicited and unsolicited, to bishops. They expected bishops (even those in ancient sees who held the higher status of patriarch) to heed their instruction, although they did not use this power to make any public challenges to the church hierarchy.[4] Rather, they used their authority to buttress that of the bishops and to influence their governance of the church. Instead of competing with civic and ecclesiastical powers for dominance, Barsanuphius and John sought to influence the manner in which all parties exercised authority in the city and surrounding countryside. Their words penetrated the bishops' residences in the cities of Jerusalem and Gaza and shaped the conversations of leading citizens.

ECCLESIASTICAL POLITICS

At the Council of Chalcedon in 451 the see of Jerusalem had gained patriarchal status, eclipsing the metropolitan see of Caesarea as head of the church in Palestine. The see of Jerusalem became the lightning rod for controversy in the sixth-century. Cyril of Scythopolis depicted emperors and monks contending for control of the bishopric. In 516 the emperor Anastasius sent the military commander (*doux*) of Palestine, Olympus of Caesarea, with an imperial force to depose Patriarch Elias for his Chalcedonian stance (he had refused to recognize the anti-Chalcedonian Severus as the new bishop of Antioch).[5]

The political controversy was fueled by the accession of the new archbishop of Jerusalem. John II (516–24) succeeded to the patriarchate on the understanding that he would renounce Chalcedon. However, under the influence of Chalcedonian monks from the Judean desert, he made a public about-face and adopted his predecessor's christological position before an audience that included the governor, the emperor's nephew Hypatius, and as many as 10,000 monks. The anchorite Sabas actually mounted the pulpit with the new archbishop for his proclamation, "Anathematize the heretics and confirm the council."[6]

During this tumultuous period of ecclesiastical politics in Palestine an episcopal election took place in Gaza.[7] As in Jerusalem the election of the new bishop in Gaza followed the forcible expulsion of the previous occupant. There is no reference to his being deposed for theological reasons, although his removal occurred when the controversy was at its height. Rather, the unnamed Bishop of Gaza is described as "hated by the people." He was not deposed by the emperor, as Patriarch Elias of Jerusalem had been, but was condemned at a regional synod for "avarice and other faults." Despite his protests, the bishop was removed from his see by a "general vote" (Letter 793). The condemned bishop proceeded to appeal this decision to Emperor Anastasius.[8]

After the process of electing a new bishop was already well under way, rumor from Constantinople reached the people of Gaza that the deposed bishop, "relying on his riches," had won his case (Letter 802). The citizens of Gaza were afraid to appeal to the emperor, and they turned to Barsanuphius, who urged them to send their own account of the bishop's legal removal to the emperor. Having hesitated to carry out this command, the townspeople panicked when they learned that the deposed bishop had returned to reclaim his see, bearing imperial orders for the governor. Barsanuphius reprimanded the people of Gaza for their negligence in not presenting their case to the emperor, but comforted them with the assurance that God would not allow the deposed bishop to enter the city (Letter 803). As a holy man, Barsanuphius was not dependent on the normal channels of appeal in the late antique empire. Although he encouraged people to make use of the systems in place for handling grievances, he recognized God's sovereignty over all political maneuverings. The bishop had been justly removed by the church, and Barsanuphius was confident that no expenditure of money or leveraging of patronage could reverse a verdict with divine sanction. As the deposed bishop was presenting his imperial mandate to the governor for enforcement, word reached the city that the emperor had died, making the judgment in favor of the bishop void. Finding his access to imperial support cut off, the bishop was furious that he had spent his money in vain. The deposed bishop found the normal routes to power rendered useless. Barsanuphius' message was clear: neither the emperor of Byzantium nor gold could change the future ordained by God and foreseen by the anchorite.

The city of Gaza was deeply divided over whom to choose as the new bishop. Custom dictated that the clergy and lay people of a see choose three candidates from whom the patriarch and local bishops would elect and consecrate the new bishop.[9] The inhabitants of Gaza nominated three candidates. Wishing to further influence the bishops' choice but finding themselves unable to agree on whom to recommend, they wrote to Barsanuphius seeking his advice on the candidates. It is possible that the people's appeal to Barsanuphius was an attempt to circumvent episcopal authority, perhaps motivated by the problems experienced under the previous bishop. Although the people of the city solicited Barsanuphius' active intervention in the debate, the holy man refused to endorse any candidate or party. Instead of exploiting the influence the laity granted him, Barsanuphius carefully cooperated with the church hierarchy. Affirming the decisions of church councils and bishops, Barsanuphius urged the people of Gaza to follow the will of the patriarch in Jerusalem (Letter 793).[10] Barsanuphius refused to allow his spiritual authority as anchorite to replace episcopal authority. Instead, he used the power that accrued to him through the support of the people to augment the authority of the church and the patriarch of Jerusalem. Barsanuphius reassured troubled lay Christians in Gaza that God's will would be accomplished in the election despite the machinations of competing factions.

One layman continued to question Barsanuphius at length about the manner in which God worked through the election process, revealing the extent of public dissension. The man wondered how God would respond to rival factions within the Christian community. Barsanuphius declared that if the people could come together in "common accord," God would give them "an angel from heaven" as their bishop (Letter 794). As such agreement seemed unlikely, the layman continued to question, asking if God would give the city the best candidate or the one requested by the faction with the strongest faith. He marveled that in the midst of much controversy those with the strongest faith might ask for a poor candidate and God might reward those with evil hearts, because they had sided with the best man for unworthy reasons (Letters 794–801).

These musings point to a high level of uncertainty in the community over the change in leadership. Although it is not possible to completely understand the issues that divided the various factions, it is possible that the current christological and Origenist controversies rampant in Palestine played a role in the episcopal succession in Gaza. Barsanuphius' primary concern was that the people of Gaza accept the man chosen by Patriarch John of Jerusalem, rather than risk a break with the church leadership of Palestine.[11] Barsanuphius' intervention as an anchorite into episcopal matters in Gaza correlates with the machinations of the monks of the Judean desert in the episcopal politics of Jerusalem.

Although there is no direct reference in these letters to Christology or Chalcedon, this incident helps us place Barsanuphius in a debate in which many other anchorites and bishops were deeply involved. Since the patriarchate of Jerusalem remained pro-Chalcedonian in this period, Barsanuphius effectively supported the Chalcedonian side in the debate. His insistence that the patriarch choose the new bishop of Gaza reveals his christological position, one that otherwise remains ambiguous throughout much of his writing. Barsanuphius did not have the pro-Chalcedonian fervor of someone like Sabas, the anchorite who persuaded a new patriarch to switch sides despite strong imperial pressure. Nor did Barsanuphius have the rancor of a neighboring bishop, the anti-Chalcedonian

John Rufus. During the time of the episcopal election in Gaza, John Rufus was actually serving as bishop of Gaza's port city, Maiouma, only a few miles away. Although he himself was a bishop, John Rufus' writings are full of references to holy monks and anchorites who fought against the "betrayal" of Palestinian bishops who acquiesced to Chalcedon.[12] We can be certain that John Rufus would not have approved of the patriarch's choice of a Chalcedonian bishop for Gaza or Barsanuphius' support of the patriarch.

In this tense environment of sixth-century Palestine, where a monk chose his spiritual father as much for his stance on ecclesiastical debates as for his manner of life, it is unusual to find an important anchorite who deliberately pursued a moderate course, avoiding both extremes in the christological controversy. Barsanuphius refused to engage openly in the debate over Chalcedon. He would affirm only his allegiance to the Council of Nicaea. Barsanuphius shared the rhetoric of the non-Chalcedonian faction, which appealed to the authority of Nicaea alone. Yet Barsanuphius was determined to remain in the middle of the christological continuum, endorsing neither radical pro-Chalcedonian nor anti-Chalcedonian agendas. His ultimate acceptance of the Council of Chalcedon is evident not from any discussion of Christology, but in his steadfast support of the Chalcedonian patriarch. Barsanuphius continually taught that God carried out his will through the decisions of the church. The Great Old Man's allegiance to Patriarch John II of Jerusalem confirms his moderate stance, accepting Chalcedon while maintaining sympathy for those in the non-Chalcedonian camp. He consistently directed his disciples not to engage in doctrinal disputes but to keep their attention focused on their own sin.

What does this episode have to say about the relationship between the spiritual authority of anchorites and that of bishops? First, the people of Gaza looked to the anchorite in the midst of a troubled transition. They expected the anchorite both to protect them from the deposed bishop and to guide them in the choice of a new bishop. Second, Barsanuphius employed his own spiritual authority to support the established church hierarchy in Jerusalem. Instead of advocating a particular candidate, he encouraged his petitioners to defer to the patriarch's judgment. Barsanuphius was far more interested in fostering unity and obedience within the church than in espousing any specific theological view or aiding any particular faction.

BISHOP MARCIAN

Barsanuphius approved of the candidate eventually chosen to be Bishop of Gaza, writing to him after his ordination to assure the man that God's will had brought about his succession (Letter 804).[13] Information about the new bishop, Marcian, is preserved in two major sources, the orations of his classmate, the rhetor Choricius, and the letters of Barsanuphius and John. The authors of these texts, an urbane orator of elite society and two elderly anchorites adorned only with ascetic virtue, came from opposite ends of the spectrum of Christian experience in Gaza; yet, in their discussion of Marcian, the writers deal with some of the same incidents, producing a far richer composite picture than either source does alone.

The new bishop seems to have been far removed from the heated contest over Christology in Jerusalem. He came from an elite family of Gaza that produced a government official, a lawyer, a teacher, and two other bishops.[14] Marcian himself was well educated, having studied in the prestigious rhetorical school of Gaza, which he then helped to administer after the death of Procopius of Gaza. Both Procopius and Choricius of Gaza addressed encomiums to the bishop.[15] After praising Marcian's classical virtues, Choricius added that the bishop was also well trained in scripture.[16] The figure of Marcian reveals close connections between the rhetorical school at Gaza and the monastic community of Tawatha that are not obvious from other sources. In Bishop Marcian the exercise of Christian leadership blended perfectly with the ideals of classical *paideia*.[17] Like Augustine's first impression of Ambrose in Milan, Marcian exemplified civility and delighted others with his rhetoric.[18]

A passing pilgrim articulated the qualities coveted by the citizens: "Gaza is a lovely and renowned city, with noble people distinguished by every kind of liberal accomplishment. They are welcoming to strangers."[19] Marcian conscientiously strove to live up to the high expectations of the citizens of Gaza. In contrast to the previous bishop, who had used his wealth for his own personal aggrandizement and had provoked the hostility of the people, Marcian focused on beautifying the city through the construction of churches dedicated to St. Sergius and St. Stephen.[20] His eulogizer, Choricius, carefully avoided the charge that excessive building might indicate selfishness by reminding the people of Gaza that, in addition to building lavish churches and baths, Marcian also erected homes for the poor: "Although you keep your mind busy with decoration of the church, you also have room for that concern which defends against the greatest of evils, old age and poverty."[21]

The concern of Bishop Marcian for the welfare of the city is evident in both the orations of Choricius and the letters of Barsanuphius and John, although the orator highlighted works of marble and the holy men works of compassion. In both orations praising Marcian, Choricius not only recorded elaborate descriptions of the churches that the bishop had built (or rebuilt) but also that he had fortified the city walls. "Believing that daily expectation of enslavement was the same as [actual] slavery," the bishop rebuilt the wall that protected the city.[22] It had deteriorated so much, that the wall was, "just a name, for most of the enclosed space had opened to intruders, while even the rest of it could be crossed, because of the heaps of rubble."[23] For this task Marcian secured imperial funds as well as financial support from leading citizens.

The election of Marcian as bishop of Gaza occurred before John the Prophet had joined Barsanuphius at Tawatha. The correspondence between Barsanuphius and John of Beersheba (whom I argue is John the Prophet) mentions the relationship between anchorites and bishops. When John had completed his training to become an anchorite and leader of the monastery, Barsanuphius granted him the authority to direct others, in particular bishops (Letter 51). This was the ultimate sign of approval for John's exercise of spiritual authority. The questions to him from bishops in the Correspondence (including two asking if they should carry out their episcopal duties or flee the responsibility) demonstrate John's spiritual authority over bishops (Letters 788 and 789).[24] Once John's spiritual authority was established, Bishop Marcian of Gaza joined those who sought him out as a spiritual advisor.

In the system of spiritual authority established in sixth-century Gaza, holy men exercised authority over bishops. However, Barsanuphius and John did not use this power to challenge members of the ecclesiastical hierarchy openly but rather to influence the actions of church leaders. Likewise, the anchorites wielded some power over civic leaders. Bringing together monastic and episcopal authority, the holy men worked with the bishop to restrain the actions of civil officials, effectively serving as a check on secular power.

CIVIL AUTHORITY

Military disturbances in the region elicited the intervention of Barsanuphius and John, who demanded the cooperation of the bishop. Justinian's edict against the Samaritans triggered a rebellion in 529, beginning in Neapolis with the killing of a Christian bishop and spreading significant unrest throughout Palestine.[25] Imperial soldiers were dispatched to the region of Gaza under the military commander, the *doux*, of Palestine I, Aratius.[26] In the course of suppressing the revolt, the soldiers began to harass local peasants.[27] Choricius described these soldiers as "having coarse minds, tongues which outrun their intelligence, and their right hands outstretched further than their tongues."[28] The rhetor placed the blame for the farmers' distress upon the soldiers and upon the merchants collecting provisions for the troops who kept some of the supplies for themselves. From the letters of Barsanuphius and John we learn that the people of Gaza blamed another party—the *doux* (Letter 831). With the bishop, the leading citizens of Gaza approached the holy men about the incident. They wanted to inform the emperor of the situation but feared retribution from the *doux*. It is not surprising that in his account Choricius passed over this influential figure without reproach, since he would go on to address an oration praising Aratius' military efforts aimed at suppressing the Samaritans.[29]

In contrast to the accommodating approach of the rhetor, Barsanuphius and John had no compunction about ordering the powerful in Gaza to fight on behalf of the poor. The anchorites rebuked Bishop Marcian for his silence over the issue and urged him to stand up to both *doux* and emperor (Letters 831–33).[30] Apparently at a loss over how to approach the *doux*, Marcian asked John to dictate a letter for him. In the course of his request, the bishop revealed that Aratius had only recently become a Christian, "by the zeal of the Christian emperor," Justinian (Letter 834).[31] In the letter he composed, John urged the newly converted *doux* to bear spiritual fruit. The message of the holy men must have eventually reached the *doux* through the reluctant agency of the bishop, for Choricius credited Marcian with bringing the unfortunate incident to a successful conclusion.[32]

Sometimes the balance of classical and Christian virtues for which Choricius praised Marcian disintegrated into open discord. Marcian sought John's advice on dealing with another figure prominent in the public arena of Gaza—the provincial magistrate, Archon Stephanus (Letter 836).[33] The bishop complained that Stephanus ignored the church's prohibitions on theater performances and pagan festivals. John instructed Marcian to remind the archon that in his role as a high government official he acted as a minister of God (Rom. 13:6). In striking contrast to this critique from the holy men, Choricius praised Stephanus by asking whether he were god or man.[34] The rhetor, articulating the sentiments of many in the community, lauded the ruler for constructing a theater in Gaza. Stephanus enjoyed both pagan festivals and Christian feast days; Choricius commended him for his role in the festival marking the consecration of the church of St. Stephanus. The archon "intermingled a certain gracefulness with piety," being neither too solemn, nor too carefree.[35] Stephanus delighted many townspeople, although he disturbed the spiritual authorities of Gaza.

INSTRUCTION ON ORDINATION

In contrast to Choricius' picture of Marcian as a classical patron of civic arts, and Barsanuphius and John's ideal of a church leader censuring erring government officials, the bishop himself appeared preoccupied with recruiting clergy. Marcian repeatedly sought instruction from the holy men as he went about his task of selecting suitable men to ordain as priests. This was a major responsibility, which weighed heavily on the new bishop. In this endeavor ascetic values could conflict with classical norms, and Marcian was often hesitant to act on the advice of the holy men.

Although Gaza was Marcian's native city, when choosing men to ordain he still depended on the recommendations of those who knew individual candidates well. There being many groups eager to influence the process, John urged the bishop to trust the recommendations of the local monastic fathers without seeking out corroborating testimony (Letter 806). On one occasion Marcian sent a list of men to John, asking which of them he should ordain to the diaconate. The bishop was surprised by the men John chose; they were, "from the human point of view, inept at administration" (Letter 808).[36] When the bishop questioned the Old Man about the unlikely candidates, John asserted that the names were from God. So that Marcian would not take this statement as a self-aggrandizing boast, John added that God could speak even through the mouth of an ass.

This assurance that the list of candidates was divinely inspired did not calm Marcian's concerns over the candidates. The bishop shared the values of the late Roman upper class, who equated authority with the rhetorical skill acquired through a common educational background.[37] Bishop Marcian wanted to know how inarticulate men could adequately carry out the work of the church; he feared that without skill in speaking they would only invite disdain. Recognizing the source of the bishop's concern, John countered that men who were "mute and without intelligence," God would make "more formidable than magistrates" (Letter 809). If, on the other hand, Marcian sent a rhetorician to plead his own cause, he would return the same as he went out—without the benefit of divine transformation. Marcian may have interpreted this as a reproach for his close association with Choricius and his colleagues at the School of Gaza, since he protested defensively that it was churchgoers he feared to scandalize by such appointments. The bishop tried to soften his continued resistance to John's candidates by prefacing his statement with assurances that he knew John's words came from God and that he would carry them out immediately (Letter 811).

A personal connection eventually helped Marcian accept John's warning not to allow public opinion to dictate his ordinations. Marcian wanted to ordain his own secretary, but he feared negative public reaction. John encouraged him to ignore human considerations and act in the fear of God (Letter 812). In this case it was the bishop's own confidence in the person's qualifications that allowed him to act against the expectation of others. He had not yet made the leap to accepting recommendations from the holy man that ran counter to both public opinion and his own.

Although the Bishop of Gaza struggled to balance the wisdom of the holy man with the expectations of other groups within the city, more powerful bishops deliberately sought out John's guidance on such issues. Peter, Patriarch of Jerusalem (524–52), addressed many questions to the Old Man about whom to ordain. Like Marcian, Peter felt pressure from various groups to ordain certain candidates. In one instance a layman, a close friend of the patriarch who represented the interests of the church before powerful people, suggested a candidate for ordination. John instructed Peter to ordain the man only if his own evaluation found the candidate worthy. Although the anchorite had given direct instructions to Marcian, in this case John made the patriarch decide for himself. According to John, while bishops should trust the advice of monastic fathers without question, they should carefully weigh the recommendations of lay persons (Letter 819).

The patriarch of Jerusalem recognized that pressure from the community influenced him to choose men for ordination based upon standards of civic rather than spiritual success. He had already ordained a man as priest, skipping the intermediate step of deacon, because the man had been a respected lawyer (Letter 813), and later regretted the ordination.[38] In one village he was pressed to choose between a rich candidate who had remarried after his wife's death and a poor one who had not (Letter 816).[39] Other clergy whom he had chosen at the demand of powerful men were now overburdened with civic responsibilities that impinged on their clerical ones (Letter 817). In one rural place, Peter knew of no one to ordain, so John permitted him to act upon the nominations of the residents; in another place the inhabitants wanted more clergy ordained than the town needed (Letters 814 and 815). The anchorite patiently led the patriarch through these and other dilemmas, responding to each of the bishop's requests for guidance.

The patriarchate of Jerusalem was not a peaceful see, and Peter felt pressured about more matters than doctrinal controversy and the choice of men for ordination. Trying to balance competing demands without creating enmity, he wrote to Barsanuphius of numerous trials. Government agents passing through the city demanded frequent welcome gifts (Letter 830).[40] The patriarch knew this was a poor use of the church's resources, but he did not want complaints to reach the magistrates. Peter was already worried about the church's ability to cover its expenses (Letters 828 and 829). In despair at having made enemies of powerful men, he considered abandoning his office and wrote to ask for the holy man's prayers (Letters 823 and 824). Throughout this turmoil, Barsanuphius continually encouraged the patriarch to resist fear and temptation.

The Great Old Man did more than comfort. In one instance, when Peter succumbed to outside pressure, Barsanuphius recalled him to his duty as bishop. Trying to please others, the patriarch had set aside some of the traditional privileges of the church. The monk who compiled the Correspondence added that negative consequences followed, "by the permission of God" (Letter 825). Barsanuphius easily made the transition from encourager to critic, warning the patriarch to examine his behavior. Funding the church's needs was often a concern for church leaders, and when citizens of Gaza urged their bishop to levy a new tax on ships,

Barsanuphius and John insisted that bishops should guard the traditional prerogatives of the church without becoming obsessed with innovative ways to improve revenue (Letter 835).[41]

The citizens of sixth-century Gaza lived in a world governed by multiple value systems. The city's reputation was enhanced both by the School of Gaza and the monastery at Tawatha. Figures like Bishop Marcian, who emerged from the urban aristocracy and sought association both with rhetors and anchorites, held in tension the competing world views of the urban elite and the ascetic prophets. Barsanuphius and John's interactions with bishops and government officials reveal the radical differences of interpretation that lay beneath the surface of everyday civic life. These competing outlooks did not, however, prevent the bishop and anchorites from working together for a number of causes, including outfitting a church with buildings and clergy, providing for the poor, and limiting the arbitrary power of the state over the lives of local inhabitants.

Bishops and anchorites were closely connected in sixth-century Palestine. They were sometimes trained in the same monasteries. While anchorites showed deference to the ecclesiastical honor of the episcopate, they were not reluctant to make demands on the policies and behavior of a bishop. Anchorites saw themselves as having spiritual authority over bishops, and bishops sought the advice of anchorites. Barsanuphius and John expected the recipients of their letters to heed their direction, although they did not use their power to challenge publicly the church hierarchy. The letters of Barsanuphius and John show anchorites and bishops cooperating to govern the Christian community. Despite their physical isolation in monastic cells, the anchorites were intimately involved in the controversies that preoccupied the inhabitants of the region and freely instructed ecclesiastical leaders on their episcopal duties and their proper relationship with civil authority.

CHAPTER 6

Aelianos
Leader for the Next Generation

Under the leadership of Barsanuphius, John, and Seridos the monastery at Tawatha experienced a long period of relative stability. The anchorites and abbot worked together closely to provide a network of spiritual authority that was flexible enough to withstand challenges from members within the monastic community and powerful enough to influence ecclesiastical politics throughout the province. The Old Men served as spiritual directors not only for monks and clergy but also for the laity of Gaza and the surrounding region. The leadership of the monastery appeared well established to the monks who lived at Tawatha while Seridos governed as abbot beneath the authority of the anchorites. The Old Men conveyed the feeling of permanence to those they oversaw; few had any reason to expect change.

When change did come to Tawatha, it came suddenly and drastically. It was precipitated by the most certain of variables—human mortality. The leaders of the monastery had prepared for their own deaths. They recognized the challenge of passing on their spiritual authority to a new generation and had sought to prepare leaders, including Dorotheos, to succeed them. The steps taken by the Old Men of Gaza in planning for passage of authority from one generation to the next reveal the mechanics of change within the community. Their efforts highlight the strengths of the governing system of the monastery under Abbot Seridos, as well as the critical challenges his successor faced.

Although the anchorites and abbot had worked together for many years to develop leaders among the monks at Tawatha, the actual transition to new leadership was in many ways surprising. Barsanuphius and John's instructions to the new abbot, Aelianos, reveal the dramatic chain of events that accelerated change at the monastery (Letters 571–98).

119

When the events occurred, circa 543, Seridos had been governing the cenobium under the supervision of Barsanuphius for several decades. John had joined them, becoming Barsanuphius' closest colleague, around 525. The three had exercised spiritual authority over the monastic community at Tawatha for almost an entire generation. This stable network of leadership came to an abrupt end.

In the immediate aftermath of the plague that ravaged the empire in the mid-sixth century, the cenobium at Tawatha faced another crisis when Abbot Seridos fell ill (Letter 599).[1] Acknowledging his imminent death, Seridos turned to the task of appointing a successor, composing a list of several names, mostly experienced members of the monastic community. The first on the list was supposed to govern until his death, and then the next, and so forth. The final name on the list was that of a layman, Aelianos, who was to succeed after the others, "if he became a monk" (Letter 574). It was this final candidate, an outsider and layman, who succeeded Seridos immediately as abbot of the cenobium.

Although not a member of the monastic community, Aelianos, a wealthy layman, was a disciple of both John and Barsanuphius. As we have seen, many laymen wrote letters to the anchorites, but Aelianos seems to have had a particularly close, personal association with Barsanuphius and John. They addressed him as child and brother. Aelianos did not write as a stranger but as one deeply interested in the monastic life. He planned to retire to the monastery, but his familial obligations troubled him. Aelianos' household consisted of an elderly lady (presumably his mother) and a number of slaves (Letter 571).[2] He intended to settle his mother with her slaves near her cousins and sell all the property that she did not need.[3] This would take some time, but he did not wish to be concerned with these worldly details after he entered the monastery. Aelianos hoped John would approve of this plan of action.

John's first response was to warn Aelianos against hesitation, reminding him of Lot's wife, who lost her salvation with a backward glance (Letter 571; Gen. 19:26). After opening with this extreme analogy, John continued in a more practical tone. Aelianos needed to fulfill his familial obligation: he should establish his mother near her cousins and provide her with sufficient land for her upkeep and that of the slaves. Because her cousins would hope to inherit the land upon her death, Aelianos could trust them to provide for his mother's needs out of the income of the land. This much, in John's eyes, was required of Aelianos. As to whether Aelianos should delay longer to oversee the disposal of his other property, John deferred to the judgment of Barsanuphius. Barsanuphius, in turn, built upon the imagery of John's warning, urging quick flight from Sodom (Letter 572); Aelianos was obliged to make provision for his mother, but he should have no further concern for his property.

In his next letter, Barsanuphius outlined the relationship of spiritual father and disciple that existed between himself and the layman. Aelianos had written again that he was unable to throw off the passions that bound him to the world and so asked Barsanuphius to intervene on his behalf before their divine master. Barsanuphius replied: "Child . . . you should know . . . that our master, the merciful and foreseeing Savior, has persuaded me to treat you truly as my spiritual son; I have entrusted to you secrets which I have not entrusted to many, this is a proof of filial adoption. Because with whom does the father confer, if not his son?" (Letter 573). Barsanuphius said that God had granted him Aelianos' salvation. He called him a "true son of my sufferings."[4] Barsanuphius committed himself to constant prayer on his son's behalf and required Aelianos to guard his father's words and not dishonor his old age.

At the time of Seridos' death, Aelianos had already established a mature relationship with John and Barsanuphius. We can assume a close relationship with Seridos, as well, since Seridos had been the intermediary between Aelianos and his self-proclaimed spiritual father. As the agent of communication between Barsanuphius and Aelianos, Seridos had both observed and participated in the process of his spiritual direction. The structure of spiritual authority at Tawatha assured that Seridos, as Barsanuphius' scribe, was always aware of developments brought before the holy man. He would have been familiar with Aelianos' desire to become a monk. His choice of Aelianos as a potential successor testified to his confidence that the layman would carry out his intention to join the monastery.

Seridos had gained sufficient insight into Aelianos' character to believe that he would make not only a good monk but also a good abbot. Aelianos' position as a man of the world, involved with property and family, made him an unusual candidate for abbot. However, these worldly qualities themselves may have recommended him to Seridos. In addition to spiritual direction, the duties of abbot included the management and distribution of resources, the supervision of interaction between the monks and their relatives, and other practical affairs relating to community living.

Following Seridos' death, the first monk named to succeed him refused "with much humility and modesty," and the others followed his example (Letter 574). The most trusted and respected members of the community, probably even John's disciple Dorotheos, chose to forgo their claim to leadership in favor of the layman. In this manner they demonstrated their own single-minded commitment to the life of humility. They also recognized that the monastery could benefit from the skills of Aelianos, who was simultaneously a trusted lay disciple of Barsanuphius, John, and Seridos and still an outsider who stood above any internal rivalries in the established hierarchy of the monastery.[5]

The sixth-century compiler's staunch support for Aelianos may indicate that there were some in the monastery who did not welcome his appointment as abbot. The choice of an outsider certainly seems unusual, but no evidence of any dissent has been preserved. If it were the compiler's intention to strengthen Aelianos' new position and silence any opposition, he succeeded as far as the written record goes. Other monastic texts offered precedents for choosing an unexpected candidate as abbot. According to the *Life of Pachomius,* the Egyptian saint's apparent spiritual heir, Theodore, was passed over twice as other men became abbot. First Pachomius chose Petronios, the head of the monastery at Tsmine, to succeed him at Tabennesi. Then when Petronios was dying he again passed over Theodore and appointed Horsiesios. In this case, the choice did cause dissension. Horsiesios was unable to consolidate his power and finally resigned in favor of Theodore.[6]

While the monks at Tawatha were reading Seridos' will, Aelianos was falling into depression. His thoughts turned to the end of the world, with its tribulations and eternal chastisements. This despair grew out of his indecision about becoming a monk. Although earlier letters indicate that his primary concern involved settling details of his worldly affairs, in John and Barsanuphius' warnings about fleeing Sodom Aelianos had found vivid motivation for concentrating on the eternal consequences of his decision. He now wrote to John that he feared for his soul (Letter 574).

Although Aelianos certainly knew of the abbot's death, he was unaware that he was named in the succession. Therefore, the manner in which John answered his letter surprised him. Aelianos had hoped for consolation, but in his reply John stressed the need for obedience to God and the subjugation of one's will to that of the heavenly Father. Nevertheless, John's words relieved Aelianos' despair. The crucial communication, when John informed Aelianos that he was the designated successor to Seridos, did not take place through the usual medium of written correspondence. Instead, John spoke to Aelianos face to face, revealing what had transpired and instructing him to assume the authority of the abbot (Letter 575). John's willingness to break his long-established custom of communicating only through letters emphasized the serious nature of this message.

We do not know Aelianos' first reaction to the news. We do, however, have his later response, written after he had returned home and reflected upon the situation: "Father, I do not understand myself better than the Spirit of God does who lives in you not me; I am afraid and I tremble, because of the peril of the situation. If you know that in this I can find mercy thanks to your protection in Christ, I do not resist, because you have full power over me, and I am in God's hands and in yours" (Letter 575).[7] Aelianos submitted to the will of his spiritual father, John. Affirming the reciprocal nature of the relationship, John pledged his commitment to Aelianos' salvation.

Aelianos received the monastic *schema* to wear,[8] was ordained a priest, and became abbot of the monastery. As he recounted these successive ranks, the compiler revealed the sources of monastic authority. It was upon the order of Barsanuphius and John that Aelianos became a monk. Aelianos embarked upon a life of asceticism at the direction of his spiritual fathers, who had been leading him in that direction for a considerable time. It was "at the general request" that the bishop ordained him priest, and he was made abbot of the monastery (Letter 575b).[9] Barsanuphius and John did not impose a leader on the monastery.[10] Instead, the community at large petitioned the bishop to ordain the candidate. This is the first time the sources mention a bishop in connection with the succession at Tawatha. Ordination by the bishop conferred clerical status to a leader already chosen by the monastic community.[11]

By requesting that the bishop ordain the man chosen by Barsanuphius, John, and Seridos, the monks participated in the installation of their new abbot. This was not, however, their first involvement in the process. They became active players in Aelianos' succession by their refusal to accept authority themselves: "With full consent they chose you to the disgrace of those who manipulate inheritances and legacies, who have a spirit that loves money like those of the world and who put earthly things before those of the kingdom of heaven" (Letter 576). This peaceful process of choosing a spiritual successor within the monastery contrasted starkly with the jealous rivalries that often took place among those who stood to inherit worldly goods.[12]

There is no evidence to suggest that either Barsanuphius or John left his seclusion to participate in the ceremonies of ordination or installation. Although they clearly influenced the choice of succession, their power resided in private relationships generated through letters. There was no need for them to play a visible, ceremonial role. By remaining in their cells, they left the bishop to demonstrate his own authority at the monastery, by ordaining Aelianos as priest. Thus, there was no possibility of competition between the ecclesiastical jurisdiction of the bishop and the charisma of the anchorites.

Aelianos' first action as abbot was to visit John in his cell. This was the second recorded physical encounter between the two men. Both incidents occurred after Seridos' death, when the absence of one of the Old Men's intermediaries encouraged closer interaction.[13] The compiler preserved John's side of the conversation in writing, as if it had been in the form of a letter rather than part of a verbal conversation (Letter 575b). Since it seems unlikely that a third person was present to record John's words, we may assume that Aelianos later wrote down the conversation or repeated it to someone at the monastery. Regardless of the manner in which John's response came to be recorded, it is clear that this meeting was important enough that an account of the conversation needed to be included in the collection.

It is worth noting that, although Aelianos was the disciple of both John and Barsanuphius, John was more accessible for personal encounters and the one Aelianos turned to first. It is also noteworthy that, although Seridos had been both abbot and the primary agent of communication for Barsanuphius, when Aelianos took his place as abbot he continued to address John first and did not take over the previous abbot's role as intermediary between Barsanuphius and the monks.

When Aelianos visited his cell, John received him as an abbot. With great humility, John asked him to say the benediction. Aelianos reluctantly complied, in order not to disobey his spiritual father. During their conversation, he marveled that the Old Men had permitted the monks named to succeed Seridos to refuse the office. Aelianos supposed that their rank should have compelled them to accept authority and that his own status as an outsider and man of the world should have disqualified him. John explained to Aelianos that Barsanuphius had predicted long ago that the layman would become the next abbot. Aelianos' succession was not an accident or an afterthought but a carefully devised plan finally brought to fulfillment by God's providence.

JOHN PREDICTS HIS DEATH

Seridos' death and Aelianos' succession were only the first two events that brought about a complete rearrangement of authority in this monastic community. Seridos' death, in addition to being the loss of a beloved abbot, also raised questions about the continuity of the entire network of leadership at Tawatha. Barsanuphius had for many years communicated with the monks only through letters carried by Seridos. When Seridos died the Great Old Man did not choose another intermediary. Rather, Barsanuphius chose to go into complete seclusion soon after Seridos' death. John was also ready to leave his disciples.

Before Seridos died, the monks at Tawatha knew that John did not expect to outlive the abbot. He had asked God to allow him to die before Seridos (Letter 599). When this did not occur, several "old men" sought to understand why God had not granted the venerable father's petition. They invoked a motif common in patristic literature, the comparison of a contemporary Christian luminary with a figure from the Old Testament. If God had revealed to the prophet Elijah the hour of his death (2 Kings 2:9–11), why had John been deprived of this foresight? This form of comparison was usually used to equate Christian saints with Old Testament heroes, but here the expected equation had broken down. John had not died before Seridos, as he had requested.

It is interesting that the men who brought forward this question were not described as young monks, or even by the ubiquitous title "brothers" (*adelphoi*), but as "old men" (*gerontes*). This title placed them in the upper ranks of the monastery as spiritual fathers in their own right. Their question gained legitimacy from their status; it was not the query of immature disciples who did not understand spiritual matters but a legitimate matter of concern for those who believed that God "always does the will of those who fear him" (Letter 599; Ps. 145:19). The monks voiced a further concern: Why did God cause Abbot Seridos to suffer with ulcers before his death? In response to these questions John invoked God's words to the premier monastic authority: "Just as it was said to Abba Antony, these are the judgments of God, and you are not able to understand them" (Letter 599).[14] John assured the monks that everything worked to God's glory.

Although God had not granted his request to die before Seridos, thoughts about John's death occupied the center of focus for the inhabitants at Tawatha. John announced that he would die within a week of Seridos' death. The members of the monastery begged their spiritual father not to leave them as orphans. John said, "If the abbot Seridos had remained, I would have remained another five years, but since God took him without my knowledge, I will remain no longer" (Letter 599b). John affirmed that his life was irrevocably linked to that of his spiritual disciple. The closeness of their deaths in time would symbolize the union of their lives.[15] Although John did not heed the general cry of the monks, the intervention of another disciple compelled him to modify his plans.

When John remained unmoved by the supplication of the monks, the new abbot approached Barsanuphius. This is the first recorded face-to-face encounter between Barsanuphius and Aelianos. Since Seridos was no longer available to carry letters, Aelianos approached Barsanuphius directly to ask "with many entreaties and tears" that Barsanuphius "give us [John]" (Letter 599b). Aelianos was interceding with one of his spiritual fathers in order to change the mind of the other. The dual leadership exercised by Barsanuphius and John made this unusual scenario possible. Monks at Tawatha considered both anchorites to be their spiritual fathers, but John also placed himself under the authority of Barsanuphius as a disciple. After John embraced solitude and became the spiritual co-director of the monastery, Barsanuphius no longer acted as John's spiritual superior. John and Barsanuphius strove to present a single voice to their disciples. As we have seen, they frequently reprimanded those who tried to solicit advice from one anchorite when they disliked the instruction offered by the other.

Although Barsanuphius did not rebuke Aelianos for interfering, neither did he order John to grant Aelianos' request. John and Barsanuphius' unique relationship, which did not rely upon verbal or written communication, preserved unity in this potentially divisive situation. Knowing "by the Spirit" what had transpired, John interviewed the monks the next day. He spoke directly to Aelianos and asked why he had gone to Barsanuphius about the matter. Buttressed by the tears of the monks gathered behind him, Aelianos made his demand, "Give me at least two weeks, in order that I might ask you about the monastery and its government" (Letter 599b).

Moved by the Holy Spirit, John took pity on the new abbot and granted him two weeks of instruction.[16]

This incident demonstrates the complexity of the father-disciple relationship in monastic circles. Aelianos had not one spiritual father but two. He tended to have more frequent interaction with John, but as the situation escalated he turned to Barsanuphius. On an earlier occasion John had referred Aelianos to Barsanuphius for advice on the question of the disposal of his property. In this second instance, Aelianos sought a personal interview with Barsanuphius, because he hoped to enlist his help in persuading John to alter his plans. Among the reasons brought forward for delaying John's departure was Barsanuphius' intention to withdraw completely and to communicate no longer, even through letters. Aelianos did not want to lose both spiritual fathers at the same time, especially because he would be taking on the administration of the monastery without them. Because John had been more accessible in the past, Aelianos assumed that he would be more willing than Barsanuphius to remain in contact with the monks a while longer. Physical death seemed more negotiable than the Great Old Man's decision to withdraw completely.

Aelianos made his request of Barsanuphius because he felt an acute need for spiritual guidance. He no longer sought help for his own salvation, but rather for the spiritual well-being of those in his care. Like John and Seridos, Aelianos was no longer merely a disciple but had become a spiritual father. He sought guidance so that he might direct others. He also hoped that John would accept the direction of their mutual spiritual father Barsanuphius in this matter. The intervention of Barsanuphius was not required, however, because Barsanuphius and John's relationship was characterized by concord.

In the subsequent interview with John, the monks surrounding Aelianos visibly accented his new status as spiritual father. The compiler of the Correspondence, speaking in the first person, said explicitly that it had been his own tears and those of the rest that had moved Aelianos to make his request. John, in order to enable his disciple to fulfill the obligations of his new fatherhood, promised to continue in his role as father a little longer. For two weeks Aelianos busily questioned him about the governance of the monastery. Despite his initial eagerness to depart, John spent this period intensively preparing Aelianos for his new role as abbot. Aelianos' concerns fell into three categories: his relationship with his new disciples, the interactions of the monastery with the outside world, and the relationship of his authority with that of those who had previously led the monastery—Barsanuphius, John, and Seridos.

THE ABBOT AND THE MONKS

Aelianos felt considerable apprehension about becoming abbot and questioned John extensively about how to establish a relationship with the monks. As a recent convert from lay life, Aelianos wondered how he could offer spiritual direction to men experienced in the monastic life: "I know nothing, what do you command me to say to the brothers?" and, "How must I behave towards them?" (Letters 577 and 579). John assured him that God would speak through him when the brothers came individually to confess their thoughts. He should behave as any true Christian in authority—as a servant: "Your rank exists that you might be merciful to all" (Letter 579).

Aelianos asked for specific advice on the formal gestures employed by an abbot. When he blessed the brothers, should he offer them his hand (to be kissed) or not? He also wondered about the appropriateness of touching the heads of the kneeling monks. These questions remind us that Aelianos never experienced living as a monk in the cenobium under the authority of an abbot; even the outward signs of monastic etiquette were foreign to him. John explained that the hand should be offered, not to oblige human conventions, but so that the monks might accrue the benefit that came in showing proper obeisance to an abbot: "He who receives a prophet in the name of a prophet will receive a prophet's reward" (Letter 578; Matt. 10:41). Aelianos should not touch the monks' heads, since that gesture conformed only to human needs.

In addition to instruction on the outward signs of his office, Aelianos needed guidance on exercising spiritual authority over his new charges. In particular, how should he correct their faults? Should correction be a private matter, between father and disciple, or should he reprimand the wrong doer before the whole community? John advised him to follow the guidelines offered in the gospel (Matt. 18:15–16). If a brother committed a serious fault he should be warned privately, "If you do not correct yourself, I must speak of it before the brothers" (Letter 581). Aelianos should both correct and punish minor faults privately.

Correction of faults was not only a major concern for spiritual directors but an obligation for all brothers. This principle was impressed upon those trained at Tawatha. Dorotheos offered his own disciples further guidelines for implementing this duty: "If someone should see his brother committing a fault, he should not despise him or let him be destroyed through silence, nor again curse him or speak against him but with compassion and the fear of God speak to someone who has power to correct him. Or he should address himself to this brother and tell him with love and humility, 'Pardon me, brother, as negligent as I am, it seems to me that in doing this, we do not do rightly.' "[17] If this first approach did not work, Dorotheos suggested bringing the matter to someone whom the brother respected, or to the abbot himself, if the fault was serious. Above all, Dorotheos insisted that the monk should keep his brother's spiritual well-being foremost in mind. He should search his heart to avoid scorn and gossip. If he found that uncharitable feelings existed, he should confess these to the abbot: "My conscience bears witness that I wish to speak for good, but I sense that some troubled thought is mixed up in it. Perhaps, at one time I had something against my brother, I do not know."[18] It was the abbot's role to draw out the brother's thoughts and then bid him speak or keep silent.

THE MONASTERY AND THE WORLD

Interaction between the members of a monastery and the outside world was a major concern for the leaders of monasteries in late antiquity.[19] Abbots had the responsibility of regulating visitors. The ascetic ideal of withdrawal was threatened each time an outsider knocked at the monastery's gate. The issue of who should have access to the brothers predominated in Aelianos' questions to John.

Acknowledging the many groups that frequented the monastery, which was so near Gaza, Aelianos asked John, "Tell me, father, how must I receive visitors, whether lay people, fathers, or brothers?" (Letter 584). In response, John outlined the behavior expected of an abbot when he entertained visitors. Although in posing the question Aelianos had distinguished between lay people, fathers, and brothers, John's answer leveled such categories, demonstrating once again that the elders at Tawatha considered the difference between lay and monastic status less significant than a person's motivation. "Whether they be lay people, brothers, or fathers," Aelianos should avoid all visitors who think, "the occasion is good for letting go to the satisfaction of the body and for filling the stomach" (Letter 584). The critical distinction was not between lay person and monk but between those who came for God and those who came for food.

The new abbot should follow the model offered by his predecessor, Seridos, of whose conduct he was "not ignorant" (Letter 584). Aelianos himself was probably one of the laymen whom Seridos had entertained with such moderation. The abbot should eat small portions, avoiding accusations of miserliness or profligacy. Visitors might pressure the abbot to indulge, saying, "if you do not drink, I will not drink; if you do not eat, then I will not eat" (Letter 584). Such arguments used the reciprocal obligation of hospitality to challenge abstinence. To counter this temptation John offered a peculiarly ascetic interpretation of Paul's injunction that, "the one who eats should not scorn the one who does not eat . . . and the one who does not eat should not judge the one who eats" (Letter 584; Rom. 14:3–6). The abbot, he said, should carefully evaluate the dispositions of his guests and avoid visitors who came frequently, desiring only a meal. These guidelines structured interactions with familiar guests, both laymen and ascetics.

In addition to the quantity of food and drink consumed, the Old Man addressed the topic of conversation at the abbot's table. John instructed Aelianos "as far as possible" not to discuss worldly subjects, "unless," he added facetiously, "a certain one does not need to hear the word of God" (Letter 584). He recommended that the abbot and his guests dwell instead on the lives of the fathers, the gospels, and the writings of the apostles and the prophets.[20] If a guest persisted in discussing worldly matters, Aelianos should say to him, "Father, the savior has said, 'Render unto Caesar that which is Caesar's, and render unto God, that which is God's'" (Letter 584; Matt. 22:21). John envisioned this reprimand being given to one called "father," not "son," or even "brother." He thus made it clear that even high rank within the community of the faithful did not guarantee single-minded devotion to spiritual things. As a new abbot, it was Aelianos' responsibility to correct even those whom he was accustomed to address as "Abba."

One category of guests could be particularly problematic for the new abbot. The abbot was responsible for regulating interaction between monks and their families. Relatives, as representatives of a system of social obligation rejected by the monks, continued to present challenges to the ascetic ideals the latter had embraced.[21] When the relatives under consid-

eration happened to be female—wives, sisters, daughters, or mothers—
the situation became even more complicated.

It was the custom of the monks at Tawatha to receive pious women and
female relatives of the brothers in an outside cell. This area had windows
that opened onto the monastery. Aelianos asked John if he should speak
to the women through these windows. Then he inquired about his own
personal ties. The worries that had preoccupied the layman Aelianos as he
struggled to become a monk had come to fruition. His mother was not
satisfied living with her cousins. She had returned to Aelianos the property he left for her upkeep and wanted to see him again. The new abbot
did not know how to deal with these obligations from his old life that
now interrupted his new responsibilities. He asked John if he should see
his mother when she came and, if so, how he should arrange the interview
(Letter 595).[22]

The presence of female visitors to the monastery did not disturb John.
This contrasts with both contemporary Western sources and the practice
in other Palestinian monasteries. Early Latin rules did not welcome
women at the monastery; some even prohibited the reception of letters
from any relatives.[23] Neither Euthymius, nor Sabas admitted female visitors to their monasteries in the Judean desert.[24] The location of the
monastery at Tawatha, so close to the large city of Gaza, guaranteed a
constant stream of visitors that a more isolated community might have
hoped to avoid. Female relatives of the monks were just one more category
of outsiders for the monastery to deal with in an appropriate manner.[25]
John advised Aelianos to continue interacting with women according to
the rule he had received from Seridos: "If on occasion you find the women
coming for God, not to see the place or for [an evil] intent but simply to
hear the word of God or to bring something to the place, and it is necessary to converse with them, converse" (Letter 595). John warned Aelianos
to guard his eyes and mind in order not to commit adultery in his heart
(Matt. 5:28) and promised that if the abbot were acting according to God,
the Lord would protect him.

John's answer alluded to the range of reasons women had for visiting
monasteries.[26] Many sources depict women traveling long distances to see
and speak with holy men.[27] Monastic authors were ambivalent about
these endeavors; sometimes the sources praised such women, but more
often they censured them. John Rufus described his spiritual father, Peter
the Iberian, going to great lengths to avoid unwanted attention from the

Empress Eudocia.[28] The monastery at Tawatha did not welcome women who came just "to see the place."

John's response to Aelianos revealed an established custom that permitted women access to the monastery at Tawatha. Women could come to the monastery in order to listen to the scriptures being read aloud. The late sixth- or early seventh-century *Life of Febronia* composed in Nisibis describes this practice. On Fridays and Sundays young married lay women came to a convent of female ascetics to hear the nun Febronia read the scriptures. Because the abbess wished to keep her from seeing their worldly dress, Febronia sat behind a curtain. The windows in the monastery at Tawatha served the same role as the curtain in Febronia's monastery: they separated the ascetics from the lay women. The system could have remarkable flexibility; Febronia's abbess did allow her on one occasion to instruct the pagan widow of a senator, as long as the woman wore the simple dress of an ascetic.[29]

John permitted women to bring things, presumably material gifts of food and clothing, to the monastery. Again, as in the case of visitation, the practice at Tawatha was more lenient than in other early monastic foundations. This did not mean that John was unaware of the problematic entanglements that could result from accepting gifts. In another instance, he advised Aelianos to refuse unneeded gifts and to repay immediately the value of a gift brought by someone hoping to gain something from the monastery (Letter 594).

John advised Aelianos to permit monks to speak with their mothers when necessary. The son of a woman who came to visit the monastery shared the abbot's responsibility to make sure the reasons for his mother's visits were necessary and not frivolous. This same principle governed Aelianos' interaction with his own mother. John required him to speak with her regularly as long as she lived and to provide for her needs. He was not critical of the woman for refusing to remain with her cousins. Indeed, he instructed Aelianos to allow her to live where she chose, either in Gaza or the nearby village.

The freedom that Aelianos was supposed to offer his mother differed markedly from the control he was to exercise over his slaves: "Do not allow them to do as they want, or you will not put them on the good path towards life. Direct them in the fear of God" (Letter 595). John instructed Aelianos to evaluate their needs carefully and to provide them with food and suitable clothing, saying to them, "Consider on your part, that you are not slaves but free. Are you not free from cares and more tranquil than those who possess riches?" (Letter 595). Aelianos' responsibility for his slaves would not end after his mother's death. John instructed him to manumit the slaves when she died and to give them an annuity.[30] Aelianos should then decide whether to settle them at the monastery or in the village. By implication, they should not remain in the city. In any case, Aelianos would continue to be responsible for their needs and behavior.[31]

THE MONASTERY AND STRANGERS

Having discussed the proper manner of entertaining friends and relatives at the monastery, Aelianos turned to the reception of strangers. Previously Aelianos and John had discussed the monastery's consumption of material goods from the standpoint of ascetic discipline. Now they considered the resources of the monastery and how they should be distributed to those outside the walls. Hospitality and charity were principal monastic virtues. The *Apophthegmata Patrum* are filled with stories of individual desert fathers acting out their love for their neighbor in private acts of almsgiving and hospitality. To enact these Christian obligations on an institutional level was more complicated.[32]

Aelianos sought from John guidelines for managing the work of charity among the poor who found their way to the monastery, only a few miles outside of Gaza: "How should we practice hospitality and charity among the poor? Is it necessary to receive all those who arrive? And when they trouble us for the sake of clothes, if we have a surplus should we give? And to whom?" (Letter 587). John advised Aelianos to practice charity in a sustainable manner. He should carefully examine each person who applied for aid and respond accordingly. If the abbot determined that a person seeking charity was a thief, he should follow the model demonstrated by the desert fathers and give him a small offering and dismiss him.[33] If the abbot suspected that the newcomer sought clothing not because he was truly needy but out of greed, he should turn him away and not allow him to exploit the resources of the monastery. Through careful scrutiny the abbot should identify the worthy recipient of charity, one whose poverty came from God rather than from dissoluteness.

Aelianos' questions expressed clear anxiety about the proper response to strangers. Whether it was a matter of offering strangers charity or accepting them into the community, the abbot was responsible for judging accurately the character of the outsider and protecting the monastery from disruptive influences. These disruptions could also come in the form of a known but unsavory outsider seeking admittance to the community. If a completely unknown person arrived at the monastery he should be received (Letter 590).[34] This reception did not mean the man was welcome to join the monastery, but only that the monks should show him hospitality as a guest. The abbot should take this opportunity to observe and evaluate the stranger before allowing him to join the community. John advised that no one should be admitted permanently without a preliminary period, "lest he become a trial and you are afflicted, unable to support him" (Letter 590).[35]

There was one category of visitors that Aelianos knew he was not supposed to receive—wandering monks (Letter 588).[36] He wrote asking for explication and confirmation of this rule. John agreed with this prohibition. Monks who wandered continuously from place to place would only bring troubles into the settled community of Tawatha.[37] In a community directed by two enclosed anchorites, the ascetic value of wandering found little sympathy. In the turbulent theological climate of the mid-sixth century, John may have feared that wandering monks, driven out of certain cities, might bring unwelcome doctrines.[38] Aelianos feared that it might not be easy to deny entry to these wandering monks. What should he do if they were insistent (Letter 589)? John maintained that they should not gain entry, but that Aelianos could give them a small offering and dismiss them. Thus, wandering monks should be dealt with in the same manner as the thieves mentioned earlier. The sooner the abbot sent them on their way, the better.

Unknown visitors posed potential threats to monastic discipline, but there were also people seeking association with the monastery whom the abbot knew to be troublemakers. Among these was a certain ordained monk, who "coming to the monastery, scandalized the brothers by his words and by his acts" (Letter 591). Aelianos and John were both circumspect in their correspondence as to the nature of the scandal, but his disturbing behavior seems to have been recurrent. Aelianos wanted to know how to deal with this troublesome person. Apparently the priest in question had settled within two miles of the monastery, along the road used by the brothers. Aelianos wanted to know how far his authority extended. Could he forbid the priest to live in the neighborhood, or should he be satisfied with keeping him out of the monastery itself?

John recommended a firm stance, cushioned by the polite respect due to a member of the clergy. Aelianos himself should take the man aside privately (his priestly office merited a face-to-face conversation with the abbot) and forbid him to enter the monastery, saying something like this: "Lord, Abba, you have scandalized the brothers. You have no need to enter here to scandalize them again. Do not think it is hate that makes us turn you away . . . but it is because of the scandal. You cannot live in the neighborhood, on account of the injury to the brothers" (Letter 591). Aelianos should address the misguided priest courteously, using both "Lord" and "Abba" as terms of respect. At the same time he should be confident in his own authority, even when exercising jurisdiction over the neighborhood around the monastery. The abbot should not allow the priest to remain in the vicinity of the monastery or to speak with the brothers on the road.

In his dealings with those outside the monastery, Aelianos was mindful of the triangular relationship between himself, the previous abbot, and the disciples to whom he responded. He was aware of existing precedents for the decisions he faced. He strove to maintain consistency in the office of abbot but was concerned about the need for flexibility. Among his questions about outsiders are two that deal with men whom Seridos had expelled from the monastery.

CHALLENGES TO THE NEW ABBOT

In his own time as abbot, Seridos had dealt with divisive monks. There was a brother who had lived at the monastery during Seridos' life who "did not benefit the brothers" (Letter 593). He had left the monastery but later returned. Seridos had refused to readmit him, saying, "Even if I wished to, I could not injure the consciences of the brothers, because there would be trouble if I accepted you. It is impossible" (Letter 593).[39] We know that Aelianos was well aware of these details, because he restated the events for John. Early in Aelianos' rule, the man returned, hoping that the new abbot would prove more lenient and let him back into the community. Aelianos looked to the anchorite for help in dealing with the difficult situation. John's reply revealed that he was familiar with the case. He added to Aelianos' account that the man in question had spoken to Seridos about readmittance not once but twice. Aelianos should respond patiently but firmly, addressing him personally as a brother but warning him, "Do not hope to live here, now or in the future." If the man should return again, he should be soundly rebuked, "Does your conscience not reproach you?" (Letter 593). Aelianos should uphold the decision of Seridos and prevent this man from rejoining the monastery.

Although Aelianos made only glancing reference to the specific misdeeds of the scandalous priest and the returning brother, he clearly identified, in a letter to John, the sin of another man whom Seridos had banished from the monastery: "Another came to the monastery and did a disloyal and inadmissible thing. He took objects in the name of the blessed abbot without him knowing it. When the abbot found out, he told him not to return to the monastery. But having heard this, [the man] entered the court from the side. The porter realized it and brought him to the abbot who said, 'Put him out.' [The porter] put him out, and he left the place for good" (Letter 592). Aelianos outlined the fault of this man, not because his crime was worse than those of the others, but because his misdeed was a deliberate affront to Abbot Seridos. To take items in the name of the abbot was a conscious attempt to usurp his authority. The man's deceit threatened the internal governance of the monastery. To compound his error, after Seridos had expelled him from the monastery, he returned surreptitiously through a side entrance. He refused to accept the discipline of the abbot. Proper authority within the monastery prevailed because of the obedience of the porter.[40]

Neither Aelianos nor John indicated the exact position of this man within the monastery (they did not call him a brother, monk, or father). The cursory introduction, "he came to the monastery and did a disloyal and inadmissible thing," might suggest a new member of the monastery or a visitor. Aelianos asked John if he should grant this man entrance. This could mean allowing him to rejoin the monastery, or merely welcoming him as a visitor. Whatever the man's station, Aelianos feared that he might return.

The return of men who had been expelled by Seridos made Aelianos aware that some viewed the accession of a new abbot as an opportunity to test the rulings of the previous abbot. As the new abbot, Aelianos should not be taken off guard when old challenges to the office resurfaced. John gave careful advice for how to deal with the unwanted visitors. Some merited a personal word with the abbot, before he sent them sent away. The man who stole using Seridos' name did not deserve this treatment; Aelianos, said John, should dismiss him through an intermediary.

THE NEW STRUCTURE OF SPIRITUAL AUTHORITY

In a very short time Aelianos made the transition from pious layman to monk and from friend of the monastery to abbot. He faced several significant challenges during this period. The loss of his own spiritual fathers, his new responsibilities as the highest spiritual authority in the monastic community, and the disappearance of the cooperative leadership network that had governed the monastery were each daunting changes for the new leader. The monastery that Aelianos had observed during the years in which he had contemplated becoming a monk was headed not by a single man but by a three-person hierarchy of leadership. Unlike the previous abbot, Seridos, who could bring his concerns to the Old Men for consultation, Aelianos would need to be confident enough to make decisions on his own for the entire community.

Although there was significant change in the governance of the monastery, Aelianos attempted to provide continuity for the community by connecting his own authority with that of his spiritual fathers, though they would no longer be physically present. The new abbot did not wish to transgress the directives of his fathers even after death separated them. This desire for continued obedience had motivated his earlier questions about readmitting men expelled by Seridos. Aelianos explicitly asked for help correlating his own authority and that of this predecessors: "If it seems necessary to me to lay aside some of your instructions, should I do so or not? If it is not necessary, and I am giving way as a human, what should I do?" (Letter 596). He repeated this query regarding the regulations of Seridos, asking John, "If I envisage changing something set up by the blessed Abba or reforming something in the monastery do you permit me to or not?" (Letter 597).

Eager to maintain the guidelines established by his predecessors, Aelianos also knew that an abbot needed to respond to changing circumstances. He recognized that his own spiritual authority rested upon that of his fathers, so he feared to transgress their decrees. Poignantly aware that soon he would no longer have recourse to the Old Men, Aelianos tried to envision the challenges he would face when they were gone. John counseled Aelianos to analyze his own motives when considering any change. If circumstances truly necessitated the change, he should not hesitate to adjust established practices. If human motives tempted him, he should resist. The most difficult case John foresaw was one in which there actually was a need for change but Aelianos realized that he was being influenced by questionable motives. In such a situation, Aelianos should seek forgiveness from God for his unworthy thoughts but proceed soberly with the change.

The necessity that the new abbot make difficult decisions by himself underlines the fundamental shift in spiritual authority at Tawatha. In the first administration, authority was divided between practical governance and a higher moral authority. As abbot, Seridos had made the managerial choices that ensured the smooth running of the monastery. However, when a conflict arose or he doubted his own motivations, he could defer to the higher spiritual authority of Barsanuphius and John, as he did when he encountered criticism for his negotiation of a land purchase (Letter 570c). When Aelianos became abbot and John and Barsanuphius relinquished their positions as spiritual advisors, the structure of authority changed. One man was now responsible for both making practical decisions and evaluating their moral ramifications. There was no longer a higher human authority to consult. Both John and Aelianos recognized the difficulties the new abbot would face as the sole arbiter in a community accustomed to a complex network of spiritual authority. Aelianos feared that one man, particularly one so new to the monastic vocation, could not provide the same level of leadership offered by three accomplished ascetics.

Aelianos' final question to John captured the disciple's anguish at being deprived of his fathers, as well as his apprehensions regarding his new responsibilities: "Master, as you have announced to us in advance your death, I am in fear and sadness. Will God not abandon us because of my unworthiness? Give me, I pray, the assurance that the support we received during your life we will continue to receive after you depart to God" (Letter 598). Aelianos feared the consequences for the whole community should his leadership prove inadequate. He sought assurance that death would not sever the father-disciple relationship. John repeated the promises of scripture that God would not abandon his children, adding, "We believe in God, that he will do more than when we were among you." He concluded with a final blessing: "Our Lord Jesus Christ, who for our salvation descended from the throne of his Father, he himself will save, will restore, will guard [you] from evil, with our cooperation, by the prayers of the saints. Amen" (Letter 598). John reminded Aelianos that, although he would exercise sole leadership in the monastery, spiritually he remained one member of a network of authority. Aelianos inherited a place in the heavenly hierarchy of fatherhood. According to John's vision, Christ, descended from the Father, through the prayers of the saints and with the "cooperation" of Barsanuphius and John, would support Aelianos. It was this invisible network which would enable Aelianos to serve as the visual representative of fatherhood for the monks at Tawatha.

With the death of Abbot Seridos, change came to the monastery at Tawatha. Not only did it receive a new abbot, but it also gained a leader who was a newcomer to the monastic life. As an outcome of Seridos' last instructions, the wealthy layman and friend of the monastery Aelianos became monk, priest, and abbot in rapid succession. But this was not the full extent of the change. Following Seridos' death, Barsanuphius and John announced their plans to leave the community, the former by complete withdrawal and the latter by physical death. The newly appointed abbot discovered that his rule would oversee the establishment of a new system of spiritual authority at Tawatha. No longer would the abbot, in the course of his daily supervision of the monastery, have recourse to the anchorites. The exceptionally stable three-person hierarchy established by Barsanuphius would be replaced by a single leader, responsible for overseeing both cenobitic and anchoritic life at Tawatha.

Even as a layman, however, Aelianos had benefited from the father-disciple relationship he shared with Barsanuphius and John. As a disciple of the Old Men of Gaza, he had a basis for his own authority. He came to his new position as leader with the full support of the anchorites. Barsanuphius and John were as instrumental as Seridos in making him abbot. After Aelianos' appointment, John continued to serve as his spiritual director. The new abbot and his spiritual father embarked upon an intensive training course, during which time Aelianos questioned John carefully about the governance of the monastery. John also offered guidance intended to help Aelianos provide spiritual direction to the monks, oversee interaction between the monastery and the outside world, and establish his own authority in relation to that of the monastery's previous leaders.

There is little evidence to evaluate Aelianos' performance as abbot. Aside from the works of Dorotheos, no further writings survive from the inhabitants of the monastic community at Tawatha. Certainly Aelianos' task of governing as abbot without the ongoing support of the Great Old

Men was formidable. He had to establish a new system of spiritual authority in response to the end of a long and successful one. If he governed alone, he did so without the concrete help and spiritual oversight that Seridos had found in Barsanuphius and John. It is possible that Aelianos sought out help from among the established fathers of Tawatha, including Dorotheos, replicating somewhat the system of cooperation between anchorite and abbot under which the monks of Tawatha had long flourished. While it remains uncertain how Aelianos chose to exercise the spiritual authority he had inherited, we do know that the letters of the anchorites to the new abbot, to the brothers of the monastery, to the lay Christians of the wider community, and to the bishops of the region were preserved for use by later generations.

EPILOGUE: JOHN'S DEPARTURE

The bustle of activity following the death of the Abbot Seridos—the reading of his will, the monks refusing high office, the ordination of Aelianos, John's intensive instruction of the new abbot—all this came to an end with the peaceful death of John. Unlike the richly descriptive hagiographic accounts of the deaths of other monastic leaders, the Correspondence does not reveal any details about John's burial or any posthumous acts of sanctity.[41] The monk who compiled the letters presented the end of the anchorite's life in a simple, anticlimactic manner.

Among Aelianos' questions to John during the last weeks of the holy man's life was the seemingly simple request that the Old Man speak to the brothers about endurance and obedience (Letter 583). John complied. The text does not indicate whether this entailed a personal interview between John and the monks, or if Aelianos read the letter from John to the gathered brothers. In either case, an open message directed to the entire community was unusual among the letters written by Barsanuphius and John. Despite advice that frequently sounds universally applicable, most letters addressed specific individuals or small groups involved in particular circumstances. An open letter read to the entire community would have stood out from the daily routine of the monastery as much as if John actually spoke to the assembly in person.

John's address to the brothers made little reference to the monastery or its new leader. His words were urgent and personal, reminding the monks that the call to follow Christ entailed affliction and distress, not comfort.

If they were obedient to Christ, he would be with them. If they rejected him, he would reject them. Eternal life required keeping Christ's commands and submitting their will to God.

Although it is uncertain if John spoke directly to the monks on this occasion, on the day of his death he did summon "all the brothers and all those who were found in the monastery" to his bedside (Letter 599b). He bid farewell to each person individually and then dismissed them all before he died. The solitude and mediated communication that had characterized his life was deliberately set aside at his death. John removed all barriers, to allow intimacy at the final interview. Not only did he invite to his bedside all of the members of the monastery, but he also summoned others who were gathered at the monastery. This group may have included a large number of pious lay people who had written to him over the years, clergy, and visitors from other monasteries. John had requested those attending him not to publicize his approaching death until the day arrived (Letter 599b).[42] This seems like a futile gesture towards privacy, in view of of ample evidence that many in the monastery knew of the expectations, negotiation, and instruction that preceded John's death. It is easy to imagine news spreading throughout the countryside around Gaza and a large number of visitors attending the Old Man's death and burial. At his death John embraced the same wide community of Christians that he had served during his life.

Conclusion

The writings of two elderly monks who deliberately chose to deny themselves face-to-face contact with others as a form of ascetic discipline seem
a surprising vehicle by which to explore the complexities of urban and
rural life in the sixth century. Yet the Correspondence of Barsanuphius
and John serves as a remarkably revealing window into late antique society. In the questions posed to these spiritual directors and their instructions to the petitioners, we meet a broad cross section of humanity:
monks, lay Christians, clergy, residents of city and village, rich and poor.
Even those whose own voices are not preserved in the Correspondence—
heretics, Jews, pagans, lepers, slaves, and women—appear as the subject of
many queries. The petitioners brought their concerns about a wide range
of matters to the anchorites, whose guidance was not limited to overtly
religious matters but holistically encompassed all areas of their disciples'
lives, including financial and legal matters, political and ecclesiastical disputes, and relationships with family, friends, servants, and neighbors. The
letters reveal Barsanuphius and John's belief that God was concerned with
all facets of a person. They taught that the disciple needed to submit
everything to the scrutiny of his spiritual father in order for him to serve
effectively as God's instrument in the disciple's life.

The Correspondence, detailing life in this community, illuminates features characteristic of the broader monastic movement flourishing in
sixth-century Byzantium. The governing system of the monastery at
Tawatha, based on the close cooperation between two levels of leaders,
anchorites and abbot, was exceptionally effective. In many other respects,
however, the picture of life in the monastery at Tawatha is illustrative of
Palestinian and Egyptian monasticism as a whole and its influence on
society in the eastern Mediterranean.

Conclusion

The leadership of the monastic community at Tawatha proved both stable and flexible. Through their partnership, Barsanuphius and John presented a unified voice of spiritual authority to their disciples. Although they always affirmed each other's instructions, they focused on different aspects of the process of spiritual direction. John frequently dealt with the practical questions of proper interaction with others in the community, while Barsanuphius addressed the more abstract principles of spiritual discipline. Together they directed individual disciples and guided the city's leaders in making decisions for the community.

Close cooperation with Abbot Seridos allowed Barsanuphius and John to practice the anchoritic life while they simultaneously oversaw the direction of the monastery. The Old Men's accessibility, while limited to written correspondence, was open to a surprisingly large number of petitioners from a wide range of positions in society. This combination of generosity and regulation of access served to augment the Old Men's authority. Seridos' role as Barsanuphius' scribe strengthened the abbot's own practical authority in the community. He was always aware of the concerns that petitioners brought to the Great Old Man, and he was able to invoke the higher authority of Barsanuphius when monks challenged his decisions as abbot. The three-person system of authority at Tawatha provided a safe outlet for the complaints of disgruntled members of the monastic community. Although Barsanuphius, John, and Seridos consistently affirmed one another's authority, a monk frustrated with the leadership of a particular father could turn to one of the others to vent his problems and work through possible solutions. Their cooperation absorbed tensions that had the potential to tear a monastic community apart.

The interactions of Barsanuphius with his disciples reveal the ongoing process of spiritual direction and the efforts of the Old Men to develop a new generation of spiritual leaders for the community. The anchorites frankly addressed problems within the community and even challenges to their own authority. Some of the same disciples who openly displayed their contentiousness, hesitation, and other spiritual shortcomings eventually exercised considerable authority within the community. The inhabitants of the village of Tawatha and the monastery emerge from the Correspondence not as static characters but as dynamic human beings, shaping and being shaped by their social environment. Barsanuphius and his colleagues discipled individual monks and lay persons, granting them more practical authority as they matured spiritually. The change over time in individual disciples that the letters reveal is striking. John, who quarreled fiercely with the abbot as soon as he arrived at the monastery, became a staunch supporter of Abbot Seridos and the closest colleague of the holy man who had appointed him. Dorotheos evolved from a naïve and socially awkward novice into a leader in the cenobium and a monastic father revered for his own teaching. The vacillating layman Aelianos succeeded Seridos as abbot and became the sole spiritual leader of the monastery.

On the institutional level, change is also apparent. The sixth-century monastic compiler of the Correspondence emphasized the continuity of spiritual authority and the stability of the three-person system of leadership at the monastery. Still, an observer cannot escape the conviction that the form of governance carefully crafted by Barsanuphius was fundamentally altered by the transfer of authority to the next generation, despite the Old Men's efforts to preserve stability. During the transition in the community after Seridos' death, there is no mention of other anchorites taking on the roles vacated by John and Barsanuphius. As abbot, Aelianos, newly converted from lay life, lacked the institutional support of the anchorites that had supported Seridos' rule. The position of abbot expanded to fulfill the functions of both the anchorites and the leader of the cenobium.

This change in leadership reveals the fragility of monastic communities in late antiquity, whether headed by a single abbot or the combined leadership of anchorites and abbot. The character and organization of spiritual authority within a monastery depended on the divine charisma granted to its leaders. Within his lifetime, a leader could strengthen the institutional structures of authority within a monastery. Barsanuphius augmented the authority of the position of abbot by communicating with all his disciples through Seridos. Leaders also strove to prepare new leaders to take their place. Barsanuphius, John, and Seridos tried to transmit their own spiritual authority to the next generation of monastic leaders. They encouraged talented laymen such as Dorotheos and Aelianos to join the monastery. They carefully trained certain monks, including Dorotheos, to assume leadership positions. Monks being prepared for leadership held various positions in the cenobium, such as porter, master of the guesthouse, and head of the infirmary, which required practical skills and good judgment. Spiritual directors allowed monks who had advanced in asceticism to withdraw from the cenobium and live as anchorites. While physically separate, these men were still active members of the community, fully integrated into the monks' life of prayer. As part of their continued training, mature monks were given the task of providing spiritual direction to disciples of their own. It was from this group of fathers that Seridos named the first individuals who should succeed him.

When the succession process at the Tawatha monastery yielded a new abbot who lacked this careful training, John agreed to instruct him in monastic governance. Aelianos' period of training for leadership was necessarily intense, limited as it was by John's impending death. Over the course of a fortnight John tried to pass on to the new abbot both the accumulated wisdom of the monastery's earlier leaders and the confidence in his own judgments that Aelianos would need to carry on their work by himself. John encouraged Aelianos to keep those customs that had proved successful for the monastic community in the past but not to fear introducing new policies that might be useful. Despite these accommodations, it is easy to imagine that the new abbot's authority was not as effective as that of the balanced hierarchy established by Barsanuphius. Aelianos exercised alone the power previously shared by anchorites and abbot. The succession of the inexperienced layman immediately following the crisis of the plague is an example of the vulnerability of the monastic community.

In addition to establishing spiritual authority within the monastery, Barsanuphius and John exercised leadership within the wider Christian community. Its location on the outskirts of a large metropolitan center allowed the monastery to maintain contact with the regional civil and ecclesiastical authorities. Rather than remaining closed to visitors from "the world," the monastery's leaders encouraged close interaction between monks and laity. Barsanuphius and John served as spiritual directors for lay people with a range of vocations, including both ones who adopted ascetic lifestyles and interacted closely with monastic fathers and others who brought very worldly issues to the attention of the anchorites. The potential of the monastery to influence the larger community is evident in Barsanuphius' response to a controversial episcopal election in Gaza. The dialogue between the anchorites and the bishops of Gaza and Jerusalem demonstrates both the authority of the holy men over the bishops and the close cooperation between episcopal and monastic sources of spiritual authority in Palestine.

A sixth-century traveler stopping in Gaza would find every convenience readily accessible. Refreshing himself at the public baths, buying supplies in the market, or stopping to worship at one of the city's splendid churches, the traveler would converse with the city's friendly inhabitants. He might inquire about the recent uprising of the Samaritans or the position of the local bishop on the various theological questions creating division in the church. He might bring new rumors of the ominous plague that had appeared in the East or gossip about the emperor's legislative attempts to suppress paganism. He might ask for help negotiating a sales contract or seek medical treatment for a member of his entourage. In any number of possible conversations the traveler might be told, "Listen, this is what the Great Old Man had to say about that," or "That is something to write to the Old Men about!" If the traveler settled in the city, he might find himself composing a letter to the anchorites, and in doing so, becoming part of the fabric of the community in Gaza.

Notes

ABBREVIATIONS IN NOTES AND BIBLIOGRAPHY

CSCO   *Corpus scriptorum christianorum orientalium*
CSEL   *Corpus scriptorum ecclesiasticorum latinorum*
PG   *Patrologia cursus completus, series graeca.* Edited by J.-P. Migne. Paris,
        1857–66.
PL   *Patrologia cursus completus, series latina.* Edited by J.-P. Migne. Paris,
        1844–80.
PO   *Patrologia orientalis.* Edited by R. Graffin and F. Nau. Paris, 1904–.

PREFACE

1. See Douglas Burton-Christie, *The Word in the Desert: Scripture and the Quest for Holiness in Early Christian Monasticism* (Oxford: Clarendon, 1993); and Graham Gould, *The Desert Fathers on Monastic Community* (Oxford: Clarendon Press, 1993).

2. See Yizhar Hirschfeld, *The Judean Desert Monasteries in the Byzantine Period* (New Haven: Yale University Press, 1992); John Binns, *Ascetics and Ambassadors of Christ: The Monasteries of Palestine, 314–631* (Oxford: Clarendon Press, 1994); and Joseph Patrich, *Sabas, Leader of Palestinian Monasticism* (Washington, DC: Dumbarton Oaks, 1995).

3. *Abba Isaiah of Scetis: Ascetic Discourses,* trans. by John Chryssavgis and Pachomios (Robert) Penkett (Kalamazoo, MI: Cistercian Publications, 2002). Isaiah of Scetis was also known as Isaiah of Gaza, for the area to which he relocated.

4. François Neyt, Paula de Angelis-Noah, and Lucien Regnault, *Barsanuphe et Jean de Gaza: Correspondance,* vol. 1, tomes 1–2, vol. 2, tomes 1–2, vol. 3, Sources Chrétiennes, nos. 426, 427, 450, 451, 468 (Paris: Éditions du Cerf, 1997–2002).

5. John Chryssavgis, *Letters from the Desert: Barsanuphius and John,* a *Selection of Questions and Responses* (Crestwood, NY: St. Vladimir's Seminary Press, 2003). His full edition of the entire Correspondence in translation is forthcoming from Catholic University of America Press. Derwas Chitty published the first 124 letters in a critical edition shortly before his death, *Barsanuphius and John, Questions and Answers,* PO 31.3 (Paris: Firmin Didot, 1966). Chitty located Barsanuphius and John in the geography of Egyptian and Palestinian asceticism in his classic book on that topic, *The Desert a City* (Oxford: Blackwell, 1966). The scattered pages referring to Barsanuphius, John, and their circle of colleagues are extremely rich in layers of information about monasticism at Tawatha.

INTRODUCTION

1. By the beginning of the fifth century, Palestine had been divided into three separate provinces. The most important of the three, Palestine I, had its political capital in Caesarea. In 451 Jerusalem was raised to the rank of a patriarchate, giving it ecclesiastical authority over Caesarea and the other sees in the region.

2. For trade routes through Gaza, including the great incense road from southern Arabia, see Martin A. Meyer, *History of the City of Gaza* (New York: Columbia University Press, 1907), 163–65; and Carol Glucker, *The City of Gaza in the Roman and Byzantine Periods,* Biblical Archaeology Review International Series, no. 325 (Oxford: Biblical Archeology Review, 1987), 86–93. For Gaza's strategic geographical role in a broad historical context see Mordechai Gichon, "History of the Gaza Strip: A Geo-Political and Geo-Strategic Perspective," *Jerusalem Cathedra* 2 (1982): 282–317; and Leah Di Segni, "The Territory of Gaza: Notes of Historical Geography," in *Christian Gaza in Late Antiquity,* ed. Brouria Bitton-Ashkelony and Aryeh Kofsky (Leiden: Brill, 2004), 41–59. For the role of Palestinian ports in late antiquity, see Sean A. Kingsley, " 'Decline' in the Ports of Palestine in Late Antiquity," in *Recent Research in Late-Antique Urbanism,* ed. Luke Lavan, Journal of Roman Archaeology Supplementary Series, no. 42 (Portsmouth, RI: Journal of Roman Archaeology, 2001), 69–87.

3. See Kilian Seitz, *Die Schule von Gaza, eine litterargeschichtliche Untersuchung* (Heidelberg, 1892); Glanville Downey, "The Christian Schools of Palestine: A Chapter in Literary History," *Harvard Library Bulletin* 12 (1958): 297–319; and George A. Kennedy, *Greek Rhetoric under Christian Emperors* (Princeton: Princeton University Press, 1983), 169–77.

4. All dates are CE.

5. Choricius, *First Encomium to Marcian, Bishop of Gaza* 39, in *Choricii Gazaei*

Opera, ed. Richard Foerster (Stuttgart: Teubner, 1972), trans. Fotios K. Litsas, "Choricius of Gaza: An Approach to His Work" (Ph.D. diss., University of Chicago, 1980), 120. All quotations from Choricius cited here in English are Litsas' translations.

6. For a classic study of spiritual authority which focuses on the qualities and duties necessary for spiritual directors and their disciples, see Irenée Hausherr, *Spiritual Direction in the Early Christian East,* trans. by Anthony P. Gythiel (Kalamazoo, MI: Cistercian Publications, 1990). This contains an excellent introduction to the ascetic teachings of Barsanuphius and John, but it tends to present spiritual direction as abstract and timeless, rather than as a dynamic historical event. François Neyt is the first scholar to have explored the process of spiritual direction within the community of Barsanuphius and John, in "A Form of Charismatic Authority," *Eastern Churches Review* 6 (1974): 52–65. This article deals exclusively with letters to Dorotheos, thereby excluding the community of anchorites, bishops, and lay Christians beyond the cenobium walls. For Barsanuphius and John's letters as the basis of a "school of Christianity," see Lorenzo Perrone, "The Necessity of Advice: Spiritual Direction as a School of Christianity in the Correspondence of Barsanuphius and John of Gaza," in *Christian Gaza in Late Antiquity,* ed. Brouria Bitton-Ashkelony and Aryeh Kofsky (Leiden: Brill, 2004), 131–49.

7. Binns, *Ascetics and Ambassadors of Christ,* 43–44. Binns describes the career of the monk Theognius.

8. This danger is particularly evident in *Life of Pachomius* (Bohairic) (in *Sancti Pachomii vita bohairice scripta,* ed. and trans. Louis-Théophile Lefort, CSCO 89 [Louvain, 1925; reprint 1953]), when Theodore is passed over, first for Petronios and then for Horsiesios. See Philip Rousseau, *Pachomius: The Making of a Community in Fourth-Century Egypt* (Berkeley: University of California Press, 1985), 178–91.

9. Hagiography means literally "holy writing" and is generally used to refer to accounts of the lives of saints. Claudia Rapp correctly points out that hagiography is not a genre in itself but encompasses a variety of literary forms. " 'For Next to God, You Are My Salvation': Reflections on the Rise of the Holy Man in Late Antiquity," in *The Cult of the Saints in Late Antiquity and the Middle Ages: Essays on the Contribution of Peter Brown,* ed. James Howard-Johnson and Paul Antony Hayward (Oxford: Oxford University Press, 1999), 64–65.

10. I disagree with Glen Bowersock, who warns that the designation "late antique" implies a "new and vibrant spiritual world beginning in the fourth century," which does not characterize Palestine. See "The Greek Moses: Confusion of Ethnic and Cultural Components in Later Roman and Early Byzantine Palestine," in *Religious and Ethnic Communities in Later Roman Palestine,* ed. Hayim Lapin (Potomac: University Press of Maryland, 1998), 34. I argue that

in the sixth century Gaza typified this vibrant, new world with its accomplishments in both rhetoric and spirituality.

CHAPTER 1. GAZA

1. Mark the Deacon, *Vie de Porphyre, Évéque de Gaza* 64, ed. and trans. Henri Grégoire and M.-A. Kugener (Paris: Société d'Édition "Les Belles Lettres," 1930). All translations included from this text are from *The Life of Porphyry, Bishop of Gaza*, trans. G. F. Hill (Oxford: Clarendon Press, 1913).

2. Aryeh Kasher, "Gaza during the Greco-Roman Era," *Jerusalem Cathedra* 2 (1982), 75.

3. Raymond Van Dam, "From Paganism to Christianity at Late Antique Gaza," *Viator* 16 (1985): 7–8; and Frank Trombley, *Hellenic Religion and Christianization c. 370–529* (Leiden: E. J. Brill, 1994), 1:190. For pagan rituals in Gaza, see also Nicole Belayche, "Pagan Festivals in Fourth-Century Gaza," in *Christian Gaza in Late Antiquity*, ed. Brouria Bitton-Ashkelony and Aryeh Kofsky (Leiden: Brill, 2004), 5–22.

4. Mark the Deacon, *Vie de Porphyre* 41.

5. Jerome, *Epistula* 107.2, ed. I. Hillberg, CSEL 54–56 (1910, 1912), trans. Philip Schaff and Henry Wace in *Post-Nicene Fathers of the Church*, 2nd ser., 6:190.

6. Trombley attempts to explain this difference in religious affiliation by looking at the socioeconomic basis of each city. See *Hellenic Religion*, 1:192. For an early-twentieth-century topographical description of the port city, see Duncan Mackenzie, "The Port of Gaza and Excavation in Philistia," *Palestine Exploration Fund Quarterly Statement* (1918): 72–79.

7. Eusebius, *Vita Constantini* 5.38, in *Uber das Leben des Kaisers Konstantin*, ed. Friedhelm Winklmann (Berlin: Akademie-Verlag, 1991).

8. Sozomen, *Historia ecclesiastica* 5.3, in *Kirchengeschichte*, ed. and trans. Günther Christian Hansen (Turnhout: Brepols, 2004).

9. Ibid. 5.9. Sozomen recounted the martyrdom of Eusebius and Nestabus and the flight of Zeno, the future bishop of Gaza, to Maiouma. Sozomen's own family was forced to flee during this period. Hilarion also left the region before the leaders of Gaza could enforce a death sentence signed by Julian. Jerome, *Vita Hilarionis* 33, in *Vita di Martioi; vita di Ilarione; in memoria di Paolo*, ed. A. A. R. Bastiaensen and Jan W. Smit, trans. Luca Canali and Claudio Moreschini ([Milan ?]: Fondazione Lorenzo Valla, A. Mondadori, 1998).

10. "Who does not know of the horrors of the people of Gaza?" Gregory of Nazianzus, *Contro Giuliano l'apostata: Oratio IV* 86 (Florence: Nardini Editore, 1993). See also Meyer, *History of Gaza*, 61–65.

11. Mark the Deacon, *Vie de Porphyre* 57–58.

12. Trombley, *Hellenic Religion*, 1:273–78. His argument is based on a passage

of Sozomen that leaves unnamed the particular bishop of Gaza who tried to gain power over Maiouma. See *Historia ecclesiastica* 5.3.

13. Peter the Iberian and John Rufus, each at one time Bishop of Maiouma, rejected the Chalcedonian settlement, as did the majority of Christians in Syria and Egypt. They believed that the council did not proclaim Christ's divinity strongly enough. See John Rufus, *Plerophoriae*, ed. F. Nau, *Jean Rufus, Évéque de Maïouma, Plérophories*, PO 8.1 (1912). See also Kathleen M. Hay, "Evolution of Resistance: Peter the Iberian, Itinerant Bishop," in *Prayer and Spirituality in the Early Church*, ed. Pauline Allen, Raymond Canning, and Lawrence Cross (Everston Park, Queensland: Centre for Early Christian Studies, Australian Catholic University, 1998), 159–68. Barsanuphius encouraged the citizens of Gaza to receive a bishop named by the Chalcedonian Patriarch of Jerusalem, see Chapter 5 of this volume.

14. *Codex Justinianus* 1.11.9–10, in *Corpus Iuris Civilis*, ed. Paul Krueger (Berlin: Weidmann, 1954).

15. Egeria, *Itinerarium Egeriae*, 30–39, in *Journal du voyage: Itinéraire*, ed. and trans. Pierre Maraval, Sources Chrétiennes, no. 296 (Paris: Éditions du Cerf, 1982). For the discovery of the True Cross, see Jan Wilhem Drijvers, *Helena Augusta: The Mother of Constantine the Great and the Legend of Her Finding of the True Cross* (Leiden: E. J. Brill, 1992).

16. For the development of Christian views of Palestine, see Robert L. Wilken, *The Land Called Holy: Palestine in Christian History and Thought* (New Haven: Yale University Press, 1992), esp. 65–125. For Christian pilgrimage to the Holy Land, see E. D. Hunt, *Holy Land Pilgrimage in the Later Roman Empire, 312–460* (Oxford: Clarendon Press, 1984); and John Wilkinson, *Jerusalem Pilgrims before the Crusades* (Warminster, England: Aris and Phillips, 1977).

17. Samuel Rubenson, "The Egyptian Relations of Early Palestinian Monasticism," in *The Christian Heritage in the Holy Land*, ed. Anthony O'Mahony, Göran Gunner, and Kevork Hintlian (London: Scorpion Cavendish, 1995), 45–46; and Lorenzo Perrone, "Monasticism in the Holy Land: From the Beginnings to the Crusades," *Proche-Orient Chrétien* 45 (1995): 31–63.

18. Jerome, *Epistula* 46.13.

19. See Hunt, *Holy Land Pilgrimage*, 221–48; and Kenneth G. Holum, *Theodosian Empresses* (Berkeley: University of California Press, 1982), 184–94.

20. John of Ephesus, *Lives of the Eastern Saints* 27, ed. E. W. Brooks, in PO 17 (1923), trans. in Susan Ashbrook Harvey and Sebastian P. Brock, *Holy Women of the Syrian Orient* (Berkeley: University of California Press, 1987), 134. Susan eventually settled in a convent of women "between Ascalon and Gaza." When pro-Chalcedonian sentiment forced this group to disband, Susan withdrew to Egypt with some of her followers. John of Ephesus recounts the experience of another woman, Mary, who practiced asceticism in Jerusalem, praying at

Golgotha daily for three years, in *Lives of the Eastern Saints* 12, and *Holy Women*, 124–26.

21. For monasticism in the Judean desert, see Binns, *Ascetics and Ambassadors of Christ*; Hirschfeld, *Judean Desert Monasteries*; and Patrich, *Sabas, Leader of Palestinian Monasticism*.

22. Jerome, *Vita Hilarionis* 3, trans. Carolinne White, *Early Christian Lives* (London: Penguin, 1998), 90.

23. Chitty sets the date of Hilarion's birth at c. 293, and Jerome says that Hilarion was fifteen when he returned from Egypt (*The Desert a City*, 13–14). Athanasius' *Life of Antony* provided a model for Jerome's hagiographical account of Hilarion, and Jerome may have intentionally depicted Hilarion as greater than his spiritual father, Antony. See Aryeh Kofsky and Bruria Bitton-Ashkelony, "Gazan Monasticism in the Fourth–Sixth Centuries," *Proche-Orient Chrétien* 50 (2000): 18–23; and Philip Rousseau, *Ascetics, Authority, and the Church in the Age of Jerome and Cassian* (Oxford: Oxford University Press, 1978), 136–39.

24. Sozomen, *Historia ecclesiastica* 6.32.

25. Sozomen, *Historia ecclesiastica* 5.15. The ability of Sozomen's grandfather to interpret scriptures earned him spiritual authority in the region. See Van Dam, "From Paganism to Christianity," 9.

26. Mark the Deacon, *Vie de Porphyre* 4.

27. Chitty, *The Desert a City*, 71–72. For Silvanus, see Sozomen, *Historia ecclesiastica* 6.32; and Michel van Parys, "Abba Silvain et ses disciples. Une famille monastique entre Scété et la Palestine à la fin du IVe et la première moitié du Ve siècle," *Irénikon* 61 (1968): 313–30, 451–80.

28. Rubenson, "Egyptian Relations of Palestinian Monasticism," 41–43. For the controversy over Origenism in Egypt, see John Cassian, *Conferences* 10.2, ed. and trans. E. Pichery, Sources Chrétiennes, no. 54 (Paris: Éditions du Cerf, 1958). Cassian claimed to have been present in Scetis in 399 when Theophilus' controversial festival letter arrived. See Elizabeth A. Clark, *The Origenist Controversy: The Cultural Construction of an Early Christian Debate* (Princeton: Princeton University Press, 1992), 50–51. For the invasions, see Hugh G. Evelyn-White, *The Monasteries of the Wadi'n Natrun Part II: The History of the Monasteries of Nitria and of Scetis* (New York: Metropolitan Museum of Art, 1932), 151–59.

29. Lucien Regnault, "Les Apotegmes des pères en Palestine aux Ve–VIe siècles," *Irénikon* 54 (1981): 320–30.

30. *Life of Isaiah*, ed. by E. W. Brooks, CSCO. Scriptores Syri, ser. 3, vol. 25 (Paris: 1907); and Derwas Chitty, "Abba Isaiah," *Journal of Theological Studies*, n.s. 22 (1971): 47–72.

31. *Life of Isaiah* 1.24; John Rufus, *Plerophoriae* 48.

32. François Neyt has examined citations of the writings of Isaiah in the

letters of Barsanuphius and John in "Citations 'Isaiennes' chez Barsanuphe et Jean de Gaza," *Le Muséon* 89 (1971): 65–92. For other philological studies of the Correspondence, see Neyt, "Précisions sur le vocabulaire de Barsanuphe et de Jean de Gaza," *Studia Patristica: Papers Presented to the Sixth International Conference on Patristic Studies, Held in Oxford 1971* (1975): 247–53; and "L'Apsephiston chez les Pères de Gaza," in *Überlieferung Geschichtliche Untersuchungen*, 427–34 (Berlin: Akademie-Verlag, 1981).

33. For Peter's stay in Tawatha, see John Rufus, *Life of Peter the Iberian*, ed. and trans. Richard Raabe, *Petrus der Iberer: Ein Charakterbild zur Kirchen-und Sitten-geschichte des fünften Jahrhunderts* (Leipzig: 1895), 100–101, 111–23; and Chitty, "Abba Isaiah," 60. Yaron Dan argues that the village mentioned in John Rufus' text, Migdal Thautha, was distinct from the village of Tawatha where the monastery of Seridos was located. He suggests that the later village grew out of the earlier Migdal Thautha, which was a single estate in the days of Peter the Iberian. Dan, "On the Ownership of Lands in the Village of Tawatha in the Byzantine Period," *Scripta Classica Israelica* 5 (1979/1980): 258–62.

34. John Rufus, *Life of Peter the Iberian*, 65–66. While in Egypt Peter consecrated Timothy Aleurus (d. 477) as archbishop of Alexandria in 457. Usually many bishops gathered for the consecration of a new bishop, but so many of the non-Chalcedonian bishops were in hiding at the time because of imperial persecution that only one other bishop, Eusebius of Pelusium, joined Peter for the consecration.

35. See François Neyt, "La formation au monastère de l'abbé Séridos à Gaza," in *Christian Gaza in Late Antiquity*, ed. Brouria Bitton-Ashkelony and Aryeh Kofsky (Leiden: Brill, 2004), 151–63.

36. Translations of Barsanuphius and John's Correspondence are my own unless otherwise noted.

37. For the simplified image of Antony presented in the *Apophthegmata Patrum* contrasted with the information supplied by his letters, see Samuel Rubenson, *The Letters of St. Antony: Monasticism and the Making of a Saint* (Minneapolis: Fortress Press, 1995), 152–62.

38. Migne first published some letters from the Old Men of Gaza to Dorotheos and others concerning Origenism, PG 88.1811D–1822B and PG 86.1.891–902. Nikodemos Hagiorita prepared a nearly complete edition of the letters for publication from a single manuscript, *Biblos Barsanouphiou kai Ioannou* (Venice, 1816). The letters have not been widely available in the West, but the Correspondence did influence Russian Orthodox monasticism. See François Neyt, "Les lettres à Dorothée dans la correspondance de Barsanuphe et de Jean de Gaza" (Ph.D. diss., Université Catholique de Louvain, 1969), xlii–xliii. For a translation of some of the letters into English from Russian, see Seraphim Rose, *Saints Barsanuphius and John: Guidance towards Spiritual*

Life (Platina, CA: St. Herman of Alaska Brotherhood, 1990). Soterios Schoinas published a new edition of the Greek text as *Biblos psychophelestate Barsanouphiou kai Ioannou* (Volos, 1960). François Neyt, working with Lucien Regnault and Paula de Angelis-Noah, has produced a critical edition (see Preface n. 4) that incorporates the 1972 French translation (see next note).

39. For a French translation, see Lucien Regnault, Philippe Lemaire, and Bernard Outtier, *Barsanuphe et Jean de Gaza: Correspondance* (Sablé-sur-Sarthe: Abbaye Saint Pierre de Solesmes, 1972). For a German translation, see Matthias Dietz, *Vom Reichtum des Schweigens: Ein Zeugnis der Ostkirche: Geistliche Antwortbriefe der Schweigemönche Barsanuph und seines Schülers Johannes (G. Jahr)* (Zurich: Thomas Verlag, 1963). For an Italian translation, see M. Francesca Teresa Lovato and Luciana Mortari, *Barsanufio e Giovanni di Gaza: Epistolario* (Rome: Città Nouva Editrice, 1991). For an English translation of selected letters, see John Chryssavgis, *Letters from the Desert: Barsanuphius and John*. His translation of the full letter collection is forthcoming from Catholic University of America Press.

40. The manuscript tradition is quite extensive. For a summary, see Chitty, *Questions and Answers*, 450–52, and Neyt, de Angelis-Noah, and Regnault, *Correspondance*, vol. 1, tome 1, 131–44, 149–55.

41. John Moschus, a younger contemporary of the Old Men's disciple Dorotheos, in the early seventh century recorded the last description of Palestinian monasticism before the arrival of the Persians and subsequently the Arabs. See *Le pré spirituel*, ed. and trans. M.-J. Rouet de Journel, Sources Chrétiennes, no. 12 (Paris: Éditions du Cerf, 1946). The value of Barsanuphius' teaching on spiritual direction was recognized in the eleventh century, although in a very different social context: St. Cyril Phileotes recommended the wisdom of Barsanuphius to a lay woman, probably Anna Dalassena. See Rosemary Morris, *Monks and Laymen in Byzantium* (Cambridge: Cambridge University Press, 1995), 100. For the changes brought to the region by the Islamic conquests, see Hugh Kennedy, "Islam," in *Late Antiquity: A Guide to the Postclassical World*, ed. G. W. Bowersock, Peter Brown, and Oleg Grabar (Cambridge: Harvard University Press, 1999), 219–37.

42. See Chapter 2, n. 32, below.

43. Compare with Basil's "rules," which developed from his answers to particular questions addressed to him by monks. Basil of Caesarea, *Ascetica: Regulae fusis tractae*, PG 31.889–1052, *Regulae brevius tractae*, PG 31.1080A–1305B. Some letters in the Correspondence were more appropriate for this purpose than others. See especially the letters to Aelianos discussed in Chapter 6 of this volume.

44. Translation is by Chitty (*Questions and Answers*, 457). I have used Chitty's English translations when quoting from the prologue.

45. The total number of letters is dependent on the manner in which some longer sections of the Correspondence are divided. For the numeration of the letters see François Neyt, "Les lettres à Dorothée," xlvi–xlvii.

46. Siméon Vailhé, "Les lettres spirituelles de Jean et de Barsanuphe," *Echos d'Orient* 7 (1904): 273. Vailhé, the first scholar of the twentieth century to study the letters of Barsanuphius and John, counted 396 letters from Barsanuphius and 446 from John.

47. The study of spiritual direction has traditionally focused on the spiritual formation of monks. This reflects the pool of sources—mostly hagiographic—which tend to recount the stories of men and women who belonged to the spiritual elite. When the spiritual direction of an individual lay person is recorded, he or she usually is connected to those in the highest level of political power. Barsanuphius' contemporary, John of Ephesus, also paid close attention to lay piety. See Susan Ashbrook Harvey, *Asceticism and Society in Crisis: John of Ephesus and* The Lives of the Eastern Saints (Berkeley: University of California Press, 1990).

48. Neyt describes them thus: "Free on the whole from the literary trends prevailing in more intellectual circles, they give a faithful image of the 'opening of the heart' as practiced by the Palestinian monks" ("A Form of Charismatic Authority," 52–53).

49. Athanasius, *Vie d'Antoine* 14, 49, ed. and trans. G. J. M. Bartelink, Sources Chrétiennes, no. 400 (Paris: Éditions du Cerf, 1994).

50. Claudia Rapp has placed Barsanuphius and John within the broader context of letter-writing holy men. See "'For Next to God, You Are My Salvation.'" For letter-writing fathers in Egypt, see also Bernadette McNary-Zak, *Letters and Asceticism in Fourth-Century Egypt* (Lanham, MD: University Press of America, 2000).

51. "It was once revealed to him with regard to the hermitages under his direction that some of them did not maintain a strict observance. He wrote letters to them all through the priest, saying that these were lax and those were zealous for virtue. And it was found that what he said was true. He also wrote to their superiors, saying that some of them were negligent about the salvation of the brethren, while others encouraged them satisfactorily, and he declared the rewards and punishments of each." Rufinus of Aquileia, *Historia monachorum in Aegypto: Édition critique du texte grec,* ed. A. J. Festugière (Brussels: Société des Bollandistes, 1961), 11, 430D–431C, English trans. Norman Russell, *The Lives of the Desert Fathers* (Kalamazoo, MI: Cistercian Publications, 1980), 94.

52. The letters to the monk Paphnutius preserved in papyri document the social world of Egypt in the mid-fourth century. Paphnutius' diverse petitioners included slaves and women. The collection is much smaller than the

Correspondence of Barsanuphius and John and includes only letters to Paphnutius, not responses from the holy man. See Paphnutius, *Letters*, in H. I. Bell, *Jews and Christians in Egypt* (London, 1924), 100–120, trans. Robert Boughner and James Goehring, "Egyptian Monasticism (Selected Papyri)," in *Ascetic Behavior in Greco-Roman Antiquity: A Sourcebook*, ed. Vincent Wimbush (Minneapolis: Fortress Press, 1990), 456–63.

53. *Das Archiv des Nepheros und verwandte Texte*, ed. B. Kramer, J. C. Shelton, and G. M. Browne (Mainz: P. von Zabern, 1987).

54. See Pachomius, *Letters*, in *Die Briefe Pachoms: Griechischer Text der Handschrift W. 145 der Chester Beatty Library*, ed. Hans Quecke, Textus Patristici et Liturgici, no. 11 (Regensburg: Friedrich Pustet, 1975). The letters of Pachomius, Theodore, and Horsiesios are translated by Armand Veilleux in *Pachomian Koinonia*, vol. 3 (Kalamazoo, MI: Cistercian Publications, 1982).

55. Rubenson, *The Letters of St. Antony*, 46–47. Rubenson notes of the audience, "What is evident is that they were monks, but the lack of references to a communal life, to superiors, or to monastic rules makes it impossible to tell whether or not they belonged to organized monasteries."

56. St. Antony, Letter 6, trans. Rubenson, in *The Letters of St. Antony*, 216. The identification of Antony's Christian audience with the "Israelite children" is repeated in Letter 7, 225.

57. Rubenson, *The Letters of St. Antony*, 48–49.

58. Jerome, *Vita Hilarionis* 24. Jerome also mentioned St. Antony's seven letters in *De viris illustribus* 88, ed. E. C. Richardson and O. von Gebhardt, *Texte und Untersuchungen zur Geschichte der altchristlichen Literatur* 14.1 (Leipzig: J. C. Hinrichs, 1896).

59. Athanasius, *Vie d'Antoine* 81, 86. The emperors were Constantine and his sons Constantius and Constans.

60. *Sancti Pachomii vita bohairice scripta* 127, ed. and trans. Louis-Théophile Lefort, CSCO 89 (Louvain, 1925; reprint 1953), English trans. Veilleux, *Pachomian Koinonia*, 1:184.

61. For Cyril of Scythopolis, see Bernard Flusin, *Miracle et histoire dans l'oeuvre de Cyrille de Scythopolis* (Paris: Études Augustiniennes, 1983), 76–83; and Patrich, *Sabas*, 331–48. Controversy over Origenism erupted in both the fourth and sixth centuries. For the fourth-century debate, see Clark, *The Origenist Controversy*. For Origenism in the sixth century, see F. Diekamp, *Die Origenistischen Streitigkeiten im sechsten Jarhundert und das fünfte allgemeine Concil* (Münster: Aschendorff, 1899); and Antoine Guillaumont, *Les 'Képhalia Gnostica' d'Évagre le Pontique et l'histoire de l'Origénisme chez les Grecs et chez les Syriens* (Paris: Éditions du Seuil, 1962), 124–70; and Daniël Hombergen, *The Second Origenist Controversy: A New Perspective on Cyril of Scythopolis' Monastic Biographies as Historical Sources for Sixth-Century Origenism* (Rome: Studia Anselmiana, 2001).

62. *Life of Cyriacus* 14, in *Kyrillos von Skythopolis*, ed. and trans. Eduard Schwartz (Leipzig: J. C. Hinrichs, 1939), 230.31; and *Life of Sabas* 83, in *Kyrillos von Skythopolis* 188.18.

63. For the continuing discussion on Origenism among Barsanuphius, John, and their disciples, see Letters 601–7. See also the discussion of these letters by Guillaumont in *Les 'Képhalia Gnostica'* (124–28) and by Daniël Hombergen in "Barsanuphius and John of Gaza and the Origenist Controversy" (*Christian Gaza in Late Antiquity*, ed. Brouria Bitton-Ashkelony and Aryeh Kofsky [Leiden: Brill, 2004], 173–81). For the possible influence of Evagrian theology on Dorotheos, see P. Cavinet, "Dorothée de Gaza est-il un disciple d'Évagre?" *Revue des Études Greques* 78 (1965): 336–46.

64. John concurred with Barsanuphius that such teachings should be avoided. He vehemently denounced them as coming from the devil (Letter 601). However, later he admitted that a monk could read Evagrius for what was useful, discarding the rest (Letter 602). Barsanuphius was willing to discuss the nature of the resurrected body (Letter 607).

65. For John Rufus, see Jan-Eric Steppa, *John Rufus and the World Vision of Anti-Chalcedonian Culture* (Piscataway, NJ: Gorgias Press, 2002); Volker Menze, "Die Stimma von Maiuma: Johannes Rufus, das Konzil von Chalkedon und die wahre Kirche," in *Literarische Konstituierung von Identifikationsfiguren in der Antike*, 215–32, eds. Barbara Aland, Johannes Hahn, and Christian Ronning (Tübingen: Mohr Siebeck, 2003); and Jennifer Hevelone-Harper, "The *Plerophoriae* of John Rufus and Spiritual Authority Based on Discipleship," paper presented at the Syriac Symposium III, University of Notre Dame, Notre Dame, IN, June 18, 1999. For Sabas, see Patrich, *Sabas*, 301.

66. John Rufus, *Plerophoriae* 47.

67. Nestorius was the Patriarch of Constantinople from 428 through 431. He became involved in conflict with Cyril of Alexandria over Christology. Emphasizing the humanity of Christ according to the Antiochene school, Nestorius objected to the title *theotokos* or "God-bearer" for the Virgin Mary. He was condemned at the Council of Ephesus. In exile in Egypt, Nestorius approved the Chalcedonian settlement before his death. See Nestorius, *Liber Heraclides*, trans. F. Nau, *Le Livre d'Héraclide de Damas* (Paris: Letouzey et Ané, 1910).

68. John Rufus identified Chalcedonians with Nestorians throughout the *Plerophoriae*.

69. For Barsanuphius and John's understanding of sin placed within the broader context of Gazan monasticism, see Aryeh Kofsky, "Aspects of Sin in the Monastic School of Gaza," in *Transformation of the Inner Self in Ancient Religions*, ed. J. Assman and G. G. Stroumsa, 421–37 (Leiden: Brill, 1999); and Aryeh Kofsky, "The Byzantine Holy Person: The Case of Barsanuphius and

John of Gaza," in *Saints and Role Models in Judaism and Christianity*, ed. Marcel Poorthius and Joshua Schwartz, 261–85 (Leiden: Brill, 2004).

70. Both Latin martyrologies and Greek synaxaries include Barsanuphius. In the West he is commemorated on June 11 and in the East on February 6, along with his disciples John and Dorotheos. The Russian monastery of St. Panteleimon on Mt. Athos had an office for Barsanuphius and John. Relics of Barsanuphius were translated in the ninth century to Oria, a town in southern Italy near Brindisi, and the Gazan saint was credited with protecting the town from war. At the end of the twelfth or the beginning of the thirteenth century, a clerk at the church at Oria composed a Latin hagiographic account of Barsanuphius, see Neyt, de Angelis-Noah, and Regnault, *Correspondance*, vol. 1, tome 1, 27–32

71. Leontios of Neapolis, *Vita S. Johannis Eleemosynarii*, PG 93.1645 B8; ed. Heinrich Gelzer, *Leontios' von Neapolis, Leben des heiligen Johannes des Barmherzigen, Erzbischofs von Alexandrien*, Sammlung Ausgewählter kirchen und dogmengeschichtlicher Quellenschriften von G. Kruger, 5 (Freiburg: Mohr P. Siebeck, 1893), c. 69.21 and 75.13. See also Hippolyte Delehaye, "Une vie inédite de saint Jean l'Aumonier," *Analecta Bollandiana* 45 (1927): 5–74.

72. Evagrius Scholasticus, *Historia ecclesiastica* 4.33, ed. J. Bidez and L. Parmentier (London, 1898). See also Neyt, "Les lettres à Dorothée," xvii.

73. For Eustochius' anti-Origenist activities, see John Meyendorff, *Imperial Unity and Christian Divisions: The Church 450–680 A.D.* (Crestwood, NY: St. Vladimir's Seminary Press, 1989), 234–35.

74. See Siméon Vailhé, "Saint Barsanuphe," *Echos d'Orient* 8 (1905): 14–15; and Aryeh Kofsky, "What Happened to the Monophysite Monasticism of Gaza?" in *Christian Gaza in Late Antiquity*, ed. Brouria Bitton-Ashkelony and Aryeh Kofsky (Leiden: Brill, 2004), 183–94.

75. PG 87.3.3192–3193.

76. PG 99.1028, A14–B1, and 1816.

77. Lucien Regnault and J. de Préville, *Dorothée de Gaza: Oeuvres spirituelles*, no. 92, Sources Chrétiennes (Paris: Éditions du Cerf, 1963), 106–9. See also Neyt, de Angelis-Noah, and Regnault, *Correspondance*, vol. 1, tome 1, 24–25. Neyt says the preface belongs to a manuscript dating to the fifteenth century or later. He gives citations for an anti-Chalcedonian Barsanuphius, possibly a bishop.

78. Regnault and Préville, *Dorothée de Gaza: Oeuvres spirituelles*, 108.

79. Simon Tugwell, *Ways of Imperfection* (Springfield, IL: Templegate Publishers, 1985), 87.

80. In his introduction to the writings of Cyril of Scythopolis, John Binns notes that Cyril records ninety-four miracles while the *Historia monachorum*

contains sixty-two and the *Life of Antony* twelve. Cyril of Scythopolis, *The Lives of the Monks of Palestine,* trans. R. M. Price (Kalamazoo, MI: Cistercian Publications, 1991), xxxii.

CHAPTER 2. TAWATHA

1. See Michael Avi-Yonah, *The Madaba Mosaic Map* (Jerusalem: Israel Exploration Society, 1954); M. Piccirillo, *The Mosaics of Jordan* (Amman, 1993).

2. Jerome, *Vita Hilarionis* 2–3. Sozomen, *Historia ecclesiastica* 3.14.

3. For Isaiah and Peter, see Chapter 1, nn. 30, 33.

4. Massimo Capuani, *Christian Egypt: Coptic Art and Monuments Through Two Millennia* (Collegeville, MN: Liturgical Press, 1999), 74–79. For monastic cells in Egypt, see also Yvette Mottier and Nathalie Bosson, *Les Kellia: ermitages coptes en Basse-Egypte* (Geneva: Éditions du Tricorne, 1989); and Rodolphe Kasser and Jean-Marie Alès, *Survey archéologique des Kellia (Basse-Egypte)* (Louvain: Éditions Peeters, 1983).

5. Chitty, *Questions and Answers,* 453–54. See Letters 59–71, addressed to Euthymius.

6. Chitty translates: "And he sat still, and God sent us to him" (*Questions and Answers,* 475). This letter is addressed to John of Beersheba, who, as I will argue later in the chapter, should be identified with Barsanuphius' colleague John.

7. François Neyt uses this passage in Letter 17 to argue that Seridos was already the head of a monastery that welcomed Barsanuphius and that other abbots competed for this privilege, *Correspondance,* vol. 1, tome 1, 37. The alternative pattern of a charismatic monk withdrawing to an isolated spot, attracting disciples, and building a monastery was common in Palestinian monasticism. For contemporary evidence of this type of development in the Judean desert, see Hirschfeld, *Judean Desert Monasteries,* 69–70.

8. Yizhar Hirschfeld has recently proposed that Abbot Seridos' monastery be identified with that excavated at Dier e-Nuserat. For a brief description of these impressive remains, see Yizhar Hirschfeld, "The Monasteries of Gaza: An Archaeological Review," in *Christian Gaza in Late Antiquity,* ed. Brouria Bitton-Ashkelony and Aryeh Kofsky (Leiden: Brill, 2004), 76–77.

9. For burial places in other Palestinian monasteries, see Hirschfeld, *Judean Desert Monasteries,* 130–43.

10. For water systems, see Hirschfeld, *Judean Desert Monasteries,* 148–61.

11. Patrich, *Sabas,* 189–92.

12. *Novella* 5.3.3–40, in *Corpus Iuris Civilis,* ed. Paul Krueger (Berlin: Weidmann, 1954). See also Patrich, *Sabas,* 163–64; and Hirschfeld, *Judean Desert Monasteries,* 94–96, 176–77.

13. For the monks' diet, kitchen duty, and monastic bakeries, see Patrich, *Sabas,* 179–81, 185–86, and 207–10; and Hirschfeld, *Judean Desert Monasteries,* 82–91, 106–11.

14. Neyt recognized the uniqueness of the rule of three fathers at Tawatha—"the only example of its kind in the history of monastic texts"—in "A Form of Charismatic Authority," 63.

15. *Vie de saint Dosithée* 1.6–8, in Regnault and Préville, *Dorothée de Gaza: Oeuvres spirituelles,* explains that this title was given to him because of the gift of discernment he received from God. See Siméon Vailhé, "Jean le prophet et Seridos," *Echos d'Orient* 8 (1905): 157.

16. See Letter 599b and Letter 54, the final letter in a series of letters addressed to John of Beersheba, who should be identified with John the Prophet, see text section below. Compare also Letters 224 and 784.

17. Compare with Pachomius' knowledge of the behavior of his monks, also seen as directly inspired by God. Philip Rousseau, *Pachomius,* 107–8.

18. Chitty argues against conflating the two Johns, *Questions and Answers,* 453. Lorenzo Perrone assumes they are different men, "La lettere a Giovanni di Beersheva nella corrispondenza di Barsanufio e Giovanni di Gaza," *Studia Ephemeridis "Augustinianum"* 27 (mémorial Dom Jean Gribomont [1920–1986]) (1988), 467 n. 7; as does Neyt, de Angelis-Noah, and Regnault, *Correspondance,* vol. 1, tome 1, 62. J.-M. Sauget assumed that John the Prophet was John of Beersheba, "John the Prophet," *Encyclopedia of the Early Church,* ed. Angelo Di Berardino (Oxford: Oxford University Press, 1992). His Grace Bishop Sava of Troas first suggested to me that John of Beersheba might be John the Prophet, and I find the case convincing. A change of name for a monk who relocated would not be unusual, e.g. Isaiah of Scetis became Isaiah of Gaza.

19. Letter 5 is actually to Seridos regarding John of Beersheba's expected arrival.

20. Both Chitty and Perrone see this series as one of the earliest parts of the collection, see *Questions and Answers,* 453, and "La lettere a Giovanni di Beersheva," 466. I would suggest that Letters 59–71, to Euthymius, pre-date those to John of Beersheba and were written without the help of Seridos.

21. The compiler introduces John as Abba John of Beersheba. This title could mean that he was the abbot of a monastery at Beersheba, as some have suggested. See Neyt, de Angelis-Noah, and Regnault, *Correspondance,* vol. 1, tome 1, 62. The title "abba" could also be used for a monk with high spiritual status who did not hold an administrative position. There is no evidence in the Correspondence that John served as the abbot of a cenobium at Beersheba, although he may have exercised leadership within a monastery there in another capacity. There is a reference to trouble among the monks of Beersheba, but the site is called only the "place where John was living before

he came to the cenobium," Letter 4. If John had left a post as abbot, it seems likely that the subject would have merited additional discussion. For the town of Beersheba, including possible sites for a monastery located there, see Pau Figueras, "Beersheva in the Roman-Byzantine Period," *Boletín de Asociación Española de Orientalistas* (1980): 135–62.

22. See Chitty, *Questions and Answers*, 460. Chitty suggested that the name Euthymius was a later addition intended to make the identification of John of Beersheba and John the Prophet possible. Compare Neyt, de Angelis-Noah, and Regnault, *Correspondance*, vol. 1, tome 1, 166, which does not mention the possibility that Euthymius authored Letter 3.

23. In Letter 57 Barsanuphius refers to the solitary Paul as his "*homopsychos.*" In Letter 10 Barsanuphius refers to Seridos as John of Beersheba's "*homopsychos.*" For John the Prophet's description of the close relationship that existed between himself and Seridos, see Chapter 6.

24. Letters 13 and 16 concern building, Letters 30 and 31 his trip to Egypt to find manual labor. In Letter 42 he asked Barsanuphius if he should advise the brothers who were making another trip to Egypt. For the relationship between monks and laborers in sixth-century Palestine, see Binns, *Ascetics and Ambassadors of Christ*, 94–95. For the economic interactions of monasteries with surrounding communities, see James E. Goehring, "The World Engaged: The Social and Economic World of Early Egyptian Monasticism," in *Ascetics, Society and the Desert: Studies in Early Egyptian Monasticism* (Harrisburg, PA: Trinity International, 1999), 39–52.

25. The significance of the term "son" should not be underestimated. It denotes a very specific relationship. Barsanuphius used it only to refer to Seridos and later his successor Aelianos. See Letters 189 and 573, discussed in Chapter 6. Barsanuphius used the address "child" for Seridos in Letters 9 and 17, Aelianos in Letter 573, and Dorotheos in Letter 253, as discussed in Chapter 3.

26. For letters to bishops, see Chapter 5.

27. In Letters 36 and 49 Barsanuphius said to John of Beersheba that he had written to him, "from Alpha to Omega." Barsanuphius repeated many times the message that he had written John sufficiently and that John should now meditate on his words, see Letters 9–11, 13, 19, 21, 27, 28, 32, 36, 43, 49, and 53.

28. See also Letter 40, in which Barsanuphius condemned speaking in riddles, because it encouraged individualism. For Barsanuphius' own enigmatic treatise on the letter "eta," in Letter 137b, see Paula de Angelis-Noah, "La méditation de Barsanuphe sur la lettre êta," *Byzantion* 53, fasc. 2 (1983): 494–506.

29. For concern that monks using their native language might hide het-

erodoxy, see Sabas' instruction that Armenian monks should sing the Tri-sagion in Greek, in Cyril of Scythopolis, *Life of Sabas* 32, in *Kryillos von Sky-thopolis,* ed. and trans. Eduard Schwartz (Leipzig: J. C. Hinrichs, 1939).

30. In his refusal to see the monk, Barsanuphius paraphrased a text famil-iar to the Egyptian monk, *Apophthegmata Patrum,* Alphabetical Collection, Arse-nius 8: "If I opened to you, I would open to all."

31. Palestinian monks also used stone couches. See Hirschfeld, *Judean Des-ert Monasteries,* 93–94; and Patrich, *Sabas,* 221, 223. Sleeping on the floor without a mattress or covering was considered a form of *askesis.*

32. This was not the only time that Barsanuphius offered a sign to doubt-ing monks. When a few monks dared to suggest that the anchorite was only a prop invented by Seridos to assert his own authority, Barsanuphius came forward to wash the disciples' feet (Letter 125). By reenacting the service of Christ on the eve of his betrayal, the Great Old Man affirmed both his own spiritual authority and that of the abbot. See also Letter 464 for John's expla-nation of Jesus' washing Judas' feet.

33. Note that this test would not have proved Barsanuphius' existence if the deacon had believed that the Great Old Man was Seridos' creation, as did the monks cited above in Letter 125.

34. The deacon was not the only monk to complain that the abbot prac-ticed favoritism. In Letter 488 a monk complained that his requests for a window and some quicklime had been passed over, while the abbot had given such things to others. For the construction of windows in monasteries, see Hirschfeld, *Judean Desert Monasteries,* 67–68.

35. In a similar instance of discord, Barsanuphius intervened, hoping to reconcile a monk to the abbot. He stressed that the monk's disobedience could damage the father-son relationship that should exist between abbot and monk: "I have asked the abbot to receive you as his own, as before. For he had been paralyzed by your disobedience and stubbornness, and I have per-suaded him to receive you, in the fear of God, as a legitimate son and not as a bastard," Letter 614. See also Letters 615–16, to the same monk.

36. In Letter 244 Barsanuphius offered encouragement to another deacon who feared to serve at the altar because of his sins.

37. There is no suggestion in the Correspondence that Barsanuphius, John, or Seridos was ordained. For the presence of clergy in Egyptian monas-teries, see Ewa Wipszycka, "Les clercs dans les communautés monastiques d'Égypte," *Journal of Juristic Papyrology* 26 (1996): 135–66; and for tensions between ordained clergy and monks, see Henry Chadwick, "Bishops and Monks," *Studia Patristica* 24 (1993): 45–61.

38. Lay people frequently subsidized monastic building projects. For other examples at Tawatha, see *Vie de saint Dosithée* 1, discussed in Chapter 3.

39. See J.-N. Biraben and Jacques Le Goff, "The Plague in the Early Middle Ages," in *Biology of Man in History*, ed. Robert Forster (Baltimore: Johns Hopkins University Press, 1975), 58; Pauline Allen, "The 'Justinianic' Plague," *Byzantion* (1979) 49:5–20; and Timothy L. Bratton, "The Identity of the Plague of Justinian," *Transactions and Studies of the College of Physicians of Philadelphia*, n.s. 5, vol. 3 (1981): 113–24, 174–80. For inscriptions from Gaza that may refer to victims of the plague, see Glucker, *Gaza in the Roman and Byzantine Periods*, 124–27.

40. Chitty identified the crisis referred to in this letter as the plague that struck Palestine in 542 (*The Desert a City*, 138). For contemporary descriptions of this epidemic, see Procopius of Caesarea, *History of the Wars* 2.22–3, ed. and trans. H. B. Dewing (Cambridge: Harvard University Press, 1914); and Evagrius Scholasticus, *Historia ecclesiastica* 4.29.

41. John of Ephesus, *Lives of the Eastern Saints*, 37, PO 18:640, trans. Harvey, *Asceticism and Society in Crisis*, 86.

42. Cyril of Scythopolis, *Life of Cyriacus* 10, in *Kyrillos von Skythopolis*, ed. and trans. Eduard Schwartz (Leipzig: J. C. Hinrichs, 1939).

43. Each parish or monastery had a canonarch, who was responsible for preserving canonical order in the liturgy and assuring that the cycle of feasts in the liturgical calendar was correctly observed.

44. I have not yet discovered a satisfactory explanation of who these men were or why Barsanuphius chose to mention them. The names do serve to highlight the geographic breadth of Barsanuphius' connections and his belief that the fate of Gaza was connected to that of people in distant cities.

45. Although there is no explicit mention of the nature of the difficulties Seridos speaks of in the letter, the reference to the Passover account in Exodus would be appropriate if the crisis were the outbreak of the plague. I suggest that Letters 567–69 are closely related and were grouped together by the compiler because they related to the same events.

46. The Great Lavra, founded by Sabas in 483, had a cenobium as well as cells dispersed along the valley. The monastery of Choziba consisted of a cenobium with anchorites living alongside it in the Cells of Choziba (Hirschfeld, *Judean Desert Monasteries*, 25–26, 36–38). See also Antony of Choziba, *Vita sancti Georgii Chozibitae auctore Antonio Chozibita*, ed. C. House, *Analecta Bollandiana* 7 (1888): 95–144; and Tim Vivian and Apostolos Athanassakis, *Life of Saint George of Choziba and the Miracles of the Most Holy Mother of God at Choziba* (San Francisco: International Scholars Publications, 1994), 9–19.

47. For the moral and intellectual characteristics a spiritual director should possess see Hausherr, *Spiritual Direction*, 51–115.

48. Regnault argued that the monk so instructed was Dorotheos (*Oeuvres spirituelles*, 11). Neyt admits this as a possibility ("Les lettres à Dorothée," 98–101). Characteristics such as the monk's poor health and his lack of submis-

sion to the abbot make the identification attractive, but the sources about Dorotheos give no indication that he left the cenobium to serve a father in his early years at Tawatha. Furthermore, in contrast to this monk, who feared to leave the cenobium, Dorotheos tired of interaction with the brothers and desired the solitary life.

49. In Letter 503 a monk asked about his daily schedule and expressed concern because his father's behavior seemed unfitting to him.

CHAPTER 3. DOROTHEOS

1. François Neyt established which letters in the Correspondence were addressed to Dorotheos in "Les lettres à Dorothée." These include letters 252–338 and possibly 247–51, 359–60, and 544–45. For my discussion of Dorotheos I have relied only on 252–338 and the two letters addressed to the porter, 359 and 360. For discussion of the recipient of letters 247–51, see Chapter 2.

2. Regnault and Préville, *Oeuvres spirituelles*, 33.

3. His correspondence, of which sixteen letters are extant, is considerably shorter than that of his spiritual fathers. See ibid., 488–535.

4. The critical edition and a French translation of the *Discourses* is included in Regnault and Préville, *Oeuvres spirituelles.* The notes indicate when I have quoted from Eric P. Wheeler's English translation, *Dorotheos of Gaza: Discourses and Sayings* (Kalamazoo, MI: Cistercian Publications, 1977); on all other occasions translations are my own (cited simply as *Discourses*). Other scholars have explored Dorotheos' teachings on spiritual direction See T. Spidlik, "Le concept de l'obéissance et de la conscience selon Dorothée de Gaza," *Studia Patristica* 11, no. 2 (1972): 72–78; and Nicolas Egender, "Dorothée de Gaza et Benoît de Nursie," *Irénikon* 66 (1993): 179–98, an interesting comparison of Dorotheos with Western monastics.

5. The Dominicans and Jesuits utilized the *Discourses*. See Lucien Regnault, "Monachisme orientale et spiritualité ignatienne: L'influence de S. Dorothée sur les écrivains de la Compagnie de Jésus," *Revue d'Ascétique et de Mystique* 33 (1957): 141–49. For the place of the *Discourses* in Eastern and Western monastic tradition, see Regnault and Préville, *Oeuvres spirituelles*, 94–97.

6. François Neyt characterized the situation thus: "The truth is that Dorotheos, sensitive by nature, refined further by good education and advanced studies, had become part of a community where the majority of the brothers were of simple origin and a somewhat rough disposition." See "A Form of Charismatic Authority," 55–56. Dorotheos faced the classic problem of intellectually gifted youth, fitting in socially with their less intellectually inclined peers.

7. See Neyt, "Les lettres à Dorothée," xxx n. 16; and Regnault and Préville, *Oeuvres spirituelles,* 12 n. 1.

8. *Discourses* 10.105, trans. Wheeler, *Dorotheos of Gaza,* 164. See also *Discourses* 2.36.

9. Neyt points out the significance of the vocative case and the uniqueness of this address in place of the more common "brother," adding that the blessing of a spiritual father ratified the authenticity of a candidate's vocation ("Les lettres à Dorothée," 38–39). Compare Cyril of Scythopolis, *Life of Sabas* 75. Barsanuphius describes Seridos as his "child" and his "true son" (Letters 9, 17, 48; discussed in Chapter 2). Dorotheos and Seridos shared an important task: they both served as letter carriers for the Old Men.

10. See Neyt, "Les lettres à Dorothée," 39–40. Compare with Letters 571–72 to Aelianos, discussed in Chapter 6.

11. Athanasius, *Vie d'Antoine;* and Gregory of Nyssa, *Vie de sainte Macrine,* ed. and trans. Pierre Maraval, Sources Chrétiennes, no. 178 (Paris: Les Éditions du Cerf, 1971). For Macrina's divestment of family property, see Susanna Elm, *Virgins of God: The Making of Asceticism in Late Antiquity* (Oxford: Clarendon Press, 1994), 84–91.

12. These books included Basil's *Ascetica,* Letters 318–19, and works on medicine, Letter 327.

13. His allowance of clothing included two thick tunics, a cape, two mantles, and a shirt for winter; two thin tunics, a frock, a hood, and a lighter mantle for summer; and two blankets, one thick and one thin. This clothing allowance was generous and may have been influenced by a concern for Dorotheos' weak health. For a description of monastic clothing, see Hirschfeld, *Judean Desert Monasteries,* 91–93; and Patrich, *Sabas,* 210–20. Dorotheos' clothing may have caused envy among the brothers; in one letter Dorotheos asked what to do if someone requested one of his possessions, Letter 317.

14. For Dorotheos' interpretation of Christ's command to sell all one's goods and give the money to the poor (Matt. 19:27) see Neyt, "Les lettres à Dorothée," 55–58.

15. *Vie de saint Dosithée* 1.

16. *Discourses* 1.25, trans. Wheeler, *Dorotheos of Gaza,* 91.

17. "The abbot established you at the gate, saying, 'Give me an account of all men who arrive.'" Dorotheos noted that Seridos gave him this responsibility at the advice of Barsanuphius and John (*Discourses* 11.119). See also Letter 262, in which Dorotheos said he had been given a position of responsibility and asked Barsanuphius to pray that he would know when to speak and when to be quiet. Letters 287, 289–93, and 300 to Dorotheos also deal with knowing when to speak and when to keep silent.

18. Dorotheos, *Discourses* 11.119, trans. Wheeler, *Dorotheos of Gaza,* 177. For

Dorotheos' concern about speaking with visitors, see Letters 308–10, and about speaking with important fathers, see Letter 360.

19. Dorotheos gave his own disciples advice about how to correct someone and when to tell the abbot of another's fault (*Discourses* 4.54). Letter 592 speaks of an unnamed porter, possibly Dorotheos, who had to report to the abbot the return of a monk who had previously been expelled from the monastery (discussed in Chapter 6).

20. *Vie de saint Dosithée* 1. Until this time there had apparently been no facilities to care for the sick in this monastery. Compare also Letter 570c for a layman criticizing Seridos' plans to build a church and a guesthouse, discussed in Chapter 2.

21. *Discourses* 4.57, trans. Wheeler, *Dorotheos of Gaza*, 118.

22. Ibid.

23. See also *Discourses* 7.80 for an account of another monk in the community who was targeted by the brothers for insults. Palladius records the physical abuse directed at a female monastic believed to be mad in *The Lausiac History of Palladius* 34, ed. Cuthbert Butler (Nendeln, Lichtenstein: Kraus Reprints, 1967, 1898).

24. For Barsanuphius' teachings about healing, see Chapter 4.

25. John permitted Dorotheos to excuse himself from the infirmary when possible, to attend the liturgy or to retreat to his cell.

26. Later in his life, Dorotheos wrote to a correspondent who oversaw monks, advising him to deal patiently with a monk who resisted his authority. See Dorotheos of Gaza, *Letters* 2.185, in *Dorothée de Gaza: Oeuvres spirituelles*, ed. and trans. Lucien Regnault and J. de Préville, Sources Chrétiennes, no. 92 (Paris: Éditions du Cerf, 1963).

27. *Discourses* 11.121. Compare with Barsanuphius granting John of Beersheba permission to direct others, as discussed in Chapter 2.

28. *Discourses* 11.121.

29. *Vie de saint Dosithée* 2. The same fear of hiding criminals is expressed in the *Rule of St. Pachomius* 49, in *Oeuvres de s. Pachôme et de ses disciples*, ed. and trans. Louis-Théophile Lefort, CSCO 159 (Louvain, 1956), English trans. Veilleux, *Pachomian Koinonia* 2:153. Dorotheos did not adopt Seridos' caution on this issue, for John Moschus related the story of a murderer who hid in a monastery with Dorotheos' permission, in *Le pré spirituel* 166.

30. *Vie de saint Dosithée* 4. Compare with Sabas, who, to avoid the opportunity for sexual temptation, did not accept youths into his lavra but sent them to be trained at the cenobium of Theodosius. See Cyril of Scythopolis, *Life of Sabas* 29. Seridos' statement seems to indicate that Dositheos was younger than the average novice at the cenobium.

31. *Vie de saint Dosithée* 4.

32. Ibid.

33. "He had never heard the word of God" (ibid., 3). This is confirmed by *Discourses* 1.21.

34. *Vie de saint Dosithée* 3.

35. Ibid. 2 and 11.

36. Ibid. 9.

37. Ibid. 8.

38. Ibid. 7. Dorotheos and Seridos were even concerned that studying scripture might create intellectual pride in Dositheos.

39. Ibid. 10. For the connection of these prayers with the Jesus prayer, see Kallistos Ware, "The Origins of the Jesus Prayer: Diadochus, Gaza, Sinai," in *The Study of Spirituality*, ed. Geoffrey Wainright and Edward Yarnold Cheslyn Jones (Oxford: Oxford University Press, 1986), 175–84.

40. *Vie de saint Dosithée* 10.

41. Ibid. 13. Dorotheos also mentioned this vision in *Discourses* 1.21.

42. *Vie de saint Dosithée* 6.

43. Neyt says that John wrote his letters himself, and Dorotheos served him only as a letter carrier, while Seridos took dictation from Barsanuphius ("Les lettres à Dorothée," xlvii). The details of Barsanuphius' dictation to Seridos are described in his earliest letters to John of Beersheba and discussed in Chapter 2; however, it is unclear why Neyt dismisses the possibility that John dictated his letters to Dorotheos.

44. For the length of his service to John, see *Discourses* 4.56.36.

45. Ibid., 4.56.

46. Neyt, "Les lettres à Dorothée," 49–52.

47. *Discourses* 4.56.

48. Ibid. 5.66. I have placed Dorotheos' hesitation to disturb John during the time when Dorotheos served him as disciple, although it is possible that it occurred when Dorotheos was only communicating with John by letters.

49. Siméon Vailhé, "Saint Dorothée et Saint Zosime," *Echos d'Orient* 4 (1901): 360–61; and Chitty, *The Desert a City*, 140.

50. Regnault and Préville, *Oeuvres spirituelles*, 146.

51. Although surprised that Dorotheos would leave Tawatha, Regnault was certain that he did: "Après tout ce que Dorothée avait entendu dire par Jean at Barsanuphe de la vertu attachée à ce saint lieu où Seridos avait établait son monastère, il peut suprenant qu'il ait pu un jour le quitter, pour s'en aller founder à son tour un monastère. Pourtant, le fait est certain. Nous en avons l'attestation dans le titre des *Instructions*, tel que nous le donnent les manuscrits anciens" (ibid., 26). Regnault and Préville do not list or date the manuscripts that include this title. The oldest manuscripts they mention are the Arabic ones, which they date to the ninth or tenth century (ibid., 84).

52. *Discourses* 7.80.2. Regnault translates, "Il y avait au monastère, avantque je le quitte." (*Oeuvres spirituelles,* 290).

53. John Moschus, *Le pré spirituel* 166.

54. For the dating of Dorotheos' death see Neyt, "Les lettres à Dorothée," xxxvi. For the beginning of John Moschus' career, see John Wortley, *The Spiritual Meadow* (Kalamazoo, MI: Cistercian Publications, 1992), xvii–xviii.

55. Compare Wheeler, *Dorotheos of Gaza,* 60–67. Wheeler is concerned to demonstrate that Dorotheos did not leave Tawatha, because that would imply a break with the teachings of Barsanuphius and John.

56. Dorotheos, *Letters* 2.

57. This possibility was suggested to me by His Grace Bishop Sava of Troas.

58. It is unlikely that Seridos compiled the text himself, since many of the letters are connected with events surrounding his death (see Chapter 6); however, it is possible that he commissioned Dorotheos or others to begin the project.

59. See Chapter 2 n. 32.

CHAPTER 4. LAY DISCIPLES

1. I use the term "lay" to designate a person who is neither a monk nor a member of the clergy.

2. Functional literacy in the ancient and medieval world required that one either read and write or be able to afford the services of those who could perform those activities. For the role of literacy in late antique society, see Alan K. Bowman and Greg Woolf, eds., *Literacy and Power in the Ancient World* (Cambridge: Cambridge University Press, 1997); and Robert Browning, "Literacy in the Byzantine World," *Byzantine and Modern Greek Studies* 4 (1978): 39–54.

3. See Letters 128–30, 571–72, 595, 646, 661, and 662.

4. Bowersock, "The Greek Moses," 45. For the presence of Jews in Gaza, see A. Ovadiah, "Excavations in the Area of the Ancient Synagogue at Gaza (Preliminary Report)," *Israel Exploration Journal* 19 no. 4 (1969): 193–98.

5. See Zvi Ma'oz, "Comments on Jewish and Christian Communities in Byzantine Palestine," *Palestine Exploration Quarterly* 117 (1985): 65.

6. See the Council of Elvira (first decade of the fourth century), Canon 50, in Charles Joseph Hefele, *A History of the Councils of the Church from the Original Documents,* 5 vols. (Edinburgh: T. and T. Clark, 1896), 1:250; and the *Apostolic Constitutions* 2.61; 5.17; 8.47, 65, 70 in *Les constitutions apostoliques,* ed. and trans. Marcel Metzger, Sources Chrétiennes, nos. 320, 329, 336 (Paris: Les Éditions du Cerf, 1985–1986). The Canons of Laodicea 37–38, in Hefele, *History of the*

Councils of the Church, 2:318, prohibited celebrating festivals with the Jews and receiving gifts from them, and Canon 39 forbade Christians to participate in pagan festivals.

7. It was the archon Stephanus whom the bishop needed to reprimand (see Chapter 5). For the attraction of Christians to Jewish festivals and traditions in late antiquity, see Robert L. Wilken, *John Chrysostom and the Jews: Rhetoric and Reality in the Late Fourth Century* (Berkeley: University of California Press, 1983), 66–94.

8. *Codex Justinianus* 1.11.9–10.

9. Even Aratius, *doux* of Palestine I, converted to Christianity because of Justinian's legislation (Letter 834, see Chapter 5). The Patriarch of Jerusalem also asked John what to do about Manichaeans, who in order to "escape danger" were going elsewhere to seek baptism. John said it was the patriarch's duty to write ahead and warn the clergy, for many churches did not take the process of catechism as seriously as they ought (Letter 820).

10. Choricius, *Second Encomium to Marcian, Bishop of Gaza* 61, in *Choricii Gazaei Opera*, ed. Richard Foerster (Stuttgart: Teubner, 1972), trans. Litsas, "Choricius of Gaza: An Approach to His Work," 148. For the rhetor's descriptions of the sumptuous Christian festivals in Gaza, see in the same edition *First Encomium to Marcian*, 10–14, 83–94; and *Second Encomium to Marcian*, 58–75. See also Fotios K. Litsas, "Choricius of Gaza and His Descriptions of Festivals at Gaza," *Jahrbuch der Österreichischen Byzantinistik* 32 no. 3 (1982): 427–36.

11. Earlier John had urged the same layman not to pledge a security on another's behalf (Letter 731). This could have implied either a financial or a spiritual commitment.

12. John quotes from the *Apophthegmata Patrum* that if a person sees another drowning in a river, he should hand him a stick, rather than his arm, so as not to be drowned. See Systematic Collection, trans. Lucien Regnault, *Les sentences des pères du désert, nouveau recueil* (Sablé-sur-Sarthe: Abbaye Saint-Pierre de Solesmes, 1970), 74.

13. Compare with John Rufus, who saw asceticism rather than ecclesiastical office as the true test of orthodoxy. See Hevelone-Harper, "The *Plerophoriae* of John Rufus."

14. Compare Dorotheos: "To respect our conscience towards our neighbor means not to do anything that we think may trouble or harm our neighbor in deed, or word, or gesture, or look. For there are gestures . . . which hurt our neighbors and there are looks capable of wounding him and . . . whatever a man does readily, knowing it gives his neighbor a bad thought stains his own conscience, because it means that he is ready to harm or trouble his neighbor," *Discourses* 3.44, trans. Wheeler, *Dorotheos of Gaza*, 106–7.

15. Holy men in Gaza had been recommending holy water for animals for

some time. A Christian who kept horses for the circus had persuaded Hilarion to bless his endeavors, since the man's rivals had recourse to magicians. Water from Hilarion's cup sprinkled on the horses secured their victory in the races, causing crowds to cry out, "Marnas is conquered by Christ!" Jerome, *Vita Hilarionis* 20.

16. Compare this emphasis on being responsible for the behavior of one's servants with John's charge to Aelianos that he would still be responsible for his slaves, even after their eventual manumission (Letter 595).

17. For Barsanuphius' extended correspondence with a sick monk, see Letters 72–123.

18. In Letter 725 John urged another lay person to reconcile quickly rather than press a lawsuit. John was more flexible in a case involving property belonging to God. If the litigation threatened to harm the soul, it should be abandoned. If action could be undertaken without any harm, then it would be negligent not to proceed, Letter 748. For corruption and other evils associated with law courts, see Chadwick, "Bishops and Monks," 53 n. 65.

19. Dorotheos admitted that it might be better to lie than to hand a murderer over to the police, although it would be necessary later to repent of the lie (*Discourses* 9.102). Compare also *Apophthegmata Patrum*, Alphabetical Collection, Alonios 4.

20. John recalled the biblical prohibition against charging interest (Ps. 15:5). One's own financial circumstances determined if it were necessary to ask for repayment of a loan from a poor man. Letter 726 to another layman also deals with settling a debt.

21. The man asked how to interpret Exod. 23:3, "Do not show favoritism to a poor man in his lawsuit." Barsanuphius replied that although a judge could invite someone to show pity towards a poor opponent, he should decide the case fairly, disregarding the economic status of the persons involved.

22. See Letters 734, 735, and 714, discussed below.

23. Letter 722 may relate to the same situation. The correspondent asked if he should correct an elderly or important person who made mistakes when reading aloud. John replied that he should correct the person only if he could do so humbly and if he knew the person would accept the criticism graciously.

24. See Kevin Uhalde, "The Expectation of Justice A.D. 400–700" (Ph.D. diss., Princeton University, 1999), chap. 3, for the functions and ambiguities of oath swearing (including the issue of "necessity"), with emphasis on the teachings of Augustine.

25. See Gerontius, *Vita Melaniae Junioris*, ed. and trans. D. Gorce, *Vie de sainte Mélanie*, Sources Chrétiennes, no. 90 (Paris: Les Éditions du Cerf, 1962).

For kinship and ascetic practice, see Philip Rousseau, "Blood-relationships among Early Eastern Ascetics," *Journal of Theological Studies* 23 (1972): 135–44.

26. In the preceding letter, 675, the man asked how to "rejoice with those who rejoice, and weep with those who weep" (Rom. 12:15). On the death of children within the Roman family, see Richard Saller, "Slavery and the Roman Family," in *Classical Slavery*, ed. Moses I. Finley (London: Frank Cass and Co., 1987), 80–81; Mark Golden, "Did the Ancients Care When Their Children Died?" *Greece and Rome* 35, no. 2 (1988): 152–63; and Suzanne Dixon, *The Roman Mother* (Norman: University of Oklahoma Press, 1988), 111–14, 201, 212–14.

27. For the impact of slaves on Roman family life, see Richard Saller, "Pietas, Obligation, and Authority in the Roman Family," in *Alte Geschichte und Wissenschaftsgeschichte: Festschrift für Karl Christ zum 65. Geburtstag*, ed. Peter Kneissl and Volker Losemann (Darmstadt: Wissenschaftliche Buchgesellschaft, 1988), 393–410.

28. During the grape harvest, hospitality and frugality could easily come into conflict. Hilarion once passed through a vineyard where guards had been set to prevent visitors from taking grapes. This crop produced only vinegar, but the vineyard of a host who shared his grapes with the holy man produced three times more wine than expected (Jerome, *Vita Hilarionis* 26–27).

29. Compare John's advice to Aelianos about his responsibility for his slaves, in Chapter 6.

30. Even monks had difficulty distributing their alms in person. In Letter 324 Dorotheos asked if he could give his alms to the abbot to distribute among the brothers.

31. Compare Jerome, *Vita Hilarionis* 18.

32. For another layman who offered lodging to fathers, see Letter 691.

33. John also advised Aelianos about receiving wandering monks at the monastery (Chapter 6).

34. Compare with the *Regula magistri* 79, in *La règle du maître*, 3 vols., ed. and trans. Adalbert de Vogüé, Sources Chrétiennes, nos. 14–16 (Paris: Les Éditions du Cerf, 1964–65). The guest quarters of the monastery should not contain anything valuable, in case the guests proved to be thieves.

35. For a father's refusal or willingness to dine with laity, see Letter 455.

36. The *schema* was the habit that distinguished a monk.

Compare this advice to Letter 251, in which Barsanuphius advised a young monk to obey the old man with whom he lived and say the blessing over the food, although the older monk was a priest and the younger monk was not.

37. John recommended that he say, "By the prayers of the holy fathers, the Lord deals with us. Amen." The layman next asked if the bread should be

placed on the table before the blessing was said. John said the bread should be placed on the table first, since one prayed "Bless that which is set before [us]," Letter 719.

38. The Trisagion (literally "thrice holy") is an ancient hymn that was common to all Greek Orthodox and some other early Christian liturgies, including the Gallican liturgy: *Agios o Theos. Agios ischyros. Agios athanatos, eleison imas* (O Holy God. Holy, Strong. Holy, Immortal, have mercy on us).

39. In the next letter, Letter 713, the man asked if he were alone but had something in his lap that prevented his rising, could he remain seated. John replied that he should not worry about this but act with a spirit of discernment.

40. Dorotheos related a vision in which the angel of God visited a monastery church and marked with his seal those present from the beginning of the liturgy, those who stayed until the end, and the places of those who were absent by permission of the abbot (*Discourses* 11.118).

41. Choricius, *First Encomium to Marcian, Bishop of Gaza* 22, trans. Litsas, "Choricius of Gaza: An Approach to His Work," 116–17.

42. Choricius, *Second Encomium to Marcian, Bishop of Gaza* 66, 69. Jerome expressed a similar concern about night vigils in *Epistula* 107.9.

43. See also Letter 433 for the proper manner for laity to venerate relics.

44. The man countered John's rebuke by asking about Paul's injunction not to eat food sacrificed to idols if it was a stumbling block to a weaker brother (1 Cor. 8:4–13) (Letter 772).

45. For an example of false visions deceiving even priests, see John of Ephesus, *Lives of the Eastern Saints* 15, PO 17:220–28, discussed in Harvey, *Asceticism and Society*, 118–20.

46. For the transition of laymen to monastic life, see the letters to Dorotheos, discussed in Chapter 3, and to Aelianos, discussed in Chapter 6.

CHAPTER 5. BISHOPS AND CIVIL AUTHORITIES

1. See Chadwick, "Bishops and Monks," 45–61.

2. This latent conflict is evident in another sixth-century text composed in Gaza, John Rufus' *Plerophoriae*. See Hevelone-Harper, "The *Plerophoriae* of John Rufus."

3. Athanasius, *Vie d'Antoine* 69, trans. Robert C. Gregg, in *Life of Antony and the Letter to Marcellinus* (New York: Paulist Press, 1980), 82.

4. For Barsanuphius' polite deference to a bishop, see Letter 791, in which a bishop requested an exhortation from the holy man.

5. Cyril of Scythopolis, *Life of Sabas* 56. See also Derwas Chitty, "Jerusalem after Chalcedon, A.D. 451–518," *The Christian East*, vol. 2, n.s. no. 1, (1952): 22–32; and Meyendorff, *Imperial Unity and Christian Divisions*, 202–6.

6. Cyril of Scythopolis, *Life of Sabas* 151.21f. For an alternative view of these events that neglects Sabas' contribution see Theodore of Petra, *Life of Theodosius* 61.26–62.20, ed. Hermann Usener, *Der heilige Theodosius: Schriften des Theodoros und Kyrillos* (Hildesheim: H. A. Gerstenberg, 1975). These different views are discussed by Binns, *Ascetics and Ambassadors of Christ*, 45. For Sabas' work in defense of Chalcedon see Patrich, *Sabas*, 301–10.

7. The election of the new Bishop of Gaza discussed in the letters of Barsanuphius took place sometime in the second decade of the sixth century, either at the end of Elias' tenure or at the beginning of the patriarchate of John II.

8. The name of the emperor is not given. I have dated this episode to the end of the reign of Anastasius I (491–518), because this series of letters does not mention John the Prophet, who joined Barsanuphius around 525. Marcian had become Bishop of Gaza by the late 510s according to Choricius of Gaza. See Litsas, "Choricius of Gaza," 67.

9. This method of episcopal selection would be confirmed by legislation in 528 in the *Codex Justinianus* 1.3.41. The alternative practice of bishops choosing three candidates, and the clergy and people choosing the bishop was also acceptable according to the Council of Arles (c. 450), Canon 54. See Meyendorff, *Imperial Unity and Christian Divisions*, 44, and A. H. M. Jones, *The Later Roman Empire, 284–602* (Norman: University of Oklahoma Press, 1964), 2:919, 1384 n. 121.

10. In this letter Barsanuphius urged them not to elect anyone, but to accept the one given by the bishop. In Letter 795 Barsanuphius used the word "archbishop." He therefore was referring not to a candidate suggested by the deposed bishop but to one named by the Patriarch of Jerusalem. Before the Council of Chalcedon, the Bishop of Jerusalem consecrated only the metropolitan, who consecrated other bishops (Jones, *Later Roman Empire*, 2:893). When at the end of the fourth century the people of Gaza could not decide on a new bishop, they asked the Metropolitan of Caesarea to appoint one. See Mark the Deacon, *Vie de Porphyre* 16. After 451 the Patriarch of Jerusalem was responsible for ordaining the metropolitans of Caesarea, Scythopolis, and Petra and the bishops of Palestine I. Siméon Vailhé, "L'érection du Patriarcat de Jérusalem, 451," *Revue de l'Orient Chrétien* 4 (1899): 55. For sees under the jurisdiction of Jerusalem, see F.-M. Abel, *Géographie de la Palestine* (Paris: Librarie Lecoffre, 1938), 2: 199–202. For the role of the congregation, clergy, and local bishops in electing a new bishop, see Jones, *Later Roman Empire*, 2:875, 915–20; and Meyendorff, *Imperial Unity and Christian Divisions*, 44. For conflict between the laity and bishops in the process of electing a bishop see Chadwick, "Bishops and Monks," 54–55.

11. It is possible that Elias was still Patriarch of Jerusalem when the elec-

tion of the new Bishop of Gaza took place. Elias was deposed in 516 and Anastasius died in 518. Patriarch Elias and his successor, John II (516–24), both supported the Chalcedonian settlement.

12. For John Rufus' views on Chalcedon, see *Plerophoriae.* See also Steppa, *John Rufus;* Chitty, *The Desert a City,* 103–5; and W. H. C. Frend, *The Rise of the Monophysite Movement: Chapters in the History of the Church in the Fifth and Sixth Centuries* (Cambridge: Cambridge University Press, 1972), 149–51.

13. The bishop wrote back to Barsanuphius that he was unworthy of the sacred functions of a bishop and inept at administration, so he planned to resign. This was probably a display of humility, thought appropriate for a new bishop.

14. Litsas, "Choricius of Gaza," 67–68, 246 n. 17. For the virtues attributed to Marcian's family, see the funeral oration for his mother, Choricius, *Funeral Oration to Maria,* in *Choricii Gazaei Opera.* Marcian's brother Anastasius became the bishop of the neighboring city, Eleutheropolis. Litsas argues that Marcian's uncle was Aeneas, Bishop of Gaza, who taught at the rhetorical school. See Choricius, *Second Encomium to Marcian* 8.

15. Choricius composed more than the two orations that survive. Procopius' oration is no longer extant. See Litsas, "Choricius of Gaza," 68 n. 4.

16. Choricius, *First Encomium to Marcian* 7.

17. See Peter Brown, *Power and Persuasion in Late Antiquity* (Madison: University of Wisconsin Press, 1992), 121. In the Greco-Roman world *paideia* encompassed the traditional educational ideals of pagan rhetorical training valued by elite society. Brown adds, "It was an open secret that many Christian bishops owed their prestige in society at large to the fact that they had once been rhetors," 75. For the classical education of clergy in Gaza, see Yakov Ashkenazi, "Sophists and Priests in Late Antique Gaza according to Choricius the Rhetor," in *Christian Gaza in Late Antiquity,* ed. Brouria Bitton-Ashkelony and Aryeh Kofsky, 195–208 (Leiden: Brill, 2004).

18. Augustine, *Confessions* 5.13, ed. James O'Donell (Oxford: Clarendon Press, 2000).

19. Piacenza Pilgrim, *Travels* 33, ed. P. Geyer, CSEL 39, 159–91 (Vienna, 1898), trans. John Wilkinson in *Jerusalem Pilgrims Before the Crusades* (Warminster, England: Aris and Phillips, 1977), 85. Wilkinson dates this visit to about 570.

20. For the architecture of the churches of St. Stephen and St. Sergius, see Henry Maguire, "The 'Half-Cone' Vault of St. Stephen at Gaza," *Dumbarton Oaks Papers* 32 (1978): 319–25; R. W. Hamilton, "Two Churches at Gaza, as Described by Choricius of Gaza," *Palestine Exploration Quarterly* (1930): 178–91; and E. Baldwin Smith, *The Dome: A Study of the History of Ideas* (Princeton: Princeton University Press, 1950), 38–40. For the recent discovery in the Gaza

strip of a church dedicated to John the Baptist, see Ross Dunn, "Sixth-century Byzantine Church Discovered in Gaza Strip," Presbyterian News Service, 18 March 1999, http://www.pcusa.org/pcnews/oldnews/1999/99110.htm. Inscriptions date the building of the church to 544–50.

21. Choricius, *First Encomium to Marcian* 78, trans. Litsas, "Choricius of Gaza," 129. For bishops criticized for excessive building see Brown, *Power and Persuasion,* 120. For a recent argument that church building represented control of wealth by the new clerical elite, see William Bowen, "A New Urban Elite? Church Builders and Church Building in Late-Antique Epirus," in *Recent Research in Late-Antique Urbanism,* ed. Luke Lavan, Journal of Roman Archaeology Supplementary Series, no. 42 (Portsmouth, RI, 2001), 57–68. Choricius also attributed works of charity to Marcian's mother Maria, saying that she urged her children to grant the petitions of the needy, *Funeral Oration to Maria* 17–19.

22. Choricius, *First Encomium to Marcian* 7, trans. Litsas, "Choricius of Gaza," 112. Choricius' rhetorical exaggeration of the danger of enemy invaders in the first half of the sixth century seems to foreshadow the more concrete threat faced later in the century with renewed Persian hostilities.

23. Choricius, *Second Encomium to Marcian* 16, trans. Litsas, "Choricius of Gaza," 138. For an inscription in the wall that may date to this reconstruction, see Glucker, *Gaza in the Roman and Byzantine Periods,* 140–41.

24. John encouraged the men to exercise their episcopal duties rather than become monks, although a similar letter from Barsanuphius, Letter 790, yields advice that is less clear.

25. *Codex Justinianus* 1.5.12–14, 17. For the Samaritan revolt, see James A. Montgomery, *The Samaritans: The Earliest Jewish Sect* (New York: Ktav Publishing House, 1968), 113–21, and Meyer, *History of the City of Gaza,* 66, 71–72 n. 106. For a good treatment of Samaritan goals see Kenneth G. Holum, "Caesarea and the Samaritans," in *City, Town, and Countryside in the Early Byzantine Era,* ed. Robert Hohlfelder (Boulder: East European Monographs, 1982), 65–73.

26. For the office of *doux* in Palestine I under Justinian, see Jones, *Later Roman Empire,* 1:281–82; and Neyt, d'Angelis-Noah, and Regnault, *Correspondance,* vol. 3, 309 n. 2. Under Justinian, civil and military authorities were kept distinct in Palestine I, despite reorganization in many other provinces that combined these powers. For more on Doux Aratius, see Litsas, "Choricius of Gaza," 71–75.

27. The episode is mentioned in both the Correspondence, Letter 831, and the *Second Encomium to Marcian* 24. Choricius adds that the soldiers had harassed neighboring cities as well. The traditional assumption shared by both Meyer and Litsas that the soldiers were dispatched to deal with Samaritan disturbances in the Gaza region has recently been challenged by Leah Di Segni in "The Samaritans in Roman-Byzantine Palestine: Some Misap-

prehensions," in *Religious and Ethnic Communities in Later Roman Palestine*, ed. Hayim Lapin (Potomac, MD: University Press of Maryland, 1998), 53. Di Segni cites the difficulty in distinguishing between the presence of Jews and Samaritans from material evidence. Cyril of Scythopolis records disturbances similar to those in Gaza, explicitly naming the Samaritans as the cause. In response Justinian ordered the counts Theodore and John to lead an army against the Samaritans. Sabas traveled to Jerusalem to appeal for financial assistance to rebuild churches burned by the Samaritans, *Life of Sabas* 70–73.

28. Choricius, *Second Encomium to Marcian* 23, trans. Litsas, "Choricius of Gaza," 140.

29. Choricius, *Encomium to Doux Aratius and Archon Stephanus* 10–13.

30. In Letters 831–32 Barsanuphius chastised the leaders of Gaza, including the bishop, for ignoring the situation. Letter 833 is from John to Marcian directly. For the challenge that a bishop could pose to secular authority see Chadwick, "Bishops and Monks," 55–56.

31. The *doux* probably converted as a result of Justinian's legislation against paganism in 529 (*Codex Justinianus* 1. 11. 9–10). The legislation against the pagans closely followed the edicts aimed at Jews and Samaritans in 527 that had triggered the Samaritan revolt. Aratius' status demonstrates the high position in the military that pagans could attain in the early sixth century.

32. Choricius, *Second Encomium to Marcian* 24.

33. The bishop's letter identified him only as the archon. For more on Archon Stephanus, who would eventually be killed in violence with the Samaritans, see Litsas, "Choricius of Gaza," 75–80. For the use of the title "*archon*" in Gaza, see Meyer, *History of the City of Gaza*, 56.

34. Choricius, *Encomium to Doux Aratius and Archon Stephanus* 2.

35. Ibid. 65, trans. Litsas, "Choricius of Gaza," 171. For the theater and other entertainments in Gaza, see Zeer Weiss, "Games and Spectacles in Ancient Gaza: Performances for the Masses Held in Buildings Now Lost," in *Christian Gaza in Late Antiquity*, ed. Brouria Bitton-Ashkelony and Aryeh Kofsky, 23–39 (Leiden: Brill, 2004).

36. Deacons performed numerous responsibilities for the bishop. For an inscription dating to 540 mentioning a deacon's oversight of the paving of part of a church, see Glucker, *Gaza in the Roman and Byzantine Periods*, 142–43.

37. See Robert A. Kaster, *Guardians of Language: The Grammarian and Society in Late Antiquity* (Berkeley: University of California Press, 1988), 11–31.

38. The fact that the man had renounced the world to become a monk did nothing to mitigate Peter's regret. John admitted that he should not have been swayed by the man's status as a lawyer but urged him not worry about past decisions.

39. For disparity in the financial positions of clergy, see Jones, *Later Roman*

Empire, 2:904–10. Ecclesiastical custom held that clergy should marry only once.

40. Regnault translates *praktores* as "agents d'exécution," but it may mean more specifically "tax collectors."

41. When the "illustrious people of the city" wanted the bishop to levy a tax on ships, John discouraged the church from gaining revenue in such a secular manner. This letter is generally assumed to be addressed to the Bishop of Gaza, but the tax on ships might suggest the Bishop of Maiouma. This letter may reflect ongoing struggle between the bishops of the two cities (see Chapter 1). For imperial taxes and Palestinian ports, see Kingsley, " 'Decline' in the Ports of Palestine," 83–84.

CHAPTER 6. AELIANOS

1. It is unclear if Seridos died of the plague, but his symptoms included ulcers. For anxiety at the monastery caused by the plague, see Chapter 2.

2. Aelianos was responsible for his *graia,* meaning "old woman," and his *paides,* meaning either "children" or "slaves." Regnault understood these terms to mean "wife" and "children." From the context, "mother" and "slaves" seem more accurate.

3. Gregory of Nazianzus was also concerned with settling an older female relative on an estate. His will provided her with two slave girls to attend her. She might manumit them if she chose; otherwise the slaves, along with the property would revert to the church of Nazianzus after the woman's death. See Raymond Van Dam, "Self-Representation in the Will of Gregory of Nazianzus," *Journal of Theological Studies* 46 (1995): 118–48.

4. For the significance of the title "son," which Barsanuphius used only for Seridos and Aelianos, see chap. 2 n. 25.

5. The election of an outsider as bishop was a common theme in late antique narratives. See Neil B. McLynn, *Ambrose of Milan: Church and Court in a Christian Capital* (Berkeley: University of California Press, 1994), 1–52, for Ambrose's accession in Milan; and Raymond Van Dam, *Leadership and Community in Late Antique Gaul* (Berkeley: University of California Press, 1985), 122–28, for Martin in Tours.

6. For these events, see *Life of Pachomius* (Bohairic) 121, 130, 139.

7. The "peril" in believing oneself capable of becoming abbot is emphasized in the *Life of Pachomius* (Bohairic 94, Greek 106–107). Theodore, who was not a lay outsider like Aelianos but a favored disciple and recognized spiritual heir of Pachomius, was severely rebuked when, believing Pachomius to be dead, he allowed the other monks to elect him as abbot. There was also peril in refusing office. When Auxentius disregarded Euthymius' advice and re-

fused the humble office of muleteer, he was immediately struck down by a demon, Cyril of Scythopolis, *Life of Euthymius* 18, in *Kyrillos von Skythopolis*, ed. and trans. Eduard Schwartz (Leipzig: J. C. Hinrichs, 1939).

8. The *schema*, or habit, was the distinguishing garment of a monk. For the dress of monks, see Hirschfeld, *Judean Desert Monasteries*, 91–93; and Patrich, *Sabas*, 210–20.

9. In the West there was recognized variation in the manner of choosing a new abbot. According to Benedict, the abbot could "be the one selected either by the whole community acting unanimously in the fear of God, or by some part of the community, no matter how small, which possesses sounder judgment." The abbot might be "last in community rank," if he possessed sufficient goodness and wisdom. People outside the community (clerical, lay, or monastic) could contest the choice of the monks: "May God forbid that a whole community should conspire to elect a man who goes along with its own evil ways. But if it does, and if the bishop of the diocese or the abbots or Christians in the area come to know of these evil ways . . . they must block the success of this wicked conspiracy, and set a worthy steward in charge of God's house." Benedict of Nursia, *Regula* 64, trans. Timothy Fry in *RB 1980: The Rule of St. Benedict in English and Latin with Notes* (Collegeville, MN: Liturgical Press, 1981). Compare with the *Regula magistri* 93, in *La règle du maître*, 3 vols., ed. and trans. Adalbert de Vogüé, Sources Chrétiennes, nos. 14–16 (Paris: Éditions du Cerf, 1964–65). For imperial legislation on monasteries, including the selection of abbots, see Charles A. Frazee, "Late Roman and Byzantine Legislation on the Monastic Life from the Fourth to the Eighth Centuries," *Church History* 51, no. 3 (1982): 263–79; and Asterios Gerostergios, *Justinian the Great: The Emperor and Saint* (Belmont, MA: Institute for Byzantine and Modern Greek Studies, 1982), 168–75.

10. Cyril of Scythopolis' *Life of Euthymius* 39 offers a contemporary account of the careful interaction between a spiritual father / abbot and his monks in the process of choosing a successor. As he was dying, Euthymius gathered the "fathers" around him. He asked them whom they wished to have as a superior. They unanimously elected Euthymius' disciple Domitian, but Euthymius refused their request, explaining that Domitian would die within a week. The monks requested another man, whom Euthymius charged with responsibility as abbot. Euthymius also decreed major institutional changes, issuing detailed instructions for transforming the lavra into a cenobium.

11. Justinianic legislation published in 546 required a bishop to preside at the installation of a new abbot. See Frazee, "Legislation on the Monastic Life," 275.

12. There is no indication that any of Aelianos' previous wealth benefited

the monastery; he seems to have disposed of it at the direction of his spiritual fathers before he became abbot. On other occasions, a new monk's wealth could benefit his monastery. In Letter 252 Barsanuphius encouraged Dorotheos to distribute his goods through the intermediary of the abbot (see Chapter 3). When Sabas joined the monastery of Theoctistus he gave all his money to the abbot (Cyril of Scythopolis, *Life of Sabas* 8). When Maris joined the same monastery he donated all his property to the monastery for use in building and expansion (Cyril of Scythopolis, *Life of Euthymius* 10). As abbot, Sabas required monks who could to finance the building of their cells (*Life of Sabas* 28). For legislation on the property of monks or nuns, see *Novellae* 5.5 and 123.38, in *Corpus Iuris Civilis*.

13. Presumably Dorotheos was still serving as John's intermediary at this point.

14. See *Apophthegmata Patrum*, Alphabetical Collection, Antony 2.

15. Domitian, the beloved disciple of Euthymius, died within a week of his spiritual father. Unlike John's first pronouncement, Euthymius' prediction of Domitian's death was fulfilled within the time frame he had originally foreseen. Cyril recounts that on the night of Domitian's death Euthymius appeared to his disciple in a vision, saying, "Enter into the glory prepared for you; for Christ the Lord, in response to my entreaty, has granted me the favor of having you with me" (Cyril of Scythopolis, *Life of Euthymius* 39–41). John the Hesychast begged his spiritual father, Sabas, to intercede on his behalf, that God might allow him to follow Sabas in death, but Sabas responded that John needed to continue directing his own disciples. Cyril of Scythopolis, *Life of John the Hesychast* 16, in *Kyrillos von Skythopolis*, ed. and trans. Eduard Schwartz (Leipzig: J. C. Hinrichs, 1939). John Moschus tells of a certain hermit who died. His disciple, foreseeing his own imminent death, asked the gravediggers to make a large grave so that he could be buried with his master (*Le pré spirituel* 93). The events at Tawatha were unusual, because it was the spiritual father who wished to die with his disciple.

16. Aelianos was fortunate that his request was granted. According to Cyril of Scythopolis, Euthymius, tired of dealing with his demanding disciples, decided to flee: "On discovering this, the blessed Theoctistus assembled the brethren and got them to beg him on bended knee not to leave them. Wishing to gratify them, he promised not to depart then and there. But a few days later . . . he left the cenobium." *Life of Euthymius* 11, trans. Price in Cyril of Scythopolis, *Lives of the Monks of Palestine*, 17.

17. Dorotheos, *Discourses* 4.54.

18. Ibid., trans. Wheeler, *Dorotheos of Gaza*, 116.

19. See Benedict, *Regula* 53, and *Rule of St. Pachomius* 53.

20. These were the standard texts that a lector read aloud to monks during a meal. For the custom of reading at meals, see Benedict, *Regula* 38, and the *Regula magistri* 24.

21. In Letter 566 a monk blamed his abandoning the monastery on demons and his mother. Compare Rousseau, "Blood-relationships." Palladius records a humorous example of how a monk might try to balance his obligations to his natural family and his ascetic vows (*Lausiac History* 39). A young Egyptian ascetic had sworn he would never see any of his relatives again. After fifty years his aged sister desperately wanted to see him. He went to her house, knocked, and then covered his eyes so she could look at him, but he could not see her. In this way he met his sister's needs without breaking his vow. After she was satisfied with looking at her brother, he prayed at her threshold and returned to his cell.

22. Sabas also dealt with his elderly mother. He eventually persuaded her to renounce the world, but after her death he secured her wealth to build a guesthouse for the monastery (Cyril of Scythopolis, *Life of Sabas* 25).

23. Benedict, *Regula* 54. Neither this text nor the *Regula magistri* makes provision for female guests.

24. Cyril of Scythopolis, *Life of Euthymius* 54. This strict rule was once mitigated miraculously. The deaconess Basilina from Constantinople wished to visit John the Hesychast, but knowing that women were not permitted at the monastery, she decided to disguise herself as a man. John became aware of her plan through a vision and sent her word not to embark upon the scheme, promising that he would come to her in a dream while she slept, so that they might converse (Cyril of Scythopolis, *Life of John the Hesychast* 23–24). Male relatives were welcome to visit monks in the lavra (*Life of Euthymius* 20). Choziba may have been the only monastery in the Judean desert to welcome women as visitors. See Vivian and Athanassakis, *Life of Saint George of Choziba*, 10. The custom of receiving female visitors was justified by a story that the Virgin Mary herself first sent a woman to the monastery for healing. The noblewoman and her attendants were permitted to stay overnight in the sacristy, for lack of more suitable accommodations for women (Antony of Choziba, *Miraculi Beatae Virginis Mariae in Choziba* 1, ed. C. House, *Analecta Bollandiana* 7 [1888]: 360–70). On another occasion, the story continues, the Virgin appeared at the monastery herself in the guise of a poor woman asking to speak with the abbot (Antony of Choziba, *Vita sancti Georgii Chozibitae* 6.25). At the monastery of Theoctistus, inscriptions of women's names suggest that female visitors used a campsite outside the monastery (Hirschfeld, *Judean Desert Monasteries*, 196).

25. Pachomius recognized the need to integrate female relatives into the

monastic community. Near the monastery at Tabennesi, he established a monastery for his sister and the female relatives of other brothers. He allowed monks to have supervised visits with their female relatives (*Life of Pachomius* [Bohairic] 27). For regulations on female relatives visiting the monks, see *Rule of St. Pachomius* 52.

26. John does not mention another common motivation for women to visit monasteries: healing. Cyril of Scythopolis (*Life of Euthymius* 54) tells of a man who brought his demon-possessed wife to the Great Lavra. Since no women were allowed within and there were apparently no guesthouses for female visitors, the woman remained in front of the monastery for three days and nights, praying and fasting, before she was healed. The rules forbidding female visitors did not always prevent women from attempting to attain healing. During his lifetime, Euthymius healed a barren woman brought to him by touching her womb (ibid. 23); and after his death, oil taken from his tomb healed a girl brought by her uncle to the monastery (ibid. 52). The account says she remained there three days, but it does not specify whether she was allowed into the monastery or forced to wait outside.

27. Both Egeria and Melania the Elder traveled to see holy men. For Egeria, see *Itinerarium Egeriae.* For Melania the Elder, see Palladius, *Lausiac History* 46. Compare also *Apophthegmata Patrum,* Alphabetical Collection, Arsenius 28.

28. John Rufus, *Plerophoriae* 33.

29. *Life of Febronia* 6, in *Acta martyrum et sanctorum,* ed. Paul Bedjan (Paris, 1890–97; repr. Hildesheim, 1968), 5.577–78, trans. Sebastian Brock and Susan Ashbrook Harvey, *Holy Women of the Syrian Orient,* 155.

30. For the manumission of slaves in the Roman Empire, see K. R. Bradley, "Manumission," in *Slaves and Masters in the Roman Empire* (Oxford: Oxford University Press, 1987), 81–112.

31. John did not always advocate such prolonged responsibility. In another case John recommended that a layman dismiss a runaway slave who had returned. See Letter 653, discussed in Chapter 4.

32. Cyril of Scythopolis related a miracle that facilitated hospitality. When Euthymius was living with nine brothers, four hundred Armenians stopped to visit. Euthymius instructed his disciple Domitian to feed the guests, although there was not even enough food for the monks themselves. Miraculously, the bread, oil, and wine multiplied to feed the guests, *Life of Euthymius* 17. Compare Matt. 15:29–39. For the practice of giving a gift of money or food to a departing guest, see John Moschus, *Le pré spirituel* 42, and Theodore of Petra, *Life of Theodosius* 15.39.11.

33. The advice to give a token offering to an undesirable guest was fol-

lowed at the monastery of Euthymius even when a thief dared to steal an urn from Euthymius' burial vault. The thief was miraculously prevented from getting away and then was provisioned for the journey by the monks (Cyril of Scythopolis, *Life of Euthymius* 59). In this text the saint regularly punished theft with illness, which was relieved only by confession (ibid. 48, 50, 58). For concern that guests would steal from the monastery, see *Regula magistri* 79. For interaction between monks and robbers, see the *Apophthegmata Patrum*, Alphabetical Collection, Macarius 18; and Rufinus, *Historia monachorum* 6.2, 8.31, 9.6, 10.34–35, 15.3–4. Miracles guarded monasteries from robbers in Antony of Choziba, *Vita sancti Georgii Chozibitae* 28, and prevented other thieves from enjoying their stolen goods in Rufinus, *Historia monachorum* 10.34–35. Some monastic fathers had earlier careers as robbers (Rufinus, *Historia monachorum* 10.5; and *Apophthegmata Patrum*, Alphabetical Collection, Macarius 31).

34. Cyril of Scythopolis added the injunction from scripture that by receiving guests, one might entertain angels unawares (Heb. 13:2) (*Life of Euthymius* 17).

35. This advice corresponds with contemporary Western monastic practice, although Benedict's procedure for segregating guests was far stricter. For Benedict's recommendations on receiving new monks, see *Regula* 58. Compare also *Regula magistri* 87–91.

36. For wandering as a form of ascetic practice and a perceived threat to monasteries and the episcopal hierarchy, see Maribel Dietz, "Travel, Wandering, and Pilgrimage in Late Antiquity and the Early Middle Ages" (Ph.D. diss., Princeton University, 1997); and Daniel Caner, *Wandering, Begging Monks: Spiritual Authority and the Promotion of Monasticism in Late Antiquity* (Berkeley: University of California, 2002). See also Benedict, *Regula* 1, and *Regula magistri* 1 and 78. On wandering by Palestinian monks, see Hirschfeld, *Judean Desert Monasteries*, 214–15, 281–82 n. 7–11.

37. Pachomius eventually restricted the access of wandering monks to his communities. He established a guesthouse for them by the gatehouse to prevent them from troubling the younger monks (*Life of Pachomius* [Bohairic] 40).

38. Throughout the *Plerophoriae*, John Rufus described exiled monks spreading non-Chalcedonian teachings. For the wandering of Peter the Iberian (to Tyre, Sidon, Mt. Nebo, and the Dead Sea), see John Rufus, *Life of Peter the Iberian* 78, 76.

39. *Regula magistri* 64 allowed a brother to be readmitted up to three times.

40. It is possible that this incident occurred during the time that Dorotheos served as porter (see Chapter 3). The porter or gatekeeper held a position of great authority, since he controlled entrance to the monastery. Monastic literature recommended that the porter be a man of discernment,

vigilance, and obedience, since, as in this example, he was able either to support or undermine the abbot's decrees. See Benedict, *Regula* 66. For gates and gatekeepers in other Palestinian monasteries, see Hirschfeld, *Judean Desert Monasteries*, 161–65.

41. Compare Cyril of Scythopolis, *Life of Euthymius* 40, 42.

42. Speaking in the first person, the compiler included himself in the group John instructed not to spread the news of his imminent death.

Bibliography

EDITIONS AND TRANSLATIONS OF THE CORRESPONDENCE OF BARSANUPHIUS AND JOHN OF GAZA

Chitty, Derwas J. *Barsanuphius and John, Questions and Answers.* Partial critical edition of the Greek text with English translation. PO 31.3. Paris: Firmin Didot, 1966, 445–616.

Chryssavgis, John. *Barsanuphius and John: Questions and Responses.* English translation. 2 vols. Washington, DC: Catholic University of America Press, forthcoming.

Chryssavgis, John. *Letters from the Desert: Barsanuphius and John, a Selection of Questions and Responses.* Selected English translation. Crestwood, NY: St. Vladimir's Seminary Press, 2003.

Dietz, Matthias. *Vom Reichtum des Schweigens: Ein Zeugnis der Ostkirche: Geistliche Antwortbriefe der Schweigemönche Barsanuph und seines Schülers Johannes (G. Jahr).* German translation. Zurich: Thomas Verlag, 1963.

Hagiorita, Nikodemos. *Biblos Barsanouphiou kai Ioannou.* Greek edition. Venice, 1816.

Lovato, M. Francesca Teresa, and Luciana Mortari. *Barsanufio e Giovanni di Gaza: Epistolario.* Italian translation. Rome: Città Nouva Editrice, 1991.

Neyt, François, Paula de Angelis-Noah, and Lucien Regnault. *Barsanuphe et Jean de Gaza: Correspondance.* Vol. 1, tomes 1–2; vol. 2, tomes 1–2; vol 3. Greek edition with French translation. Sources Chrétiennes, nos. 426, 427, 450, 451, 468. Paris: Éditions du Cerf, 1997, 1998, 2000, 2001, 2002.

Regnault, Lucien, Philippe Lemaire, and Bernard Outtier. *Barsanuphe et Jean de Gaza: Correspondance.* French translation. Sablé-sur-Sarthe: Abbaye Saint-Pierre de Solesmes, 1972.

Rose, Seraphim. *Saints Barsanuphius and John: Guidance towards Spiritual Life.* Partial English translation from the Russian. Platina, CA: St. Herman of Alaska Brotherhood, 1990.

Schoinas, Soterios. *Biblos psychophelestate Barsanouphiou kai Ioannou.* Greek edition. Volos, 1960.

OTHER PRIMARY SOURCES

Antony. *Letters.* PG 40.977–1000. Translated by Samuel Rubenson, *The Letters of St. Antony: Monasticism and the Making of a Saint.* Minneapolis: Fortress Press, 1995.

Antony of Choziba. *Miraculi Beatae Virginis Mariae in Choziba.* Edited by C. House, *Analecta Bollandiana* 7 (1888), 360–70. Translated by Tim Vivian and Apostolos N. Athanassakis. *Life of Saint George of Choziba and the Miracles of the Most Holy Mother of God at Choziba.* San Francisco: International Scholars Publications, 1994.

———. *Vita sancti Georgii Chozibitae auctore Antonio Chozibita.* Edited by C. House, *Analecta Bollandiana* 7 (1888): 95–144. Translated by Tim Vivian and Apostolos N. Athanassakis. *Life of Saint George of Choziba and the Miracles of the Most Holy Mother of God at Choziba.* San Francisco: International Scholars Publications, 1994.

Apophthegmata Patrum. Alphabetical Collection. PG 65.71–440. Translated by Benedicta Ward. *Sayings of the Desert Fathers.* Kalamazoo, MI: Cistercian Publications, 1984. Systematic Collection. PL 73.851–1052. Translated by Lucien Regnault. *Les sentences des pères du désert, nouveau recueil.* Sablé-sur-Sarthe: Abbaye Saint-Pierre de Solesmes, 1970.

Apostolic Constitutions. In *Les constitutions apostoliques,* edited and translated by Marcel Metzger. Sources Chrétiennes, nos. 320, 329, 336. Paris: Éditions du Cerf, 1985–86.

Athanasius. *Vie d'Antoine.* Edited and translated by G. J. M. Bartelink. Sources Chrétiennes, no. 400. Paris: Éditions du Cerf, 1994. Translated by Robert C. Gregg. *Life of Antony and the Letter to Marcellinus.* New York: Paulist Press, 1980.

Augustine. *Confessions.* Edited by James O'Donnell, 3 vols. Oxford: Clarendon Press, 2000.

Basil of Caesarea. *Ascetica: Regulae fusis tractae.* PG 31.889–1052, *Regulae brevius tractae.* PG 31.1080A–1305B.

Benedict of Nursia. *Regula.* In *RB 1980: The Rule of St. Benedict in Latin and English with Notes,* translated by Timothy Fry. Collegeville, MN: Liturgical Press, 1981.

Cassian. *Conferences.* Edited and translated by E. Pichery. Sources Chrétiennes, no. 54. Paris: Éditions du Cerf, 1958.

Corpus Iuris Civilis. Edited by Paul Krueger, 11 vols. Berlin: Weidmann, 1954.

Choricius of Gaza. *Choricii Gazaei Opera.* Edited by Richard Foerster. Stuttgart: Teubner, 1972.

———. *Encomium to Dux Aratius and Archon Stephanus.* In *Choricii Gazaei Opera,* edited by Richard Foerster. Stuttgart: Teubner, 1972. Translated by Fotios K. Litsas in "Choricius of Gaza: An Approach to His Work." Ph.D. dissertation, University of Chicago, 1980, 154–75.

———. *First Oration to Marcian, Bishop of Gaza.* In *Choricii Gazaei Opera,* edited by Richard Foerster. Stuttgart: Teubner, 1972. Translated by Fotios K. Litsas in "Choricius of Gaza: An Approach to His Work." Ph.D. dissertation, University of Chicago, 1980, 110–32.

———. *Funeral Oration to Maria.* In *Choricii Gazaei Opera,* edited by Richard Foerster. Stuttgart: Teubner, 1972. Translated by Fotios K. Litsas in "Choricius of Gaza: An Approach to His Work." Ph.D. dissertation, University of Chicago, 1980, 204–12.

———. *Second Encomium to Marcian, Bishop of Gaza.* In *Choricii Gazaei Opera,* edited by Richard Foerster. Stuttgart: Teubner, 1972. Translated by Fotios K. Litsas in "Choricius of Gaza: An Approach to His Work." Ph.D. dissertation, University of Chicago, 1980, 133–53.

Cyril of Scythopolis. *Life of Cyriacus.* In *Kyrillos von Skythopolis,* edited and translated by Eduard Schwartz. Leipzig: J. C. Hinrichs, 1939.

———. *Life of Euthymius.* In *Kyrillos von Skythopolis,* edited and translated by Eduard Schwartz. Leipzig: J. C. Hinrichs, 1939.

———. *Life of John the Hesychast.* In *Kyrillos von Skythopolis,* edited and translated by Eduard Schwartz. Leipzig: J. C. Hinrichs, 1939.

———. *Life of Sabas.* In *Kyrillos von Skythopolis,* edited and translated by Eduard Schwartz. Leipzig: J. C. Hinrichs, 1939.

———. *The Lives of the Monks of Palestine.* Translated by R. M. Price. Kalamazoo, MI: Cistercian Publications, 1991.

Dorotheos of Gaza. *Discourses.* In *Dorothée de Gaza: Oeuvres spirituelles,* edited and translated by Lucien Regnault and J. de Préville. Sources Chrétiennes, no. 92. Paris: Éditions du Cerf, 1963. Translated by Eric P. Wheeler, *Dorotheos of Gaza: Discourses and Sayings.* Kalamazoo, MI: Cistercian Publications, 1977.

———. *Letters.* In *Dorothée de Gaza: Oeuvres spirituelles,* edited and translated by Lucien Regnault and J. de Préville. Sources Chrétiennes, no. 92. Paris: Éditions du Cerf, 1963.

Egeria. *Itinerarium Egeriae.* In *Journal du voyage: Itinéraire,* edited and translated by Pierre Maraval. Sources Chrétiennes, no. 296. Paris: Éditions du Cerf, 1982. Translated by George E. Gingras. *Egeria: Diary of a Pilgrim.* Edited by T. C. Lawler, J. Quasten, and Walter Burghardt. *Ancient Christian Writers,* vol. 38. New York: Paulist Press, 1970.

Eusebius. *Vita Constantini.* In *Über das Leben des Kaisers Konstantin,* edited by Friedhelm Winklmann. Berlin: Akademie-Verlag, 1991.

Evagrius Scholasticus. *Historia ecclesiastica.* Edited by J. Bidez and L. Parmentier. London, 1898. Translated by A.-J. Festugiére. *Byzantion* 45 (1975): 187–471.

Gerontius. *Vita Melaniae Junioris.* Edited and translated by D. Gorce, *Vie de sainte Mélanie,* Sources Chrétiennes, no. 90. Paris: Éditions du Cerf, 1962.

Gregory of Nazianzus. *Contro Giuliano l'apostata: Oratio IV.* Florence: Nardini Editore, 1993.

Gregory of Nyssa. *Vie de sainte Macrine.* Edited and translated by Pierre Maraval. Sources Chrétiennes, no. 178. Paris: Éditions du Cerf, 1971.

Historia monachorum. In *The Lives of the Desert Fathers,* translated by Norman Russell. Kalamazoo, MI: Cistercian Publications, 1980.

Isaiah of Scetis. *Discourses.* In *Tou osiou patros hemon abba Asaiou logoi 29,* edited by Soterios Schoinas. Volos, 1962. Translated by John Chryssavgis and Pachomios (Robert) Penkett, *Ascetic Discourses.* Kalamazoo, MI: Cistercian Publications, 2002.

Jerome. *Epistulae.* Edited by I. Hillberg. CSEL 54–56 (1910, 1912).

———. *Vita Hilarionis.* In *Vitadi Martioi; vita di Ilarione; in memoria di Paolo,* edited by A. A. R. Bastiaensen and Jan W. Smit, translated by Luca Canali and Claudio Moreschini. [Milan ?]: Fondazione Lorenzo Valla, A. Mondadori, 1998. English translation by Carolinne White, in *Early Christian Lives.* London: Penguin, 1998.

———. *De viris illustribus.* Edited by E. C. Richardson and O. von Gebhardt, *Texte und Untersuchungen zur Geschichte der altchristlichen Literatur* 14.1. Leipzig: J. C. Hinrichs, 1896.

John of Ephesus. *Lives of the Eastern Saints,* PO 17–19. Paris, 1923–25.

John Moschus. *Le pré spirituel.* Edited and translated by M.-J. Rouet de Journel. Sources Chrétiennes, no. 12. Paris: Éditions du Cerf, 1946. Translated by John Wortley, *The Spiritual Meadow.* Kalamazoo, MI: Cistercian Publications, 1992.

John Rufus. *Life of Peter the Iberian.* Edited and translated by Richard Raabe. In *Petrus der Iberer: Ein Charakterbild zur Kirchen und Sittengeschichte des fünften Jahrhunderts.* Leipzig: J. C. Hinrichs, 1895.

———. *Plerophoriae.* In *Jean Rufus, Évéque de Maïouma, Plérophories,* edited by F. Nau. PO 8.1, 1912.

Leontios of Neapolis. *Vita S. Johannis Eleemosynarii.* PG 93.1645 B8. In *Leontios' von Neapolis, Leben des heiligen Johannes des Barmherzigen, Erzbischofs von Alexandrien,* edited by Heinrich Gelzer. Sammlung Ausgewählter kirchen und dogmengeschichtlicher Quellenschriften von G. Kruger, 5. Freiburg: Mohr P. Siebeck, 1893.

Life of Febronia. In *Acta martyrum et sanctorum,* edited by Paul Bedjan. Paris, 1890–97; reprint, Hildesheim, 1968. Translated by Sebastian Brock and Susan

Ashbrook Harvey, *Holy Women of the Syrian Orient*. Berkeley: University of California Press, 1987.

Life of Isaiah. Edited by E. W. Brooks. CSCO. Scriptores Syri, ser. 3, vol. 25, Paris, 1907.

Life of Pachomius (Bohairic). In *Sancti Pachomii vita bohairice scripta*, edited and translated by Louis-Théophile Lefort, CSCO 89. Louvain, 1925, reprint 1953. English translation by Armand Veilleux, in *Pachomian Koinonia*, vol. 1. Kalamazoo, MI: Cistercian Publications, 1980.

Life of Pachomius (Greek). In *Sancti Pachomii vitae graecae*, edited by François Halkin. Subsidia hagiographica, no. 19. Brussels: Société des Bollandistes, 1932. English translation by Armand Veilleux, in *Pachomian Koinonia*, vol. 1. Kalamazoo, MI: Cistercian Publications, 1980.

Mark the Deacon. *Vie de Porphyre Évéque de Gaza*. Edited and translated by Henri Grégoire and M.-A. Kugener. Paris: Société d'Édition "Les Belles Lettres," 1930. Translated by G. F. Hill, *The Life of Porphyry, Bishop of Gaza*. Oxford: Clarendon Press, 1913.

Nepheros. *Das Archiv des Nepheros und verwandte Texte*. Edited B. Kramer, J. C. Shelton, and G. M. Browne. Mainz: P. von Zabern, 1987.

Nestorius, *Liber Heraclides*. Translated by F. Nau, *Le livre d'Héraclide de Damas*. Paris: Letouzey et Ané, 1910.

Pachomius, *Letters*. In *Die Briefe Pachoms. Griechischer Text der Handschrift W. 145 der Chester Beatty Library*, edited by Hans Quecke. Textus Patristici et Liturgici, no. 11. Regensburg: Friedrich Pustet, 1975.

———. *Rule of St. Pachomius*. In *Oeuvres de s. Pachôme et de ses disciples*, edited and translated by Louis-Théophile Lefort. CSCO 159. Louvain, 1956. English translation by Armand Veilleux, *Pachomian Koinonia*, vol. 2. Kalamazoo, MI: Cistercian Publications, 1981.

Palladius. *The Lausiac History of Palladius*, edited by Cuthbert Butler. Nendeln, Lichtenstein: Kraus Reprints, [1898], 1967.

Paphnutius. *Letters*. In H. I. Bell, *Jews and Christians in Egypt*. London, 1924, 100–120. Translated by Robert Boughner, introduction by James Goehring. "Egyptian Monasticism (Selected Papyri)." In *Ascetic Behavior in Greco-Roman Antiquity: A Sourcebook*, edited by Vincent Wimbush, 456–63. Minneapolis: Fortress Press, 1990.

Piacenza Pilgrim. *Travels*. Edited by P. Geyer, CSEL 39, 159–91. Vienna, 1898. Translated by John Wilkinson in *Jerusalem Pilgrims before the Crusades*, 79–89. Warminster, England: Aris and Phillips, 1977.

Procopios of Caesarea. *History of the Wars*. Edited and translated by H. B. Dewing. Cambridge: Harvard University Press, 1914.

Pseudo-Dionysius. *Incerti auctoris chronicon anonymum psudo-Dionysianum vulgo dic-*

tum. Edited and translated by J.-B. Chabot, CSCO 91/43, 121/66, and 104/53. Louvain, 1927–49.

Regula magistri. In *La régle du maître,* 3 vols., edited and translated by Adalbert de Vogüé. Sources Chrétiennes, nos. 14–16. Paris: Éditions du Cerf, 1964–65.

Rufinus of Aquileia. *Historia monachorum in Aegypto: Édition critique du texte grec.* Edited and translated by A. J. Festugière. Brussells: Société des Bollandistes, 1961. Translated by Norman Russell. *Lives of the Desert Fathers: The Historia Monachorum in Aegypto.* Kalamazoo, MI: Cistercian Publications, 1981.

Sozomen. *Historia ecclesiastica.* In *Kirchengeschichte,* edited and translated by Günther Christian Hansen. 4 vols. Turnhout: Brepols, 2004.

Theodore of Petra. *Life of Theodosius.* In *Der heilige Theodosius: Schriften des Theodoros und Kyrillos,* edited by Hermann Usener. Hildesheim: H. A. Gerstenberg, 1975.

Vie de saint Dosithée. Edited and translated by Lucien Regnault and J. de Préville. In *Dorothée de Gaza: Oeuvres spirituelles.* Sources Chrétiennes, no. 92. Paris: Éditions du Cerf, 122–45, 1963. Edited and translated by Pierre-Marie Brun. "La vie de saint Dosithée." *Orientalia Christiana* 26, no. 78 (1932): 85–124.

SECONDARY SOURCES

Abel, F.-M. "Gaza au VIe siècle d'après le rhéteur Chorikios." *Revue Biblique* 40 (1931): 5–31.

———. *Géographie de la Palestine.* 2 vols. Paris: Librarie Lecoffre, 1938.

———. *Histoire de la Palestine depuis la conquete d'Alexandre jusque à l'invasion arabe.* Paris: Librarie Lecoffre, 1952.

Allen, Pauline. "The 'Justinianic' Plague." *Byzantion* 49 (1979): 5–20.

Ashkenazi, Yakov. "Sophists and Priests in Late Antique Gaza according to Choricius the Rhetor." In *Christian Gaza in Late Antiquity,* edited by Brouria Bitton-Ashkelony and Aryeh Kofsky, 195–208. Leiden: Brill, 2004.

Avi-Yonah, Michael. *The Madaba Mosaic Map.* Jerusalem: Israel Exploration Society, 1954.

———. "The Economics of Byzantine Palestine." *Israel Exploration Journal* 8 (1959): 39–51.

Belayche, Nicole. "Pagan Festivals in Fourth-Century Gaza." In *Christian Gaza in Late Antiquity,* edited by Brouria Bitton-Ashkelony and Aryeh Kofsky, 5–22. Leiden: Brill, 2004.

Binns, John. *Ascetics and Ambassadors of Christ: The Monasteries of Palestine, 314–631.* Oxford: Clarendon Press, 1994.

Biraben, J.-N., and Jacques Le Goff. "The Plague in the Early Middle Ages."

In *Biology of Man in History*, edited by Robert Forster, 48–80. Baltimore: Johns Hopkins University Press, 1975.

Blockley, R. C. *East Roman Foreign Policy: Formation and Conduct from Diocletian to Anastasius.* Leeds: Francis Cairns, 1992.

Bowen, William. "A New Urban Elite? Church Builders and Church Building in Late-Antique Epirus." In *Recent Research in Late-Antique Urbanism*, edited by Luke Lavan. Journal of Roman Archaeology Supplementary Series, no. 42. Portsmouth, RI: Journal of Roman Archaeology, 2001, 57–68.

Bowersock, Glen W. "The Greek Moses: Confusion of Ethnic and Cultural Components in Later Roman and Early Byzantine Palestine." In *Religious and Ethnic Communities in Later Roman Palestine*, edited by Hayim Lapin, 31–48. Potomac: University Press of Maryland, 1998.

Bowman, Alan K., and Greg Woolf, eds. *Literacy and Power in the Ancient World.* Cambridge: Cambridge University Press, 1997.

Bradley, K. R. *Slaves and Masters in the Roman Empire: A Study in Social Control.* Oxford: Oxford University Press, 1987.

Bratton, Timothy L. "The Identity of the Plague of Justinian." *Transactions and Studies of the College of Physicians of Philadelphia*, n.s. 5, vol. 3 (1981): 113–24, 174–80.

Brock, Sebastian P., and Susan Ashbrook Harvey. *Holy Women of the Syrian Orient.* Berkeley: University of California Press, 1987.

Brown, Peter. *Power and Persuasion in Late Antiquity.* Madison: University of Wisconsin Press, 1992.

Browning, Robert. "Literacy in the Byzantine World." *Byzantine and Modern Greek Studies* 4 (1978): 39–54.

Burton-Christie, Douglas. *The Word in the Desert: Scripture and the Quest for Holiness in Early Christian Monasticism.* Oxford: Clarendon, 1993.

Cameron, Alan. "On the Date of John of Gaza." *Classical Quarterly*, n.s. 43 (1993): 348–51.

Caner, Daniel. *Wandering, Begging Monks: Spiritual Authority and the Promotion of Monasticism in Late Antiquity.* Berkeley: University of California Press, 2002.

Capuani, Massimo. *Christian Egypt: Coptic Art and Monuments through Two Millennia.* Collegeville, MN: Liturgical Press, 1999.

Cavinet, P. "Dorothée de Gaza est-il un disciple d'Évagre?" *Revue des Études Greques* 78 (1965): 336–46.

Chadwick, Henry. "Bishops and Monks." *Studia Patristica* 24 (1993): 45–61.

Charlesworth, M. P. *Trade-Routes and Commerce of the Roman Empire.* New York: Cooper Square Publishers, 1970.

Chialà, Sabino, ed. *Il deserto di Gaza: Barsanufio, Giovanni e Doroteo.* Bose, Italy: Qiqajon Editions, 2004.

Chitty, Derwas J. *The Desert a City.* Oxford: Blackwell, 1966.

———. "Abba Isaiah." *Journal of Theological Studies*, n.s. 22 (1971): 47–72.

———. "The Books of the Old Men." *Eastern Churches Review* 6 (1974): 15–21.

———. "Jerusalem after Chalcedon, A.D. 451–518." *The Christian East*, vol. 2, n.s. 1 (1952): 22–32.

Clark, Elizabeth A. *The Origenist Controversy: The Cultural Construction of an Early Christian Debate.* Princeton: Princeton University Press, 1992.

Crown, A. D. "The Samaritans in the Byzantine Orbit." *Bulletin of the John Rylands Library* 69 (1986): 96–138.

Dan, Yaron. "On the Ownership of Lands in the Village of Tawatha in the Byzantine Period." *Scripta Classica Israelica* 5 (1979/1980): 258–62.

de Angelis-Noah, Paula. "La méditation de Barsanuphe sur la lettre êta." *Byzantion* 53, fasc. 2 (1983): 494–506.

Delehaye, Hippolyte. "Une vie inédite de saint Jean l'Aumonier." *Analecta Bollandiana* 45 (1927): 5–74.

De Vogüé, Adalbert. *Community and Abbot in the Rule of St. Benedict.* 2 vols. Kalamazoo, MI: Cistercian Publications, 1979.

Diekamp, F. *Die Origenistischen Streitigkeiten im sechsten Jarhundert und das fünfte allgemeine Concil.* Münster: Aschendorff, 1899.

Dietz, Maribel. "Travel, Wandering, and Pilgrimage in Late Antiquity and the Early Middle Ages." Ph.D. dissertation, Princeton University, 1997.

Di Segni, Leah. "The Samaritans in Roman-Byzantine Palestine: Some Misapprehensions." In *Religious and Ethnic Communities in Later Roman Palestine*, edited by Hayim Lapin, 51–66. Potomac: University Press of Maryland, 1998.

———. "The Territory of Gaza: Notes of Historical Geography." In *Christian Gaza in Late Antiquity*, edited by Brouria Bitton-Ashkelony and Aryeh Kofsky, 41–59. Leiden: Brill, 2004.

Dixon, Suzanne. *The Roman Mother.* Norman: University of Oklahoma Press, 1988.

Dols, Michael W. *The Black Death in the Middle East.* Princeton: Princeton University Press, 1977.

Downey, Glanville. "The Christian Schools of Palestine: A Chapter in Literary History." *Harvard Library Bulletin* 12 (1958): 297–319.

———. *Gaza in the Early Sixth Century.* Norman: University of Oklahoma Press, 1963.

Dunn, Ross. "Sixth-century Byzantine Church Discovered in Gaza Strip." Presbyterian News Service, 18 March 1999, http://www.pcusa.org/pcnews/oldnews/1999/99110.htm.

Drijvers, Jan Wilhem. *Helena Augusta: The Mother of Constantine the Great and the Legend of Her Finding of the True Cross.* Leiden: E. J. Brill, 1992.

Egender, Nicolas. "Dorothée de Gaza et Benoît de Nursie." *Irénikon* 66 (1993): 179–98.

Elm, Susanna. *Virgins of God: The Making of Asceticism in Late Antiquity.* Oxford: Clarendon Press, 1994.

Evelyn-White, Hugh G. *The Monasteries of the Wadi'n Natrun.* Part II, *The History of the Monasteries of Nitria and of Scetis.* New York: Metropolitan Museum of Art, 1932.

Festugière, A. J. *Les moines d'orient.* 2 vols. Paris: Cerf, 1961.

Figueras, Pau. "Beersheva in the Roman-Byzantine Period." *Boletín de Asociacíon Española de Orientalistas* (1980): 135–62.

Flusin, Bernard. *Miracle et histoire dans l'oeuvre de Cyrille de Scythopolis.* Paris: Études Augustiniennes, 1983.

———. *Saint Anastase le Perse et l'histoire de la Palestine au début du VIIe siècle,* 2 vols. Paris: Éditions du Centre National de la Recherche Scientifique, 1992.

Frazee, Charles A. "Late Roman and Byzantine Legislation on the Monastic Life from the Fourth to the Eighth Centuries." *Church History* 51, no. 3 (1982): 263–79.

Frend, W. H. C. *The Rise of the Monophysite Movement: Chapters in the History of the Church in the Fifth and Sixth Centuries.* Cambridge: Cambridge University Press, 1972.

Gerostergios, Asterios. *Justinian the Great: The Emperor and Saint.* Belmont, MA: Institute for Byzantine and Modern Greek Studies, 1982.

Gichon, Mordechai. "Research on the Limes Palestinae: A Stocktaking." In *Roman Frontier Studies XII,* edited by D. R. Walker and A. R. Hands, Biblical Archeology Review International Series, 843–64. Oxford: Biblical Archeology Review, 1980.

———. "History of the Gaza Strip: A Geo-Political and Geo-Strategic Perspective." *Jerusalem Cathedra* 2 (1982): 282–317.

Glucker, Carol. *The City of Gaza in the Roman and Byzantine Periods.* Biblical Archeology Review International Series, no. 325. Oxford: Biblical Archeology Review, 1987.

Goehring, James E. "The World Engaged: The Social and Economic World of Early Egyptian Monasticism." In *Ascetics, Society, and the Desert: Studies in Early Egyptian Monasticism,* 39–52. Harrisburg, PA: Trinity Press International, 1999.

Golden, Mark. "Did the Ancients Care When Their Children Died?" *Greece and Rome* 35, no. 2 (1988): 152–63.

Gould, Graham. *The Desert Fathers on Monastic Community.* Oxford: Clarendon Press, 1993.

———. "Lay Christians, Bishops, and Clergy in the *Apophthegmata Patrum.*" *Studia Patristica* 25 (1993): 396–404.

Guillaumont, Antoine. *Les "Kephalaia Gnostica" d'Evagre le Pontique et l'histoire de l'Origénisme chez les Grecs et chez les Syriens.* Patristica Sorbonensia, vol. 5. Paris: Éditions du Seuil, 1962.

Gray, Patrick T. R. *The Defense of Chalcedon in the East (451–533).* Leiden: E. J. Brill, 1979.

Grillmeier, Aloys. *Christ in Christian Tradition.* Translated by J. S. Bowden. New York: Sheed and Ward, 1965.

Hamilton, R. W. "Two Churches at Gaza, as Described by Choricius of Gaza." *Palestine Exploration Quarterly* (1930): 178–91.

Harvey, Susan Ashbrook. *Asceticism and Society in Crisis: John of Ephesus and* The Lives of the Eastern Saints. Berkeley: University of California Press, 1990.

Hausherr, Irénée. *Spiritual Direction in the Early Christian East.* Translated by Anthony P. Gythiel. Kalamazoo, MI: Cistercian Publications, 1990.

Hay, Kathleen M. "Evolution of Resistance: Peter the Iberian, Itinerant Bishop." In *Prayer and Spirituality in the Early Church,* edited by Pauline Allen, Raymond Canning, and Lawrence Cross, 159–68. Everston Park, Queensland: Centre for Early Christian Studies, Australian Catholic University, 1998.

Hefele, Charles Joseph. *A History of the Councils of the Church from the Original Documents,* vols. 1–2. Edinburgh: T. and T. Clark, 1896.

Hevelone-Harper, Jennifer. "The *Plerophoriae* of John Rufus and Spiritual Authority Based on Discipleship." Paper presented at the Syriac Symposium III, University of Notre Dame, Notre Dame, IN, 18 June 1999.

Hirschfeld, Yizhar. *The Judean Desert Monasteries in the Byzantine Period.* New Haven: Yale University Press, 1992.

———. "The Monasteries of Gaza: An Archaeological Review." In *Christian Gaza in Late Antiquity,* edited by Brouria Bitton-Ashkelony and Aryeh Kofsky, 61–88. Leiden: Brill, 2004.

Holum, Kenneth G. "Caesarea and the Samaritans." In *City, Town, and Countryside in the Early Byzantine Era,* edited by Robert Hohlfelder, 65–73. Boulder: East European Monographs, 1982.

———. *Theodosian Empresses.* Berkeley: University of California Press, 1982.

Hombergen, Daniël. *The Second Origenist Controversy: A New Perspective on Cyril of Scythopolis' Monastic Biographies as Historical Sources for Sixth-Century Origenism.* Rome: Studia Anselmiana, 2001.

———. "Barsanuphius and John of Gaza and the Origenist Controversy." In *Christian Gaza in Late Antiquity,* edited by Brouria Bitton-Ashkelony and Aryeh Kofsky, 173–81. Leiden: Brill, 2004.

Hoppe, Leslie J. *The Synagogues and Churches of Ancient Palestine.* Collegeville, MN: Liturgical Press, 1994.

Hunt, E. D. *Holy Land Pilgrimage in the Later Roman Empire, 312–460.* Oxford: Clarendon Press, 1984.

Jones, A. H. M. *The Later Roman Empire, 284–602,* 2 vols. Norman: University of Oklahoma Press, 1964.

Kasher, Aryeh. "Gaza during the Greco-Roman Era." *Jerusalem Cathedra* 2 (1982): 63–78.

Kasser, Rodolphe, and Jean-Marie Alès. *Survey archéologique des Kellia (Basse-Egypte).* Louvain: Éditions Peeters, 1983.

Kaster, Robert A. *Guardians of Language: The Grammarian and Society in Late Antiquity.* Berkeley: University of California Press, 1988.

Kennedy, George A. *Greek Rhetoric under Christian Emperors.* Princeton: Princeton University Press, 1983.

Kennedy, Hugh. "Islam." In *Late Antiquity: A Guide to the Postclassical World,* edited by G. W. Bowersock, Peter Brown, and Oleg Grabar, 219–37. Cambridge: Harvard University Press, 1999.

Kingsley, Sean A. " 'Decline' in the Ports of Palestine in Late Antiquity." In *Recent Research in Late-Antique Urbanism,* edited by Luke Lavan. Journal of Roman Archaeology Supplementary Series, no. 42. Portsmouth, RI: Journal of Roman Archaeology, 2001, 69–87.

Kofsky, Aryeh. "Aspects of Sin in the Monastic School of Gaza." In *Transformation of the Inner Self in Ancient Religions,* edited by J. Assman and G. G. Stroumsa, 421–37. Leiden: Brill, 1999.

———. "The Byzantine Holy Person: The Case of Barsanuphius and John of Gaza." In *Saints and Role Models in Judaism and Christianity,* edited by Marcel Poorthius and Joshua Schwartz, 261–85. Leiden: Brill, 2004.

———. "What Happened to the Monophysite Monasticism of Gaza?" In *Christian Gaza in Late Antiquity,* edited by Brouria Bitton-Ashkelony and Aryeh Kofsky, 183–94. Leiden: Brill, 2004.

Kofsky, Aryeh, and Brouria Bitton-Ashkelony. "Gazan Monasticism in the Fourth–Sixth Centuries." *Proche-Orient Chrétien* 50 (2000): 14–62.

Litsas, Fotios K. "Choricius of Gaza: An Approach to His Work." Ph.D. dissertation, University of Chicago, 1980.

———. "Choricius of Gaza and His Descriptions of Festivals at Gaza." *Jahrbuch der Österreichischen Byzantinistik* 32, no. 3 (1982): 427–36.

Mackenzie, Duncan. "The Port of Gaza and Excavation in Philistia." *Palestine Exploration Fund Quarterly Statement* (1918): 72–87.

Maguire, Henry. "The 'Half-Cone' Vault of St. Stephen at Gaza." *Dumbarton Oaks Papers* 32 (1978): 319–25.

Ma'oz, Zvi. "Comments on Jewish and Christian Communities in Byzantine Palestine." *Palestine Exploration Quarterly* 117 (1985): 59–68.

Mayerson, Philip. "The Wine and Vineyards of Gaza in the Byzantine Period." *Bulletin of the American Schools of Oriental Research* 257 (1985): 75–80.

McLynn, Neil B. *Ambrose of Milan: Church and Court in a Christian Capital*. Berkeley: University of California Press, 1994.

McNary-Zak, Bernadette. *Letters and Asceticism in Fourth-Century Egypt*. Lanham, MD: University Press of America, 2000.

Menze, Volker. "Die Stimma von Maiuma: Johannes Rufus, das Konzil von Chalkedon und die wahre Kirche." In *Literarische Konstituierung von Identifikationsfiguren in der Antike*, 215–32, edited by Barbara Aland, Johannes Hahn, and Christian Ronning. Tübingen: Mohr Siebeck, 2003.

Meyendorff, John. *Imperial Unity and Christian Divisions: The Church 450–680 A.D.* Crestwood, NY: St. Vladimir's Seminary Press, 1989.

Meyer, Martin A. *History of the City of Gaza*. New York: Columbia University Press, 1970.

Montgomery, James A. *The Samaritans: The Earliest Jewish Sect*. New York: Ktav Publishing House, 1968.

Morris, Rosemary. *Monks and Laymen in Byzantium*. Cambridge: Cambridge University Press, 1995.

Mottier, Yvette, and Nathalie Bosson. *Les Kellia: Ermitages coptes en Basse-Egypte*. Geneva: Éditions du Tricorne, 1989.

Neyt, François. "Les lettres à Dorothée dans la correspondance de Barsanuphe et de Jean de Gaza." Ph.D. dissertation, Université Catholique de Louvain, 1969.

———. "Citatians 'Isaiennes' chez Barsanuphe et Jean de Gaza." *Le Muséon* 89 (1971): 65–92.

———. "A Form of Charismatic Authority." *Eastern Churches Review* 6 (1974): 52–65.

———. "Précisions sur le vocabulaire de Barsanuphe et de Jean de Gaza." *Studia Patristica: Papers Presented to the Sixth International Conference on Patristic Studies, Held in Oxford, 1971* (1975): 247–53.

———. "L'Apsephiston chez les Pères de Gaza." In *Überlieferung Geschichtliche Untersuchungen*, 427–34. Berlin: Akademie-Verlag, 1981.

———. "La formation au monastère de l'abbé Séridos à Gaza." In *Christian Gaza in Late Antiquity*, edited by Brouria Bitton-Ashkelony and Aryeh Kofsky, 151–63. Leiden: Brill, 2004.

Ovadiah, A. "Excavations in the Area of the Ancient Synagogue at Gaza (Preliminary Report)." *Israel Exploration Journal* 19, no. 4 (1969): 193–98.

Patrich, Joseph. *Sabas, Leader of Palestinian Monasticism: A Comparative Study in Eastern Monasticism, Fourth to Seventh Centuries*. Washington, DC: Dumbarton Oaks, 1995.

Perrone, Lorenzo. "La lettere a Giovanni di Beersheva nella corrispondenza di Barsanufio e Giovanni di Gaza." *Studia Ephemeridis "Augustinianum"* 27 (Mémorial Dom Jean Gribomont [1920–1986]) (1988): 463–86.

———. "Monasticism in the Holy Land: From the Beginnings to the Crusades." *Proche-Orient Chrétien* 45 (1995): 31–63.

———. "The Necessity of Advice: Spiritual Direction as a School of Christianity in the Correspondence of Barsanuphius and John of Gaza." In *Christian Gaza in Late Antiquity*, edited by Brouria Bitton-Ashkelony and Aryeh Kofsky, 131–49. Leiden: Brill, 2004.

Rapp, Claudia. " 'For Next to God, You Are My Salvation': Reflections on the Rise of the Holy Man in Late Antiquity." In *The Cult of the Saints in Late Antiquity and the Middle Ages: Essays on the Contribution of Peter Brown*, edited by James Howard-Johnston and Paul Antony Hayward, 63–81. Oxford: Oxford University Press, 1999.

Regnault, Lucien. "Monachisme orientale at spiritualité ignatienne: L'influence de s. Dorothée sur les écrivains de la Compagnie de Jésus." *Revue d'Ascétique et de Mystique* 33 (1957): 141–49.

———. "Isaïe de Scété ou de Gaza? Notes critiques en marge d'une introduction au problème isaïen." *Revue d'Ascétique et de Mystique* 46 (1970): 33–44.

———. *Les sentences des pères du désert, nouveau recueil.* Sablé-sur-Sarthe: Abbaye Saint-Pierre de Solesmes, 1970.

———. "Les apotegmes des pères en Palestine aux Ve-VIe siècles." *Irénikon* 54 (1981): 320–30.

Regnault, Lucien, and J. de Préville. *Dorothée de Gaza: Oeuvres spirituelles.* Sources Chrétiennes, no. 92. Paris: Éditions du Cerf, 1963.

Rousseau, Philip. "The Spiritual Authority of the "Monk Bishop": Eastern Elements in Some Western Hagiography of the Fourth and Fifth Centuries." *Journal of Theological Studies*, n.s. 22, part 2 (1971): 380–419.

———. "Blood-relationships among Early Eastern Ascetics." *Journal of Theological Studies* 23 (1972): 135–44.

———. *Ascetics, Authority, and the Church in the Age of Jerome and Cassian.* Oxford: Oxford University Press, 1978.

———. *Pachomius: The Making of a Community in Fourth-Century Egypt.* Berkeley: University of California Press, 1985.

Rubenson, Samuel. "The Egyptian Relations of Early Palestinian Monasticism." In *The Christian Heritage in the Holy Land*, edited by Anthony O'Mahony, Göran Gunner, and Kevork Hintlian, 35–46. London: Scorpion Cavendish, 1995.

———. *The Letters of St. Antony: Monasticism and the Making of a Saint.* Minneapolis: Fortress Press, 1995.

Rubin, Ze'ev. "The Church of the Holy Sepulchre and the Conflict between the Sees of Caesarea and Jerusalem." *Jerusalem Cathedra* 2 (1982): 79–99.

Saller, Richard. "Slavery and the Roman Family." In *Classical Slavery*, edited by Moses I. Finley, 65–87. London: Frank Cass, 1987.

———. "Pietas, Obligation, and Authority in the Roman Family." In *Alte Geschichte und Wissenschaftsgeschichte: Festschrift für Karl Christ zum 65. Geburtstag*, edited by Peter Kneissl and Volker Losemann, 393–410. Darmstadt: Wissenschaftliche Buchgesellschaft, 1988.

Sauget, J.-M. "John the Prophet." In *Encyclopedia of the Early Church*, edited by Angelo Di Berardino. 2 vols. Oxford: Oxford University Press, 1992.

Seitz, Kilian. *Die Schule von Gaza: Eine litterargeschichtliche Untersuchung.* Heidelberg, 1892.

Sellers, R. V. *The Council of Chalcedon: A Historical and Doctrinal Survey.* London: SPCK, 1953.

Smith, E. Baldwin. *The Dome: A Study of the History of Ideas.* Princeton: Princeton University Press, 1950.

Spidlik, T. "Le concept de l'obéissance et de la conscience selon Dorothée de Gaza." *Studia Patristica* 11, no. 2 (1972): 72–78.

Steppa, Jan-Eric. *John Rufus and the World Vision of Anti-Chalcedonian Culture.* Piscataway, NJ: Gorgias Press, 2002.

Trombley, Frank R. *Hellenic Religion and Christianization, c. 370–529.* 2 vols. Leiden: E. J. Brill, 1994.

Tsafrir, Roram. "The Fate of Pagan Cult Places in Palestine: The Archaeological Evidence with Emphasis on Bet Shean." In *Religious and Ethnic Communities in Later Roman Palestine.* Edited by Hayim Lapin, 197–218: Potomac, MD: University Press of Maryland, 1998.

Tugwell, Simon. *Ways of Imperfection.* Springfield, IL: Templegate Publishers, 1985.

Uhalde, Kevin. "The Expectation of Justice, A.D. 400–700." Ph.D. dissertation, Princeton University, 1999.

Vailhé, Siméon. "L'érection du Patriarcat de Jérusalem, 451." *Revue de l'Orient Chrétienne* 4 (1899): 44–57.

———. "Les écrivains de Mar Saba." *Echos d'Orient* 2 (1899): 1–11, 33–47.

———. "Saint Dorothée et saint Zosime." *Echos d'Orient* 4 (1901): 359–63.

———. "Les lettres spirituelles de Jean et de Barsanuphe." *Echos d'Orient* 7 (1904): 268–76.

———. "Jean le prophète et Seridos." *Echos d'Orient* 8 (1905): 154–60.

———. "Saint Barsanuphe." *Echos d'Orient* 8 (1905): 14–25.

———. "Un mystique monophysite, le moine Isaïe." *Echos d'Orient* 9 (1906): 81–91.

Van Dam, Raymond. "From Paganism to Christianity at Late Antique Gaza." *Viator* 16 (1985): 1–20.

———. *Leadership and Community in Late Antique Gaul.* Berkeley: University of California Press, 1985.

———. "Self-Representation in the Will of Gregory of Nazianzus." *Journal of Theological Studies* 46 (1995): 118–48.

Van Esbroeck, Michel. "Une lettre de Dorothée comte de Palestine à Marcel et mari en 452." *Analecta Bollandiana* 104 (1986): 145–59.

Van Parys, Michel. "Abba Silvain et ses disciples. Une famille monastique entre Scété et la Palestine à la fin du IVe et la première moitié du Ve siècle." *Irénikon* 61 (1968): 313–30, 451–80.

Vivian, Tim, and Apostolos N. Athanassakis. *Life of Saint George of Choziba and the Miracles of the Most Holy Mother of God at Choziba.* San Francisco: International Scholars Publications, 1994.

Ware, Kallistos. "The Origins of the Jesus Prayer: Diadochus, Gaza, Sinai." In *The Study of Spirituality,* edited by Geoffrey Wainright and Edward Yarnold Cheslyn Jones, 175–84. Oxford: Oxford University Press, 1986.

Weiss, Zeev. "Games and Spectacles in Ancient Gaza: Performances for the Masses Held in Buildings Now Lost." In *Christian Gaza in Late Antiquity,* edited by Brouria Bitton-Ashkelony and Aryeh Kofsky, 23–39. Leiden: Brill, 2004.

Wheeler, Eric P. *Dorotheos of Gaza: Discourses and Sayings.* Kalamazoo, MI: Cistercian Publications, 1977.

Wilken, Robert L. *John Chrysostom and the Jews: Rhetoric and Reality in the Late Fourth Century.* Berkeley: University of California Press, 1983.

———. *The Land Called Holy: Palestine in Christian History and Thought.* New Haven: Yale University Press, 1992.

Wilkinson, John. *Jerusalem Pilgrims before the Crusades.* Warminster, England: Aris and Phillips, 1977.

Wipszycka, Ewa. "Les clercs dans le communautés monastique d'Egypte." *Journal of Juristic Papyrology* 26 (1996): 135–66.

Wortley, John. *The Spiritual Meadow.* Kalamazoo, MI: Cistercian Publications, 1992.

Index

Abba: as term of address, 18, 20, 43, 135, 160n21

abbot: authority of, 41, 44–47; as disciple of anchorites, 33–34, 36, 51–56; duties of, 121; succession of new, 76, 120–25, 177n7, 178nn9–11; training of new, 126–36. *See also* Aelianos, Abbot; Seridos, Abbot

abuse within cenobium, 66, 77, 166n23

Aelia Capitolina, 14. *See also* Jerusalem

Aelianos, Abbot: becomes abbot, 120–25; continuity with predecessors, 135–39; disciple of anchorites, 138–39, 161n25; face-to-face conversations with anchorites, 122–24, 126, 141; family of, 120–21, 177n2; ordination of, 123; trained by John, 126–36

Aeneas, Bishop of Gaza, 174n14

Alexandria, 15, 23, 107

alms and almsgiving, 63–64, 94, 95–96, 133, 165n13, 171n30

Ambrose of Milan, Saint, 112

Anastasius I, Emperor, 108, 173n8, 174n11

Anastasius, Bishop of Eleutheropolis, 174n14

anchorites: cooperation with abbot, 21–22, 36, 51–52, 76, 155n51; correspondence addressed to, 19–20; in Gaza region, 13, 15–17, 32–34; rela-

tions with bishops, 43, 106–11, 113, 114; role in monastic community, 55–57, 59, 139–40. *See also* Barsanuphius; John of Gaza

anchoritic monasticism, 4, 13, 15–17, 32–34, 55–57

Anna Dalassena, 154n41

anti-Chalcedonians. *See* non-Chalcedonians

Antioch, 15, 62

Antony of Choziba, 180n24, 182n33

Antony the Great, Saint: and episcopal power, 106–7; father of Hilarion, 15–16, 32, 152n23; letters of, 22–23; as monastic exemplar, 30, 63, 125–26

apatheia (detachment), 24, 65

Apophthegmata Patrum, 133, 170n19, 181n27, 182n33; Barsanuphius and John's use of, 17, 162n30, 169n12, 179n14; compiled in Gaza, 16; recommended for monks, 24; relationship to Correspondence, 18

Aratius, *Doux* of Palestine I, 114, 169n9, 176n31

Arcadius, Emperor, 11

archbishops. *See* bishops; patriarchate; *names of individuals*

archon, 176n33. *See also* Stephanus, Archon

Arians, 22, 106–7

201

Index

Funeral Oration to Maria (Choricius), 174n14, 175n21

Gaza: church discovered in, 174–75n20; episcopal election in, 108–12; links with Egyptian asceticism, 15–17; on Madaba map, 32, 33; persecution of Christians in, 150nn9–10; religious character of, 10–13; reputation of, 3, 112, 118; Samaritans in region of, 114, 175–76n27; and trade, 3, 32, 52, 148n2
grapes: moral questions about, 35, 82, 94, 171n28
Great Lavra, 163n46, 166n30, 180n24, 181n26
Great Old Man. *See* Barsanuphius
Greek language, 45
Gregory of Nazianzus, 25, 150n10, 177n2
Gregory of Nyssa, 25
guesthouse: in Judean desert, 180n22, 181n26; in Latin rules, 171n34; in Pachomian communities, 182n37; at Tawatha, 35, 51–52, 65, 74
guests. *See* visitors

Hadrian, Emperor, 10
Hagia Sophia. *See* Church of Hagia Sophia
hagiography, 149n9, 155n47; Antony in, 23, 106, 152n23; Correspondence contrasted with, 7–8, 21, 31, 44, 60, 84, 88, 140; Dositheos in, 61, 69; Latin *vita* of Barsanuphius, 158n70; miracles in, 158n80. *See also individual texts*
healing, 16, 22, 31, 99; absence of, 71, 84–89; visiting monastery for, 180n24, 181n26
Helena, Augusta, 14
heresy, heretics: associated with Nestorius, 27–28; Barsanuphius suspected of, 24, 29; denounced by

Antony, 107; disputing with, 83; native language and, 161–62n29; non-Chalcedonians condemned as, 108. *See also* Arians; christological controversy; Nestorians; Nestorius; Origenism
hermits. *See* anchorites
Hilarion, Saint: connection with Egyptian asceticism, 15–16, 22, 32, 152n23; and fleeing Gaza, 150n9; miracles of, 170n15, 171n28
Historia ecclesiastica (Sozomen), 150n9, 151n12, 152n25
Historia monachorum (Rufinus of Aquileia), 21, 158n80, 182n33
Holy Land, 3, 14–15, 32, 33
holy men, 5, 6, 169n15; formation of, 42, 60; in hagiography, 8, 23, 44, 49, 84, 85; as *patroni*, 53; women who visited, 181n27. *See also* anchorites; miracles
Holy Spirit, 25, 45, 55, 59, 127; facilitating communication, 39, 126
homopsychos (same soul), 40, 60, 85, 161n23
Horsiesios, 122, 149n8
hospitality, 35, 97, 129–30, 133–34, 171n28, 171n32, 181n32. *See also* visitors
humility: as ascetic virtue, 18, 24; as basis of spiritual authority, 47, 55, 59; in bishops, 174n13; in correction of others, 129; in refusing responsibility, 69, 72, 122; towards abbot, 45–46, 50
Hypatius, 108

illness, 46, 50, 84–89, 101–2, 170n17; of Dositheos, 70–72; as punishment, 182n33. *See also* healing
infirmary, 35, 57; building of, 65, 166n20; Dorotheos in charge of, 62, 65–66, 68, 69, 70, 74, 78
Isaiah of Gaza. *See* Isaiah of Scetis